Structural and Functional Aspects of Biocomputing Systems for Data Processing

U. Vignesh
Information Technology Department, Vel Tech Rangarajan Dr. Sagunthala R&D Institute of Science and Technology, Chennai, India

R. Parvathi
Vellore Institute of Technology, India

Ricardo Goncalves
Department of Electrical and Computer Engineering (DEEC), NOVA School of Science and Technology, NOVA University Lisbon, Portugal

A volume in the Advances in Computer and Electrical Engineering (ACEE) Book Series

Published in the United States of America by
IGI Global
Engineering Science Reference (an imprint of IGI Global)
701 E. Chocolate Avenue
Hershey PA, USA 17033
Tel: 717-533-8845
Fax: 717-533-8661
E-mail: cust@igi-global.com
Web site: http://www.igi-global.com

Library of Congress Cataloging-in-Publication Data

Names: Vignesh, U., 1989- editor. | Parvathi, R., 1972- editor. |
  Jardim-Gonçalves, R. (Ricardo), editor.
Title: Structural and functional aspects of biocomputing systems for data
  processing / U. Vignesh, R. Parvathi, Ricardo Jardim-Goncalves.
Description: Hershey, PA : Engineering Science Reference, [2023] | Includes
  bibliographical references and index. | Summary: "The overall aim of the
  book is to extend recent concepts, methodologies, and empirical research
  advances of various biological data mining systems through machine
  learning approaches. Covering a diverse set of research in these areas,
  this publication is ideally designed for use by technology development,
  academicians, data scientists, industrial professionals (inspection
  specialist), researchers and students interested in uncovering the
  latest innovations in the field"-- Provided by publisher.
Identifiers: LCCN 2022040868 (print) | LCCN 2022040869 (ebook) | ISBN
  9781668465233 (h/c) | ISBN 9781668465240 (s/c) | ISBN 9781668465257
  (eISBN)
Subjects: LCSH: Biocomputers. | Bioengineering--Data processing. |
  Biomedical engineering--Data processing.
Classification: LCC QA76.884 .S77 2023 (print) | LCC QA76.884 (ebook) |
  DDC 006.3/842--dc23/eng/20221109
LC record available at https://lccn.loc.gov/2022040868
LC ebook record available at https://lccn.loc.gov/2022040869

This book is published in the IGI Global book series Advances in Computer and Electrical
Engineering (ACEE) (ISSN: 2327-039X; eISSN: 2327-0403)

British Cataloguing in Publication Data
A Cataloguing in Publication record for this book is available from the British Library.

All work contributed to this book is new, previously-unpublished material.
The views expressed in this book are those of the authors, but not necessarily of the publisher.

For electronic access to this publication, please contact: eresources@igi-global.com.

Advances in Computer and Electrical Engineering (ACEE) Book Series

ISSN:2327-039X
EISSN:2327-0403

Editor-in-Chief: Srikanta Patnaik SOA University, India

MISSION

The fields of computer engineering and electrical engineering encompass a broad range of interdisciplinary topics allowing for expansive research developments across multiple fields. Research in these areas continues to develop and become increasingly important as computer and electrical systems have become an integral part of everyday life.

The **Advances in Computer and Electrical Engineering (ACEE) Book Series** aims to publish research on diverse topics pertaining to computer engineering and electrical engineering. **ACEE** encourages scholarly discourse on the latest applications, tools, and methodologies being implemented in the field for the design and development of computer and electrical systems.

COVERAGE

- Sensor Technologies
- Qualitative Methods
- Applied Electromagnetics
- VLSI Design
- Microprocessor Design
- Computer Architecture
- Optical Electronics
- Circuit Analysis
- Computer Science
- Digital Electronics

IGI Global is currently accepting manuscripts for publication within this series. To submit a proposal for a volume in this series, please contact our Acquisition Editors at Acquisitions@igi-global.com or visit: http://www.igi-global.com/publish/.

Titles in this Series

For a list of additional titles in this series, please visit:
www.igi-global.com/book-series/advances-computer-electrical-engineering/73675

Energy Systems Design for Low-Power Computing
Rathishchandra Ramachandra Gatti (Sahyadri College of Engineering and Management, India) Chandra Singh (Sahyadri College of Engineering and Management, India) P. Srividya (RV College of Engineering, India) and Sandeep Bhat (Sahyadri College of Engineering and Management, India)
Engineering Science Reference • © 2023 • 310pp • H/C (ISBN: 9781668449745) • US $270.00

5G Internet of Things and Changing Standards for Computing and Electronic Systems
Augustine O. Nwajana (University of Greenwich, UK)
Engineering Science Reference • © 2022 • 308pp • H/C (ISBN: 9781668438558) • US $250.00

Theory and Applications of NeutroAlgebras as Generalizations of Classical Algebras
Florentin Smarandache (University of New Mexico, USA) and Madeline Al-Tahan (Lebanese International University, Lebanon)
Engineering Science Reference • © 2022 • 333pp • H/C (ISBN: 9781668434956) • US $270.00

Antenna Design for Narrowband IoT Design, Analysis, and Applications
Balachandra Pattanaik (Wollega University, Ethiopia) M. Saravanan (Vel Tech Rangarajan Dr. Sagunthala R&D Institute of Science and Technology, India) U. Saravanakumar (Muthayammal Engineering College, India) and Ganesh Babu T R (Muthayammal Engineering College, India)
Engineering Science Reference • © 2022 • 261pp • H/C (ISBN: 9781799893158) • US $250.00

Handbook of Research on Advances and Applications of Fuzzy Sets and Logic
Said Broumi (Laboratory of Information Processing, Faculty of Science Ben M'Sik, University Hassan II, Casablanca, Morocco & Regional Center for the Professions of Education and Training (CRMEF), Casablanca-Settat, Morocco)
Engineering Science Reference • © 2022 • 944pp • H/C (ISBN: 9781799879794) • US $435.00

701 East Chocolate Avenue, Hershey, PA 17033, USA
Tel: 717-533-8845 x100 • Fax: 717-533-8661
E-Mail: cust@igi-global.com • www.igi-global.com

Editorial Advisory Board

Table of Contents

Detailed Table of Contents

Rahul Ratnakumar, Manipal Institute of Technology, Manipal, India &
Manipal Academy of Higher Education, Manipal, India
Shilpa K., Government Medical College, Kozhikode, India
Satyasai Jagannath Nanda, Malaviya National Institute of Technology,
Jaipur, India

Here the authors propose a simplified technique and its architecture for blind segmentation of histopathological images of lung cancer, combining the K-Means and Histogram analysis. An improved version of Otsu's algorithm is introduced for performing histogram analysis to determine the number of clusters for executing the automatic segmentation of histopathological images. The architecture is input with Biopsy images of cancer patients suffering from different stages of Lung cancer, procured from standard hospital databases to evaluate the performance. The results obtained are compared with the existing works from the literature showing considerable improvement in the overall efficiency of the image segmentation process. Segmentation output in terms of quantitative parameters like PSNR, SSIM, time of execution, etc., as well as qualitative analysis, clearly reveals the usefulness of this technique in high-speed cytological evaluation. The proposed architecture gives promising results in terms of its performance with a time of execution of 192.25ms.

Parth Birthare, Vellore Institute of Technology, India
Maheswari Raja, Vellore Institute of Technology, India
Ganesan Ramachandran, Vellore Institute of Technology, India
Carol Hargreaves, National University of Singapore, Singapore
Shreya Birthare, Vellore Institute of Technology, India, India

COVID-19 began in 2019, and by the advent of 2020, it had become widespread and adversely affected the world. In this work—Covid Live, COVID-19 data is scraped from an online website, which gives an overview of the status of the pandemic in the desired format. The authors built an application interface using a Python micro web Flask framework. The data scraping uses a multi-threading concept to reduce the program's runtime error, resulting in receiving the data quickly, and faster than existing web crawlers and scrapers. This paper focuses on dealing with storing scraped data in the desired format. It also provides options to hear the audio of the scraped data and to download the scraped data. The authors present visualizations of current trends with scraping period details and demonstrate an efficient application that does the data scraping quickly and efficiently.

Chapter 3

Raja G., Koneru Lakshmaiah Education Foundation, India
Srinivasulu Reddy U., National Institute of Technology Tiruchirappalli, India

Growth of healthcare systems has resulted in growth of personalized medicine. Genome sequencing is one of the major players that can enable personalized medicine. The huge computational requirement of this process has made this facility costly and unaffordable for many. DNA sequencing methods that can be performed at computationally low cost and with better performance are sought. The first model presents particle swarm optimization (PSO) and cuckoo search (CS) based models and analyzes their performance levels on sequencing DNA. The sequence assembly is performed using particle swarm optimization (PSO) and cuckoo search (CS). The work then analyzes the pros and cons of using PSO and CS to determine the most effective model. The second method presents the approximate matching model for DNA sequence assembly. The third technique proposes a MapReduce based highest exact matches which successfully exploits and maps between DNA sequences using parallel index method.

Chapter 4

Maheswari R., Vellore Institute of Technology, India
Pattabiraman Venkatasubbu, Vellore Institute of Technology University, India
A. Saleem Raja, University of Technology and Applied Sciences Shinas, Oman

Human analysis and diagnosis have become attractive technology in many fields. Gait defines the style of movement and gait analysis is a study of human activity to inspect the style of movement and related factors used in the field of biometrics, observation, diagnosis of gait disease, treatment, rehabilitation, etc. This work aims in providing the benefit of analysis of gait with different sensors, ML models, and also LSTM recurrent neural network, using the latest trends. Placing the sensors at the proper location and measuring the values using 3D axes for these sensors provides very appropriate results. With proper fine-tuning of ML models and the LSTM recurrent neural network, it has been observed that every model has an accuracy of greater than 90%, concluding that LSTM performance is observed to be slightly higher than machine learning models. The models helped in diagnosing the disease in the foot (if there is injury in the foot) with high efficiency and accuracy. The key features are proven to be available and extracted to fit the LSTM RNN model and have a positive outcome.

Chapter 5

    Maheswari R., Vellore Institute of Technology, India
    Prasanna Sundar Rao, Shri Sankarlal Sundarbai Shasun Jain College,
       India
    Azath H., Vellore Institute of Technology, Bhopal, India
    Vijanth S. Asirvadam, Universiti Teknologi Petronas, Malatysia

The survey on COVID-19 test kits RT-PCR (reverse transcription-polymerase chain reaction) concludes the hit rate of diagnosis and detection is degrading. Manufacturing these RT-PCR kits is very expensive and time-consuming. This work proposed an efficient way for COVID detection using a hybrid convolutional neural network (HCNN) through chest x-rays image analysis. It aids to differentiate non-COVID patient and COVID patients. It makes the medical practitioner to take appropriate treatment and measures. The results outperformed the custom blood and saliva-based RT-PCR test results. A few examinations were carried out over chest X-ray images utilizing ConvNets that produce better accuracy for the recognition of COVID-19. When considering the number of images in the database and the COVID discovery season (testing time = 0.03 s/image), the design reduced the computational expenditure. With mean ROC AUC scores 96.51 & 96.33%, the CNN with minimised convolutional and fully connected layers detects COVID-19 images inside the two-class COVID/Normal and COVID/Pneumonia orders.

Chapter 6

    Gayathri S. P., The Gandhigram Rural Institute (Deemed), India
    Siva Shankar Ramasamy, International College of Digital Innovation
       (ICDI), Chiang Mai University, Thailand
    Vijayalakshmi S., Department of Data Science, Christ University
       (Deemed), India

Clinical imaging relies heavily on the current medical services' framework to perform painless demonstrative therapy. It entails creating usable and instructive models of the human body's internal organs and structural systems for use in clinical evaluation. Its various varieties include signal-based techniques such as conventional X-ray, computed tomography (CT), magnetic resonance imaging (MRI), ultrasound (US) imaging, and mammography. Despite these clinical imaging techniques, clinical images are increasingly employed to identify various problems, particularly those that are upsetting the skin. Imaging and processing are the two distinct patterns of clinical imaging. To diagnose diseases, automatic segmentation using deep learning techniques in the field of clinical imaging is becoming vital for identifying evidence and measuring examples in clinical images. The fundamentals of deep learning techniques are discussed in this chapter along with an overview of successful implementations.

Chapter 7

The most recent technological progression has been accomplished in clinical imaging throughout the past few years. The medical services framework laid out original strategies to work on clinical information handling. One of the vast areas of exploration development addresses the progression of clinical picture handling through the interdisciplinary field. The fast improvement manages many information handling. The information to be held, from crude information to advanced picture correspondence, might give the total information stream in the cutting-edge clinical imaging framework. These days, these frameworks offer high-goal information in spatial and power aspects, and are likewise quicker in securing times. The cycle can bring about a broad measure of excellent picture information. The handled information assists with achieving precise symptomatic outcomes. Clinical imaging is a pathway to acquire images of the human body parts for clinical purposes to recognize and analyze illnesses.

Chapter 8

In reality, all homosapiens species benefit greatly from the function of ATP-binding cassette (ABC) transporter proteins. Many studies have focused specifically on the drug transporter prediction because to the recent advancements in biology. Machine learning and soft computing with data mining methodologies have been used to identify valid motif sequences from biological datasets in general. In this work, the authors analysed the research on the ABC transporter with the prediction of cellular cholesterol. This research is focused on this new area, as ABC transporters are frequently employed as pharmacological targets. In this instance, the authors have focused on the ABC transporter's legitimate signature motif involving plasma membrane cholesterol. The authors used an unique hybrid model that is rough set with random forest for the prediction of motif structure that has clinical significance for predicting relevant motif sequences.

Chapter 9

Sameer Quazi, GenLab Biosolutions Private Limited, India
Zarish Fatima, University College Lahore, Pakistan

Drug designing and repurposing is the most important field in the pharmaceutical industries and biomedical sciences. Because the challenges caused by drug such as low retention time, sensitivity can affect the efficacy of developmental process. As AI or ML has proven to be a potential activity in the health and biomedical sciences and from previous research it has found that AI can learn new data and transform it into the useful knowledge. So, in field of pharmacology, the aim is to design more efficient and novel vaccines using this method which is also cost effective. The underlying fact is to predict the molecular mechanism and structure for increased likelihood of developing new drugs. Clinical, electronic, and high-resolution imaging datasets can be used as inputs to aid the drug development niche. Moreover, the use of comprehensive target activity has been performed for repurposing a drug molecule by extending target profiles of drugs which also include off targets with therapeutic potential providing a new indication.

Chapter 10

Karthigai Selvi S., The Gandhigram Rural Institute (Deemed), India

The goal of new biocomputing research is to comprehend bio molecules' structures and functions via the lens of biofuturistic technologies. The amount of data generated every day is tremendous, and data bases are growing exponentially. A majority of computational researchers have been using machine learning for the analysis of bio-informatics data sets. This chapter explores the relationship between deep learning algorithms and the fundamental biological concepts of protein structure, phenotypes and genotype, proteins and protein levels, and the similarities and differences between popular deep learning models. This chapter offers a useful outlook for further research into its theory, algorithms, and applications in computational biology and bioinformatics. Understanding the structural aspects of cellular contact networks helps to comprehend the interdependencies, causal chains, and fundamental functional capabilities that exist across the entire network.

Preface

Structural and Functional Aspects of Biocomputing Systems for Data Processing provides insight into the structural and functional aspects of biological sequences and the pattern recognition they embed into the data processing in biocomputing systems. It extends recent concepts, methodologies, and empirical research advances of various biological data mining systems through machine learning approaches. Covering topics such as DNA sequencing, high-speed architecture, and medical image processing, this premier reference source is an essential resource for healthcare professionals, biological systems specialists, industrial professionals, PCR testing professionals, scientists, bioinformaticians, students and educators of higher education, librarians, researchers, and academicians.

Chapter 1, "A High-Speed Architecture for Lung Cancer Diagnosis," details how high sensitivity and accuracy result in detection and classification improved the chances of survival for lung cancer patients significantly. To accomplish this goal, Computer-Aided Detection (CAD) system using the CNN deep learning method has been developed.

Chapter 2, "Covid Live Multi-Threaded Live COVID-19 Data Scraper," discusses occurrences in 2019, when COVID-19 quickly spread across the world, infecting billions of people and disrupting the normal lives of citizens in every country. Governments, organizations, and research institutions all over the world are dedicating vast resources to research effective strategies to fight this rapidly propagating virus. With virus testing, most countries publish the number of confirmed cases, dead cases, recovered cases, and locations routinely through various channels and forms.

Chapter 3, "Fragment Assembly-Based Fast and Optimal DNA Sequencing," discusses how DNA fragment assembly requirements have generated an important computational problem created by their structure and the volume of data. Therefore, it is important to develop algorithms able to produce high-quality information that use computer resources efficiently. Such an algorithm, using graph theory, is introduced in the present article.

Chapter 4, "Gait Analysis using Principal Component Analysis and Long Short-Term Memory Models," talks of how machine learning approaches are increasingly successful in image-based diagnosis, disease prognosis, and risk assessment. Many scientific and practical challenges still need to be addressed to unlock their full potential, including how to train strong models on little data, how to improve access to data, how to best make use of the image structure and specific properties of medical imaging data in designing our models, how to interpret results, and how to apply these results in clinical practice.

Chapter 5, "Hybrid Deep Learning Models for Effective COVID-19 Diagnosis With Chest X-Rays," begins discussing how the novel Coronavirus is deadly for humans and animals. The ease of its dispersion, coupled with its tremendous capability for ailment and death in infected people, makes it a risk to society. The chest X-ray is conventional but hard to interpret radiographic test for initial diagnosis of coronavirus from other related infections.

Chapter 6, "Machine Learning Approaches Towards Medical Images," explains how machine learning approaches are increasingly successful in image-based diagnosis, disease prognosis, and risk assessment. Many scientific and practical challenges still need to be addressed to unlock their full potential, including how to train strong models on little data, how to improve access to data, how to best make use of the image structure and specific properties.

Chapter 7, "Overview of Recent Trends in Medical Image Processing: Overview of Recent Trends in Medical Image Processing," discusses how medical imaging and image processing domains mainly manage and process missing, ambiguous, inconsistent, complementary and information has a strong structural character. The processes of human and artificial understanding of any image involve the matching of features extracted from the image with pre-stored models.

Chapter 8, "Predicting ATP-Binding Cassette Transporters Using Rough Set and Random Forest Model," details how ATP-binding cassette (ABC) proteins play important roles in a wide variety of species. These proteins are involved in absorbing nutrients, exporting toxic substances, and regulating potassium channels, and they contribute to drug resistance in cancer cells. Therefore, the identification of ABC transporters is an urgent task.

Chapter 9, "Role of Artificial Intelligence and Machine Learning in Drug Discovery and Drug Repurposing," is about how drug repurposing provides a cost-effective strategy to re-use approved drugs for new medical indications. Several machine learning (ML) and artificial intelligence (AI) approaches have been developed for systematic identification of drug repurposing leads based on big data resources, hence further accelerating and de-risking the drug development process by computational means.

Chapter 10, "Structural and Functional Data Processing in Bio-Computing and Deep Learning: Role of ANN in Biocomputing," shows that the goal of new biocomputing research is to comprehend bio molecules' structures and functions via the lens of bio futuristic technologies. The amount of data generated every day is tremendous, data bases are growing exponentially. Majority of computational researchers have been using machine learning for the analysis of bio-informatics data sets. This chapter explores the relationship between deep learning algorithms and the fundamental biological concepts of protein structure, phenotypes and genotype, proteins and protein levels, and the similarities and differences between popular deep learning models.

U. Vignesh
Information Technology Department, Vel Tech Rangarajan Dr. Sagunthala R&D
Institute of Science and Technology, Chennai, India

R. Parvathi
Vellore Institute of Technology, India

Ricardo Goncalves
Department of Electrical and Computer Engineering (DEEC), NOVA School of
Science and Technology, NOVA University Lisbon, Portugal

Chapter 1
A High–Speed Architecture for Lung Cancer Diagnosis

Rahul Ratnakumar
Manipal Institute of Technology, Manipal, India & Manipal Academy of Higher Education, Manipal, India

Shilpa K.
Government Medical College, Kozhikode, India

Satyasai Jagannath Nanda
Malaviya National Institute of Technology, Jaipur, India

ABSTRACT

Here the authors propose a simplified technique and its architecture for blind segmentation of histopathological images of lung cancer, combining the K-Means and Histogram analysis. An improved version of Otsu's algorithm is introduced for performing histogram analysis to determine the number of clusters for executing the automatic segmentation of histopathological images. The architecture is input with Biopsy images of cancer patients suffering from different stages of Lung cancer, procured from standard hospital databases to evaluate the performance. The results obtained are compared with the existing works from the literature showing considerable improvement in the overall efficiency of the image segmentation process. Segmentation output in terms of quantitative parameters like PSNR, SSIM, time of execution, etc., as well as qualitative analysis, clearly reveals the usefulness of this technique in high-speed cytological evaluation. The proposed architecture gives promising results in terms of its performance with a time of execution of 192.25ms.

DOI: 10.4018/978-1-6684-6523-3.ch001

INTRODUCTION

In the recent years, due to the tremendous growth in computation power combined with the exponential increase in the number of 'Image/video analysis algorithms', powerful computer assisted analytic approaches have been introduced (Fatakdawala et al., 2010; Kim et al., 2006; Sont et al., 2003). The quality of diagnosis and prognosis results have been exponentially rising as the quantity of data available from the smart sensors, endoscopic gadgets and diagnostic tools developed, are rapidly increasing day by day. This has led to the evolution of very successful and powerful Computer Aided Diagnosis (CAD) tools in the field of Biomedical image processing (Ancin et al., 1996; Bilgin et al., 2007; Ortiz de Solorzano et al., 1999). One of the most challenging problems in Biomedical image processing is to segment, classify and recognize the objects as per their characteristics without having any prior medical knowledge about the characteristics (Bartels et al., 1989; Belien et al., 1997; Cillekens et al., 2000; Markiewicz et al., 2006). Diagnosis through Biopsy images are often considered as a gold standard in many cytological evaluations. Modern histopathological diagnosis techniques are quite slow to detect cells, tumors, malignant tissues and other disease specific factors from Biopsy images. The main motivation for detecting, segmenting and recognizing pathological image structures is to automatically count, measure and analyze the objects- generally nuclei or lymphocyte cells etc. which itself have good diagnostic significance for certain conditions of cancer and many other diseases like tuberculosis, and some serious pulmonary infections like Nipah, COVID-19 (SARS Cov-2) etc. Segmentation of specific blood cells, capillaries, cell structures etc. using manual inspection is tremendously difficult and demands huge computation power, time and patience along with medical expertise. Here we propose a simplified technique and architecture for blind segmentation of histopathological images of lung cancer, combining the K-Means algorithm and Histogram analysis. Even after six decades of its existence K-Means algorithm is still used in multi-disciplinary arenas and applications like recognition (Agarwal et al., 2015; Hedberg et al., 2007; Rupanagudi et al., 2015), object identification and tracking etc. because of its simplicity and versatility. Their special ability to parallelize conventional optimization techniques has made them exceptional in the field of optimization techniques (Cai & Wang, 2019; Ratnakumar & Nanda, 2021a; Ratnakumar & Nanda, 2021b; Wang et al., 2009; Yadav et al., 2021). Many of its performance on the benchmark databases have reflected the same truth. The main cons of this algorithm are (i) needs number of clusters as input, (ii) captures spherical clusters easily but performs poorly with other distributions, (iii) hardware implementation requires a divider. One of the central problems conventional clustering is to presume the exact number of clusters within the biomedical image. We use an improved version of Otsu's thresholding method to automatically find the number of clusters or regions of interest, so that the need for expert human personal is minimized. The proposed technique neither requires user interaction nor any prior knowledge to automatically segment the cells, cytoplasm, and other features in the histopathological image, so that the image is ready for recognition. Segmentation of the constituents within a biopsy image is a very important low-level-learning step in many rapidly growing areas like disease detection, biomedical, biometric forensic analysis and many other medical diagnosis and prognosis applications (Ancin et al., 1996; Bilgin et al., 2007; Hassija et al., 2022). The biomedical data provided by the sensors and instruments demand high-performance computing (HPC) platforms because of their improved spatial, spectral and temporal resolutions (Lin et al., 2007; Ratnakumar & Nanda, 2016). The standard images used are namely Histopathological (biopsy) images of Lung cancer patients taken from benchmark databases National Cancer Center, Japan.

Applying statistical analysis (Bartels et al., 1989; Belien et al., 1997; Bibbo et al., 1991) and k-means clustering in biopsy images for automatically grouping pixels within the biopsy image that are exhibiting the same chromaticity and which are different from the other groups based on the same chromatic criteria. (Bartels et al., 1989; Belien et al., 1997)

Thus, here we demonstrate the improvement in the overall efficiency and performance of Image segmentation. Segmentation output in terms of quantitative parameters like PSNR, SSIM, time of execution as well as qualitative analysis, which clearly reveal the usefulness of this technique in quick cytological evaluation (Hore & Ziou, 2010; Wang et al., 2004). The proposed architecture gives promising results in terms of its performance on software (243.29ms, 12% faster than existing techniques) as well as it is expected to be much faster on hardware implementation as well. Preliminary results in hardware clearly reveal the usefulness and simplicity of this architecture in quick cytological evaluation (Hedberg et al., 2007).

CLUSTERING

Clustering is nothing but grouping of similar data based on their intrinsic characteristics. It is an unsupervised machine learning technique (Yang et al., 2005) where- given the set of feature vectors which are unlabelled, we attempt to combine them into their natural groups called as clusters. The data-points within the same cluster are similar in majority of features considered, and the data-points of different clusters are quite dissimilar with each other. The distance criteria chosen is usually Euclidian (Ratnakumar & Nanda, 2016; Ratnakumar & Nanda, 2019a; Ratnakumar & Nanda, 2019b) (Minkowski metric with p value of two, as given in the equation 1 and 2.)

$$D(x_y, x_z) = \left(\sum_{l=1}^{d} \left| x_{yl} - x_{zl} \right|^{1/p} \right)^{p} \tag{1}$$

$$Variability(i) = \sum_{x_j \in i}^{x_k} D(\mu(i), x_j)^2 \tag{2}$$

Here the centroid is expressed as μ_i. The objective is to reduce variability within a cluster to minimum and increase similarity between different clusters, as given in the equation 3.

$$Minimise \left\langle Dissimilarity(I) = \sum_{i \in I} Variability(i) \right\rangle \tag{3}$$

K-Means Clustering Algorithm

K-Means is greedy unsupervised optimization algorithm which is simple and fast, very suited for real-time applications. One of the intrinsic disadvantages of K-Means is that the number of clusters has to be predetermined before the algorithm is run. So, the user has to understand the data that he or she is working with, thus knowing the number of clusters before-hand.

Steps of K-Means Algorithm

```
Input: data points and the number of clusters, k.
   Select k data points randomly as initial cluster centroids
While (true)
Generate m clusters by assigning each data point to the nearest
centroid
find m new centroids by computing the mean of data points
within each cluster
If  (Centroids don't shift )
End (break)
Else
                                Continue (true)
```

4

Figure 1. Distance measurement in K-means clustering Algorithm.

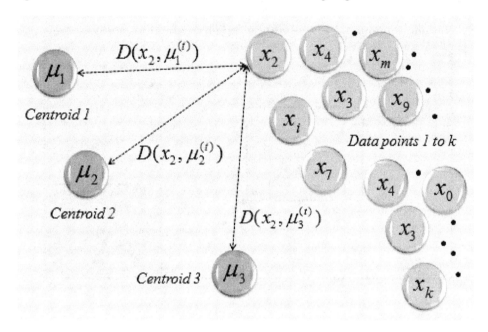

Output: Label the k data points with respect to the nearest centroid.

There are mainly two initialization methods for K-Means algorithm.

1. **Random:** Randomly assigns each data to a Cluster and proceeds to the update step, thus computing the initial mean to be the centroid of those randomly assigned points. E.g. normally used for Fuzzy K-means.
2. **Forgy:** uses randomly assigns k observations from the data itself and consider them as initial means.

Distance measurement in K-means clustering Algorithm shown in Figure. 1.

Image Segmentation

As shown in the figure 2, An Image can be expressed as a combination of k regions. These regions

$$S_1 + S_2 + ... + S_k = \sum_{i=1}^{k}(S_i) = 1 \tag{4}$$

Figure 2. The segments of an image represented by S_i.

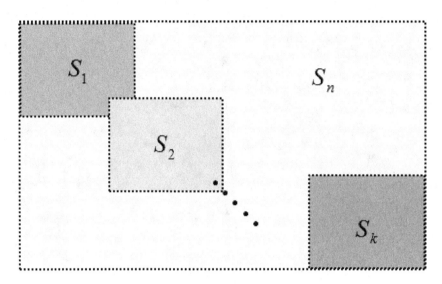

have common chromatic features. Image segmentation is the reverse process of retrieving the sub-regions from the input image based on their inherent chromatic features.

Histopathological Image Segmentation

The proposed histopathological image segmentation constitutes the following steps given below in Figure 3.

The distribution and occurrence of each pixel value is counted and frequency analysis is conducted and graphed as a statistical chart termed as histogram (Byun et al., 2006; De Solorzano et al., 2001). The calculation of thresholds is a mathematical procedure where some of the statistical parameters relating to the pixel values like median, mean, deviation etc. are extracted from the image histogram. The 'Luv' format is a three-dimensional vector which a Luminosity vector, u and v chromatic dimensions of the image 'I'. The Luminosity vector is discarded as it doesn't contain any chromatic components (Gudla et al., 2008). The histogram charts have to be plotted for both u and v dimensions. Most of the grey level images are segmented in the similar manner (Li et al., 2007).

Figure 3. Proposed histopathological image segmentation process flow.

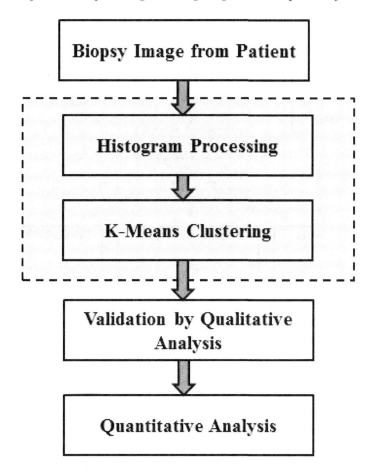

Quantitative Evaluation

Peak Signal to Noise Ratio (PSNR) of an image '**a**', in reference to an image '**b**', both having same dimensions X * Y, is given by the equation (6). Refer (Hore & Ziou, 2010; Wang et al., 2004) for deeper explanations and illustrations.

$$PSNR(a,b) = 10 \log_{10} \left(\frac{255^2}{MSE(a,b)} \right) \tag{5}$$

Where their MSE (Mean Square error) is computed by

Figure 4. The process of Biopsy, starting from sample procurement to analysis, synthesis then final results.

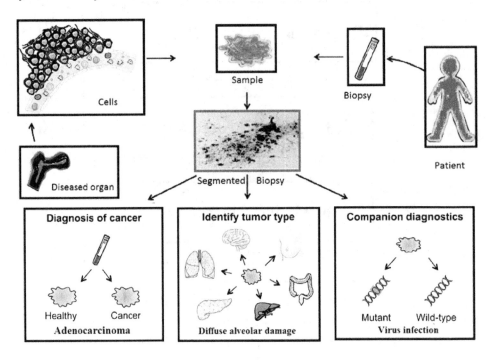

$$MSE(a,b) = \frac{1}{XY} \sum_{i=1}^{X} \sum_{j=1}^{Y} (a_{ij} - b_{ij})^2 \tag{6}$$

As the Mean Square Error improves the Peak Signal to Noise Ratio declines as inferred from the equation 6, signifying the quality degradation of the image. As the PSNR value rises higher and higher towards infinity, the MSE declines towards zero, signifying an ideal and perfect image quality. SSIM (Structural Similarity Index Measure) is another famous image quality metric determining the Structural Similarity of the image.

$$SSIM(a,b) = [l(a,b)^\alpha c(a,b)^\beta s(a,b)^\gamma] \tag{7}$$

$$l(a,b) = \frac{2\mu_a\mu_b + c_1}{\mu_a^2 + \mu_b^2 + c_1} \tag{8}$$

Figure 5. The detailed sequence of latest Liquid Biopsy process for cancer therapy (i) Primary stage or NGS (NGS-Next generation sequencing) (ii) flow cytometry (iii) Co-culturing stage (iv) isolation, pairing and sequencing (v) encoding of TCR (TCR-T-Cell receptor) (vi) re-infusion of modified T-Cells.

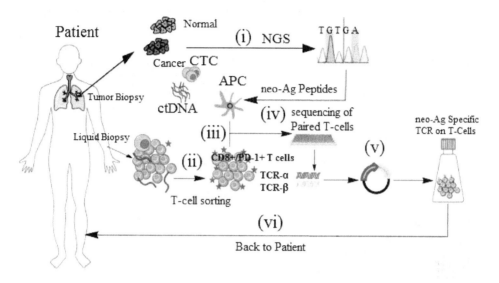

$$c(a,b) = \frac{2\sigma_a \sigma_b + c_2}{\sigma_a^2 + \sigma_b^2 + c_2} \tag{9}$$

$$s(a,b) = \frac{2\sigma_{ab} + c_3}{\sigma_a^2 + \sigma_b^2 + c_3} \tag{10}$$

The luminance, Contrast and structural comparisons between the two images are given by the functions l(a,b) in eq.(9), c(a,b) in eq.(10) and s(a,b) in eq.(11) respectively. The mean luminance of the images are denoted by μ_a and μ_b. The spread (variance) factor or the standard deviations of the pixel distribution are denoted by α_a and α_b. α_{ab} Refers to the covariance factor between the images a and b. The terms C_1, C_2 and C_3 are always positive in the view of escaping a division error. The standard Biopsy images procured from Hospital databases which are used for testing is given in the Figure. 6.

Figure 6. Biopsy images of cancer patients procured from standard hospital databases as input to the proposed methodology.

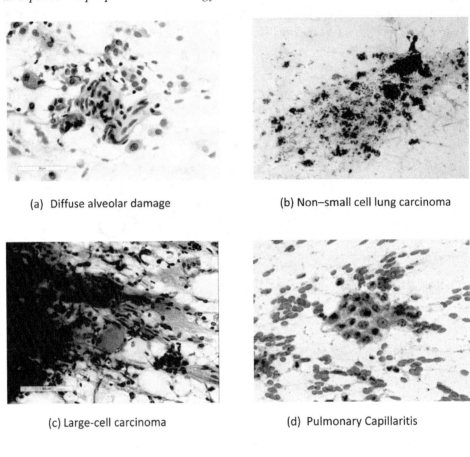

(a) Diffuse alveolar damage   (b) Non–small cell lung carcinoma

(c) Large-cell carcinoma   (d) Pulmonary Capillaritis

(e) Adenocarcinoma

Figure 7. The Proposed methodology explained with the help of a flowchart.

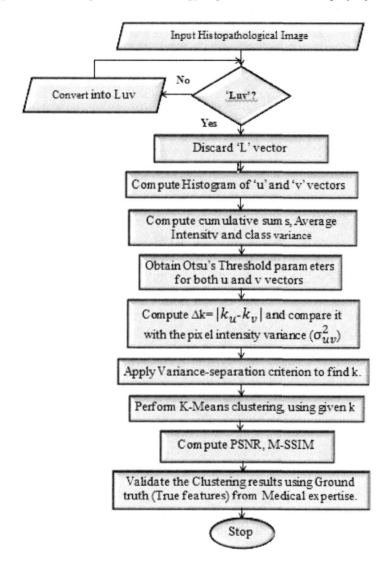

Methodology for Histopathological Image Segmentation Using K-means Clustering

This manuscript proposes a simple and an efficient methodology for histopathological image segmentation, which is represented in figures 3 and 7. The images procured from the Biopsy databases of hospitals, have to be pre-processed. The format of the raw image is usually *png* or jpeg. So, the first step is to convert input histopathological

Figure 8. The quantitative model of the new approach can be expressed as a flowchart.

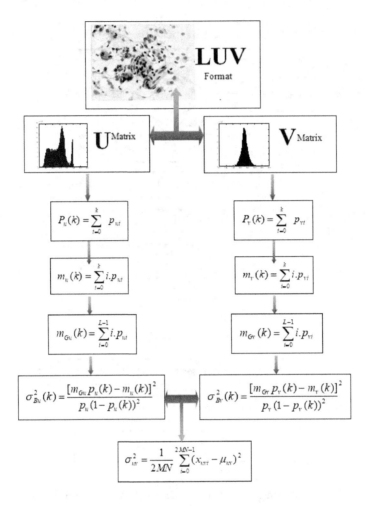

image to a format suitable for chromatic processing, then statistical parameters are computed. This is shown in figures 7 and 8.

The Process of Biopsy

A biopsy is a procedure to remove some sample of cells or tissues to get analyzed in a medical laboratory. After the prescription of a medical expert or a doctor, Biopsy is usually done to check presence of some medical conditions or diseases like cancer etc. Usually imaging tests can detect abnormality but it won't be able to confirm the presence or absence of Cancerous cells. Definitive diagnosis of cancer can only be confirmed by Biopsy only. Refer Figure. 4.

Biopsy Result Analysis

Once the sample is sent for analysis, it may be processed initially or chemically modified depending upon the type of Biopsy. The slices of that sample are then placed on a transparent medium which are in turn stained for the need for enhancing their contrast and clarity. The final process is examining the samples under a Microscope. To a Doctor or an expert medical practioner, the results of Biopsy can reveal many important details like whether cancerous cells are present or not, if affirmative what kind of cancer, where is it originated and the level of growth and its aggressiveness (represented by a scale of one to four. One being the initial stage of low-grade cancer growth and four being advanced stage -grade 4 of cancer, very aggressive.) The specific treatment choices have to be followed depending on this critical information. The Biopsy results are available in few days. But in exceptional cases like during surgeries, the pathologist after proper examination of the samples, the result is released to the concerned surgeon in few minutes. Figure.7 and 8 show the variation of the decision-making parameters used in this proposed method. The detailed sequence of latest Liquid Biopsy process for cancer therapy (i) Primary stage or NGS (NGS-Next generation sequencing) (ii) flow cytometry (iii) Co-culturing stage (iv) isolation, pairing and sequencing (v) encoding of TCR (TCR-T-Cell receptor) (vi) re-infusion of modified T-Cells. Refer Figure. 5.

Architecture for Automatic Segmentation Algorithm

The proposed architecture for the High speed Unsupervised Real time Automatic/ Blind Segmentation Algorithm is shown in Figure. 9. Here, all the data bus lines comprise of data-bus with a width of 8-bits for pixel elements and 16-bit for others (Gonzalez et al., 2012; Ratnakumar et al., 2019; Ratnakumar & Nanda, 2019a; Ratnakumar & Nanda, 2019b).

The FSM dealing with this architecture comprise of a Moore machine with 15 stages, shown in Figure.11. The input to this system includes: data points, maximum number of data points 'N' and maximum number of iterations. Forgy initializer designed using Linear-feedback-shift-Register (LFSR) (Lin et al., 2007; Ratnakumar et al., 2019). Initially the histogram analyzer will accept the image data and calculates the possible number of centroids or clusters for the same image. The rest of the hardware comprises that of a reconfigurable clustering machine whose labelled output is displayed in a VDU, after proper formatting (Gudla et al., 2008).

Figure 9. Architecture for Automatic Segmentation (Lin et al., 2007)

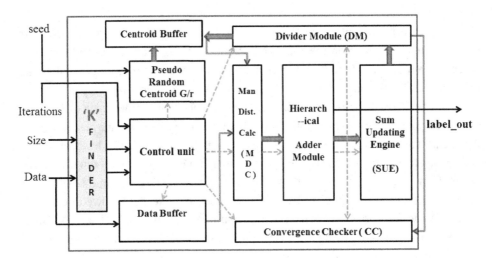

RESULTS AND DISCUSSIONS

The results of this simplified automatic segmentation technique, introduced for Biomedical/histopathological images (RGB images) of lung cancer cases (as shown in Table 1) in terms of its efficiency and speed are shown in the Table 2, plotted in the graphs, see figure.22. The overall histogram analysis of the individual biopsy images (as shown in the figures 14 to 21) and processing has been identified to ease the process of diagnosis as well as prognosis of Lung cancer using histopathological images. This method is applied on five standard Biopsy images procured from lung cancer patients taken from standard hospital database afflicted with cancer at different stages, given Fig. 6. It can be easily perceived that this technique neither requires user interaction nor any prior knowledge about the medical history to automatically segment the cells, cytoplasm, and other features within the histopathological image in a very less time (as shown in the figures 12, 14, 16, 18, 20). After that, all the segments are ready for recognition. Preliminary results in terms of PSNR, SSIM and their histogram analysis clearly reveal the usefulness of this technique in cytological evaluation. This technique can provide a faster, efficient and an economical alternative to the prevailing costlier tests and scans for medical diagnosis and prognosis. Refer Table.1 and Table.2.

Figure 10. Forgy Initializer using Linear feedback shift Register (LFSR) (Lin et al., 2007)

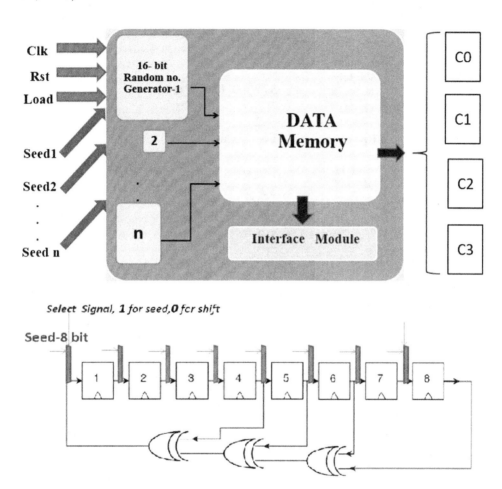

Case 1: Lung Biopsy

The Lung Biopsy of a patient taken from a Hospital database shows a peculiar condition where the WBC shown in blue color has aggregated themselves to form a cluster which represent exudative phase of diffuse alveolar damage (DAD). Refer Figure. 12. There is acute endothelial and mucosal damage with abundant edema fluid in the interstitium and alveolar lumens and abundant fibrin deposition. DAD is common among acute lung injury. Figure.15 reveals the histogram plot of the u-v matrix derived from the 'Luv' format- Lung Biopsy, histopathological image.

Figure 11. State Diagram for the architecture

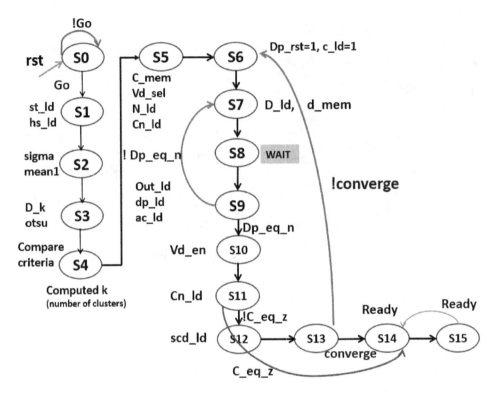

Figure 12. Image segmentation performed on a lung biopsy of patient. The input image is outlined in red color.

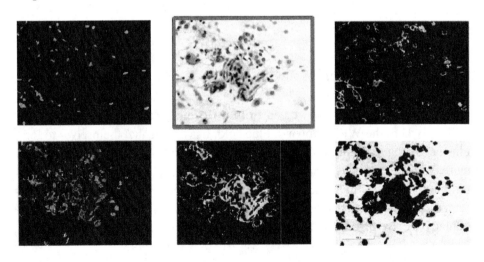

Figure 13. The Histogram plot of the u-v matrix derived from the 'Luv' format- Lung Biopsy, histopathological image

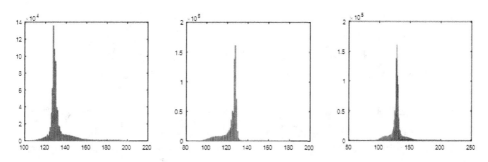

It is a cancer which originates within mucus secreting glands. Afterwards the same may spread to or develop in different parts of the human body.

Explanation of the Output

The automatic segmentation algorithm has successfully segmented all the individual chromatic zones. The first cluster comprises Red Blood Corpuscles (RBC) which is reddish in colour due to the presence of haemoglobin, the iron pigment in them. The second cluster collects all WBCs which are stained in violet colour. The other two clusters depict the proximities of RBCs and WBCs. The final cluster shows the carrying fluid part which characterized by acute endothelial and mucosal injury with resulting exudation of fluid and cells (so-called exudative phase) with varying amounts of haemorrhage and fibrin deposition, as given in Table.1.

Case 2: Sputum Biopsy

This Biopsy taken from a Cancer patient reveals the carcinogenic infection affected in the sputum secretion. Refer Figure. 14. Figure. 15 shows the Histogram plot of the u-v matrix derived from the 'Luv' format-Sputum Biopsy, histopathological image.

Explanation of the Output

The output reveals Non–small cell lung carcinoma, favor squamous cell carcinoma. This biopsy shows a solid nest of tumour cells with no clear glandular or squamous differentiation. Figure.15 captures the histogram plot of the u-v matrix derived from the 'Luv' format- Lung Biopsy-2, histopathological image. It is a histopathologic pattern that can be explained as an inflammation of the alveolar wall. This may in

Figure 14. Image segmentation performed on a Sputum biopsy of patient taken from a Hospital database. The input image is outlined in red color

turn lead to the disruption of the integrity of alveolar capillary membranes. It results in blood flooding the alveoli.

Case 3: Lung Biopsy-2

Explanation of the Output

Refer Figure. 16. Higher magnification of large cell carcinoma of the lung shows large tumor cells with pleomorphic nuclei containing prominent eosinophilic nucleoli. Diffuse alveolar damage is a histological pattern in lung disease. It is seen in acute respiratory distress syndrome transfusion related acute lung injury and acute interstitial pneumonia. The Histogram plot of the u-v matrix derived from the 'Luv' format- Lung Biopsy-2, histopathological image is given in Figure.17.

Figure 15. The Histogram plot of the u-v matrix derived from the 'Luv' format- Sputum Biopsy, histopathological image

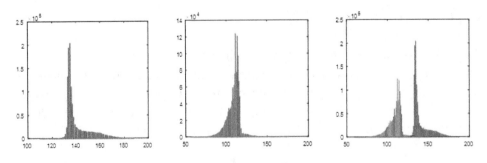

Figure 16. Image segmentation performed on a lung biopsy of patient taken from a Hospital database. The input image is outlined in red color.

Figure 17. The Histogram plot of the u-v matrix derived from the 'Luv' format- Lung Biopsy-2, histopathological image

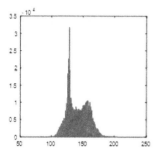 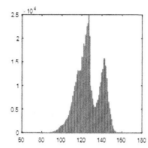 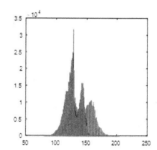

Case 4: Bronchial Biopsy

Normal test results mean that bronchial (lungs) are healthy and there are no problems with ones bronchial tubes or alveoli, which are air sacs. They also mean that one has clear secretions which

are free from any kinds of infection. The Histogram representation of u, v and combined dimensions of the Luv format of the bronchial Biopsy is shown in the figure.19.

Figure 18. Image segmentation performed on a bronchial biopsy of patient taken from a Hospital database. The input image is outlined in red color.

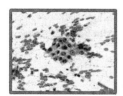  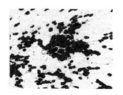 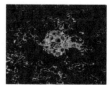

Figure 19. The Histogram plot of the u-v matrix derived from the 'Luv' format-Bronchial Biopsy, histopathological image.

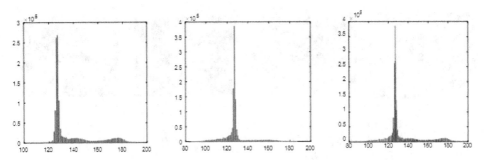

About the Biopsy Image

Pulmonary Capillaritis is characterized by acute neutrophilic infiltration that expands the alveolar septa. This is as a result of some infection which might have been initiated by viral or fungal attack. Figure.18 reveals the histogram plot of the u-v matrix derived from the 'Luv' format-Bronchial Biopsy, histopathological image.

Explanation of the Output

The automatic segmentation algorithm has successfully segmented all the individual chromatic zones. The first cluster comprises Red Blood Corpuscles (RBC) which is reddish in color due to the presence of haemoglobin, the iron pigment in them. The second cluster collects all WBCs which are stained in violet color. The other two clusters depict the proximities of RBCs and WBCs. The final cluster shows the carrying fluid part, see the figure 18. Large-cell carcinomas are a group of cancers with large cells that tend to start along the lungs' outer edges. They make up around 10 to15 percent of all lung cancers.

Case 5: Pleural Biopsy

Pleural Biopsy can diagnose many diseases constituting the visceral and the parietal pleura which may be of either malignant or inflammatory origin, mostly leading to pleural effusions. Generally, the diagnostic evaluation of pleural effusions includes chemical and microbiological studies, as well as cytological analysis, through which the etiological disease procedure is also revealed. Figure.21 shows the histogram plot of the u-v matrix derived from the 'Luv' format- Pleural Biopsy, histopathological image.

Figure 20. Image segmentation performed on a plural biopsy of patient taken from a Hospital database. The input image is outlined in red color.

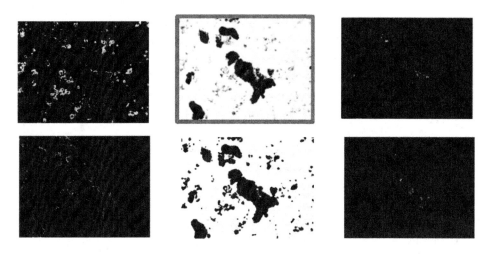

Explanation of the Output

The aggregation of RBC indicates Adenocarcinoma. The flat, cohesive sheet of uniform-appearing glandular cells has abundant clear cytoplasm filled with mucin and irregularly arranged nuclei in the "drunken honeycombing" pattern characteristic of invasive mucinous adenocarcinoma as shown in the figure 20. Lung cancer starts when cells of the lung become abnormal and begin to grow out of control. As more cancer cells develop, they can form into a tumor and spread to other areas of the body.

CONCLUSION

In this manuscript a simplified technique and its architecture for blind segmentation of histopathological images of lung cancer, combining the K-Means and Histogram analysis has been proposed. The architecture is input with Biopsy images of cancer patients suffering from Diffuse alveolar damage, non–small cell lung carcinoma, Large-cell carcinoma, Pulmonary Capillaritis, Adenocarcinoma procured from standard hospital databases like National Cancer Center, Japan to evaluate the performance of the architecture. Segmentation output in terms of quantitative parameters like PSNR, SSIM, time of execution as well as qualitative analysis clearly reveal the usefulness of this technique in high speed cytological evaluation. The proposed architecture gives promising results in terms of its performance with

Figure 21. The Histogram plot of the u-v matrix derived from the 'Luv' format-Pleural Biopsy, histopathological image.

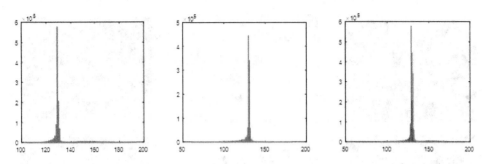

Table 1. Estimation of the PSNR, SSIM and statistical values for the biopsy cases.

Quantitative Features	Histopathological Images Procured From the Medical Database				
	Bronchial Biopsy	Sputum Biopsy	Lung_1 Biopsy	Plural Biopsy	Lung_2 Biopsy
Clusters (K)	3	6	5	5	3
PSNR	1.7179	2.2016	1.7107	1.0568	5.2917
SSIM	0.2061	0.3465	0.2637	0.2016	0.1970
Otsu_u	0.5804	0.5725	0.5608	0.5647	0.5569
Otsu_v	0.5490	0.4157	0.4627	0.4627	0.5098
D_k	0.0314	0.1569	0.0980	0.1020	0.0471

the time of execution of 192.25ms. Preliminary results clearly reveal the usefulness and simplicity of this architecture in quick cytological evaluation.

Table 2. Comparison of performance with other existing methods

Specification	Time of Execution Required for Segmentation					
Work	Hand-Gesture Identification technique (Agarwal et al., 2015)	Otsu & MoM Based (Wang et al., 2009)	Bounding-Box Based (Ratnakumar & Nanda, 2021b)	Roller-Dung beetle Algorithm (Ratnakumar & Nanda, 2021b)	Proposed Method-1	Proposed Method-2
Based on	Software	Software	Software	Hardware	Software	Hardware
Execution Time	377ms	539ms	377ms	171.31ms	320.66ms	192.25ms

Figure 22. Graph showing the comparison of execution time of the proposed method with other existing methods.

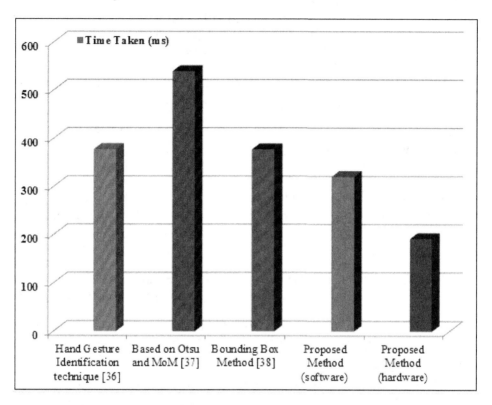

REFERENCES

Agarwal, R. K., Raman, B., & Mittal, A. (2015). Hand gesture recognition using discrete wavelet transform and support vector machine. *2nd International Conference on Signal Processing and Integrated Networks (SPIN)*. 10.1109/SPIN.2015.7095326

Ancin, H., Roysam, B., Dufresne, T. E., Chestnut, M. M., Ridder, G. M., Szarowski, D. H., & Turner, J. N. (1996, November 1). Advances in automated 3-D image analyses of cell populations imaged by confocal microscopy. *Cytometry, 25*(3), 221–234. doi:10.1002/(SICI)1097-0320(19961101)25:3<221::AID-CYTO3>3.0.CO;2-I PMID:8914819

Bartels, P.H., Bibbo, M., Graham, A., Paplanus, S., Shoemaker, R.L., & Thompson, D. (1989). Image understanding system for histopathology. *Analytical Cellular Pathology, 1*(4), 195-214.

Belien, J. A., Baak, J. P., van Diest, P. J., & van Ginkel, A. H. (1997, June 1). Counting mitoses by image processing in Feulgen stained breast cancer sections: The influence of resolution. *Cytometry*, *28*, 135–140. doi:10.1002/(SICI)1097-0320(19970601)28:2<135::AID-CYTO6>3.0.CO;2-E PMID:9181303

Bibbo, M., Kim, D. H., Pfeifer, T., Dytch, H. E., Galera-Davidson, H., & Bartels, P. H. (1991, February). Histometric features for the grading of prostatic carcinoma. *Analytical and Quantitative Cytology and Histology*, *13*, 61–68. PMID:2025375

Bilgin, C., Demir, C., Nagi, C., & Yener, B. (2007). Cell-graph mining for breast tissue modeling and classification. *Proc. 29th Annu. Int. Conf. IEEE Eng. Med. Biol. Soc. (EMBS 2007)*, 531–534. 10.1109/IEMBS.2007.4353540

Byun, J. Y., Verardo, M. R., Sumengen, B., Lewis, G. P., Manjunath, B. S., & Fisher, S. K. (2006, August 16). Automated tool for the detection of cell nuclei in digital microscopic images: Application to retinal images. *Molecular Vision*, *12*(105–107), 949–960. PMID:16943767

Cai, L., & Wang, J. (2019). Liquid biopsy for lung cancer immunotherapy (Review). *Oncology Letters*, *17*(6), 4751–4760. doi:10.3892/ol.2019.10166 PMID:31186680

Cillekens, M. J., Beliën, J. A. M., van der Valk, P., Faes, T. J. C., van Diest, P. J., Broeckaert, M. A. M., Kralendonk, J. H., & Kamphorst, W. (2000, January). A Histopathological Contribution to Supratentorial Glioma Grading, Definition of Mixed Gliomas and Recognition of Low Grade Glioma With Rosenthal Fibers. *Journal of Neuro-Oncology*, *46*(1), 23–43. doi:10.1023/A:1006496328729 PMID:10896203

De Solorzano, C. O., Malladi, R., Lelievre, S. A., & Lockett, S. J. (2001, March). Segmentation of nuclei and cells using membrane related protein markers. *J. Microsc. Oxford*, *201*(3), 404–415. doi:10.1046/j.1365-2818.2001.00854.x PMID:11240857

Fatakdawala, H., Xu, J., Basavanhally, A., Bhanot, G., Ganesan, S., Feldman, M., Tomaszewski, J. E., & Anant, M. (2010, July). (EMaGACOR): Application to Lymphocyte Segmentation on Breast Cancer Histopathology. *IEEE Transactions on Biomedical Engineering*, *57*(7), 1676–1689. doi:10.1109/TBME.2010.2041232 PMID:20172780

Gonzalez, C., Resano, J., Plaza, A., & Mozos, D. (2012). FPGA implementation of abundance estimation for spectral unmixing of hyperspectral data using the image space reconstruction algorithm. *IEEE Journal of Selected Topics in Applied Earth Observations and Remote Sensing*, *5*(1), 248–261. doi:10.1109/JSTARS.2011.2171673

Gudla, P. R., Nandy, K., Collins, J., Meaburn, K. J., Misteli, T., & Lockett, S. J. (2008, May). A high-throughput system for segmenting nuclei using multiscale techniques. *Cytometry. Part A*, *73*(5), 451–466. doi:10.1002/cyto.a.20550 PMID:18338778

Hassija, V., Ratnakumar, R., Chamola, V., Agarwal, S., Mehra, A., Kanhere, S. S., & Binh, H. T. T. (2022). A machine learning and blockchain based secure and cost-effective framework for minor medical consultations. *Sustainable Computing: Informatics and Systems*, *35*, 100651. doi:10.1016/j.suscom.2021.100651

Hedberg, H., Kristensen, F., & Öwall, V. (2007). Implementation of a Labeling Algorithm based on Contour Tracing with Feature Extraction. *IEEE International Symposium on Circuits and Systems*. 10.1109/ISCAS.2007.378202

Hore, A., & Ziou, D. (2010) Image quality metrics: PSNR vs. SSIM. In *Pattern Recognition (ICPR), 20th International Conference on* (pp. 2366-2369). IEEE.

Kim, Y. J., Romeike, B. F., Uszkoreit, J., & Feiden, W. (2006, March-April). Automated nuclear segmentation in the determination of the Ki-67 labeling index in meningiomas. *Clinical Neuropathology*, *25*, 67–73. PMID:16550739

Li, G., Liu, T. M., Nie, J. X., Guo, L., Malicki, J., Mara, A., Holley, S. A., Xia, W. M., & Wong, S. T. C. (2007, October). Detection of blob objects in microscopic zebrafish images based on gradient vector diffusion. *Cytometry. Part A*, *71A*(10), 835–845. doi:10.1002/cyto.a.20436 PMID:17654652

Lin, G., Chawla, M. K., Olson, K., Barnes, C. A., Guzowski, J. F., Bjornsson, C., Shain, W., & Roysam, B. (2007, September). A multi-model approach to simultaneous segmentation and classification of heterogeneous populations of cell nuclei in 3D confocal microscope images. *Cytometry. Part A*, *71*(9), 724–736. doi:10.1002/cyto.a.20430 PMID:17654650

Markiewicz, T., Osowski, S., Patera, J., & Kozlowski, W. (2006, October). Image processing for accurate cell recognition and count on histologic slides. *Analytical and Quantitative Cytology and Histology*, *28*, 281–291. PMID:17067010

Ortiz de Solorzano, C., Garcia Rodriguez, E., Jones, A., Pinkel, D., Gray, J. W., Sudar, D., & Lockett, S. J. (1999, March). Segmentation of confocal microscope images of cell nuclei in thick tissue sections. *Journal of Microscopy*, *193*(3), 212–226. doi:10.1046/j.1365-2818.1999.00463.x PMID:10199001

Ratnakumar, R., Chaitanya, P. V., & Gurunarayanan, S. (2019, November). An Energy Efficient Multilevel Reconfigurable parallel Cache Architecture for Embedded Multicore Processors. In *2019 International Conference on Electrical, Electronics and Computer Engineering (UPCON)* (pp. 1-6). IEEE. 10.1109/UPCON47278.2019.8980197

Ratnakumar, R., & Nanda, S. J. (2016, May). A FSM based approach for efficient implementation of K-means algorithm. In *2016 20th International Symposium on VLSI Design and Test (VDAT)* (pp. 1-6). IEEE.

Ratnakumar, R., & Nanda, S. J. (2019a). A low complexity hardware architecture of K-means algorithm for real-time satellite image segmentation. *Multimedia Tools and Applications*, *78*(9), 11949–11981. doi:10.100711042-018-6726-6

Ratnakumar, R., & Nanda, S. J. (2019b). A hardware architecture based on genetic clustering for color image segmentation. In *Soft Computing for Problem Solving* (pp. 863–876). Springer. doi:10.1007/978-981-13-1592-3_69

Ratnakumar, R., & Nanda, S. J. (2021a, January). An improved genetic clustering architecture for real-time satellite image segmentation. In *2021 International Conference on Advances in Technology, Management & Education (ICATME)* (pp. 123-128). IEEE. 10.1109/ICATME50232.2021.9732768

Ratnakumar, R., & Nanda, S. J. (2021b). A high speed roller dung beetles clustering algorithm and its architecture for real-time image segmentation. *Applied Intelligence*, *51*(7), 4682–4713. doi:10.100710489-020-02067-7

Rupanagudi, S. R., Ranjani, B., Bhat, V. G., Surabhi, K., & Reshma, P. (2015). A high speed algorithm for identifying hand gestures for an ATM input system for the blind. *IEEE Bombay Section Symposium (IBSS)*. 10.1109/IBSS.2015.7456642

Sont, J. K., De Boer, W. I., van Schadewijk, W. A., Grunberg, K., van Krieken, J. H., Hiemstra, P. S., & Sterk, P. J. (2003, June 1). Fully automated assessment of inflammatory cell counts and cytokine expression in bronchial tissue. *American Journal of Respiratory and Critical Care Medicine*, *167*(11), 1496–1503. doi:10.1164/rccm.2205003 PMID:12770855

Wang, J., Yang, C., Min, Z., & Wang, C. (2009). Implementation of Otsu's thresholding process based on FPGA. *2009 4th IEEE Conference on Industrial Electronics and Applications*, 479-483.

Wang, Z., Bovik, A. C., Sheikh, H. R., & Simoncelli, E. P. (2004). Image quality assessment: From error visibility to structural similarity. *IEEE Transactions on Image Processing*, *13*(4), 600–612. doi:10.1109/TIP.2003.819861 PMID:15376593

Yadav, S., Mehra, A., Rohmetra, H., Ratnakumar, R., & Narang, P. (2021). DerainGAN: Single image deraining using wasserstein GAN. *Multimedia Tools and Applications, 80*(30), 36491–36507. doi:10.100711042-021-11442-6

Yang, L., Meer, P., & Foran, D. J. (2005, September). Unsupervised Segmentation Based on Robust Estimation and Color Active Contour Models. *IEEE Transactions on Information Technology in Biomedicine, 9*(3), 475–486. doi:10.1109/TITB.2005.847515 PMID:16167702

Chapter 2
Covid Live Multi–Threaded Live COVID 19 Data Scraper

Parth Birthare
Vellore Institute of Technology, India

Maheswari Raja
Vellore Institute of Technology, India

Ganesan Ramachandran
Vellore Institute of Technology, India

Carol Hargreaves
ⓘ https://orcid.org/0000-0002-5522-4058
National University of Singapore, Singapore

Shreya Birthare
Vellore Institute of Technology, India, India

ABSTRACT

COVID-19 began in 2019, and by the advent of 2020, it had become widespread and adversely affected the world. In this work—Covid Live, COVID-19 data is scraped from an online website, which gives an overview of the status of the pandemic in the desired format. The authors built an application interface using a Python micro web Flask framework. The data scraping uses a multi-threading concept to reduce the program's runtime error, resulting in receiving the data quickly, and faster than existing web crawlers and scrapers. This paper focuses on dealing with storing scraped data in the desired format. It also provides options to hear the audio of the scraped data and to download the scraped data. The authors present visualizations of current trends with scraping period details and demonstrate an efficient application that does the data scraping quickly and efficiently.

DOI: 10.4018/978-1-6684-6523-3.ch002

INTRODUCTION

The COVID-19 pandemic has infected many people (Yang et al., 2020). Furthermore, in attempts to slow down the spread of the novel virus, nations imposed complete and partial lockdowns hoping to prevent further spread of the virus (Atalan, 2020). Many lives have been affected by the pandemic. Scientists and researchers are constantly analyzing the impact and devising methods to purge the spread of the virus further and predict possible variants. Therefore, positive case patterns, environmental and biological factors, and policies are crucial for COVID-19 research (Sha et al., 2021). Therefore, there should be a database for maintaining records or spatiotemporal COVID-19 records that countries publish from virus testing after the advent of 2020. As per the public data, most data come from a few international agencies, such as WHO, GHC, or CDC. The subcommittees within the organization make the data public after collecting information and producing the dataset (COVID Data Tracker, 2021).

Also, it seems that data is the new differentiation. It is the focus of market research and business strategy. Whether one has to start a new work or shake out a new strategy for an existing business, one needs to access and analyze a large amount of data for better results. Web scraping plays a role in easing up the process, and in the present scenario, large institutions are also collaborating to provide facilities to track COVID-19 in real-time. For example, Johns Hopkins University developed a COVID-19 dashboard that is regularly updated by extracting data from around eight non-government sources and publicly providing it as a single dataset (Dong, Du, & Gardner, 2020). 1Point3Acres provides a similar service, which aims to be transparent to the public about COVID-19 cases (1point3acres Global COVID-19 Tracker & Interactive Charts, 2021).

Web scraping is the process of mining data, usually unstructured data from any number of sources, efficiently and faster and storing it as structured data for further analysis (Sirisuriya, 2015). It is effortless because it does not involve visiting the web pages to copy-paste the extensive data. Data extraction can be done from any website, anywhere, no matter how large and complex the data is. Moreover, some websites may have the type of data that cannot be copied and pasted directly. For example, it can be in the form of CSV, image, or text. Web scraping can be copying, grabbing, pasting text, or parsing HTML (Sirisuriya, 2015). Further, many tools and methods are available for web scraping (Persson, Evaluating tools and techniques for web scraping, 2019; Saurkar, Pathare, & Gode, 2018). Not only in python but also in other programming languages (Easily harvest (scrape) web pages, n.d.).

Web data stored in text or CSV format is for further analysis and operations. Web scraping shortens the process of extracting data, as it is equivalent to a human interacting with the web page. It increases the interaction simulation speed by automating the process and creates easy access to the scraped data by providing it in any format (Vargiu & Urru, 2013; Breton et al., 2015; Salerno & Boulware, 2006). Web scraping is an essential process, especially when dealing with a large quantity of data, as it leads to the quick and efficient extraction of relevant information from different sources. Covid Live does the same but with some additional features. The subcommittees within the organization make the data public after collecting information and producing the dataset (COVID Data Tracker, 2021).

Also, it seems that data is the new differentiation. It is the focus of market research and business strategy. Whether one has to start a new work or shake out a new strategy for an existing business, one needs to access and analyze a large amount of data for better results. Web scraping plays a role in easing up the process, and in the present scenario, large institutions are also collaborating to provide facilities to track COVID-19 in real-time.

There are many examples of web scraping, like one where Weng and equals use web scraping to predict price fluctuation with ARIMA and RNN models (Weng et al., 2019). Also, Pawar and his equals tried to find medicinal plants and diseases in Ayurvedic System in India using web scraping (Pawar, Rajeswari, & Joshi, 2016). In the same way, Pollett and equals used web scraping methodologies to detect waves from vector-borne illnesses (Pollett, Althouse, Forshey, Rutherford, & Jarman, 2017). Using web scraping, Jang and their team made a system to control hazards related to food in Korea (Ihm et al., 2017). Similarly, Walid and their fellow mates scraped Twitter data for a long time (Shaiket, Anisuzzaman, & Saif, 2019). McGinnis and others used a similar situation in 2015 to forecast the eruption of the Zika virus (Majumder et al., 2016).

All such instances and insights gained from them are of great use for applying similar concepts to works related to the COVID-19 pandemic. For instance, Chen and their team analyzed the satisfaction level and quality of online education during the pandemic to see how much the pandemic affected the lives and minds of people (Chen et al., 2020). Also, Pham and their team gathered news data about COVID-19 in Vietnam to analyze the response from social media, science journalism, and policy for public health system sustainability during the pandemic (La et al., 2020). Similarly, Shen and their mates from China performed a quantitative analysis of public attitude, reaction, and response during the advent of the COVID-19 pandemic (Xu et al., 2020).

Covid Live is based on the same grounds as these works and scrapes data from web pages. However, scraping data also poses some privacy risks and threats. It includes a risk of the scraping algorithm extracting personal and sensitive information from web pages and publishing it to openly accessible databases (Angwin & Stecklow, 2010; Rennie et al., 2020). For example, the medical record of people.

In Covid Live, data from a website that contained the numerical data of the cases was available while preserving the data privacy regulations. Regarding the format that various websites store data, some store in XML, and some store as HTML pages. Consequently, scraping from structured and unstructured data and developing a universal scraper is a bit complex. In Brazil, COVID-19 cases were stored in XLSX format (COVID-19, 2021). Performing processing and other operations on the data require further conversion to a different format.

In Covid Live, data is scraped from specific tags of the HTML pages from different URLs directly instead of accessing it from a database. Moreover, an option for storing the data in text, CSV, and MP3 format was available. There are a variety of possibilities and features while scraping in python (Mitchell, 2018; Jarmul & Lawson, 2017). Furthermore, the multi-threading concept was applied to scrape live COVID-19 data for different countries and was stored in a text or CSV file for further processing. Multi-threading increases the speed of scraping by scraping multiple data simultaneously, which is valuable for extensive data. In Covid Live, since COVID-19 data of global countries can be scraped, it involves extracting plenty of data that may even make the application slower.

So, multi-threading plays a significant role in Covid Live, thus giving a better version of it. The time module calculated the time used for multi-threading. Multi-threading is very efficient as it enables scraping data in parallel for faster execution which is the main objective of the scraper.

In the scraping of data, the request module enables to sending of HTTP requests, and the HTTP requests will return a response object with all the response data. Then the beautifulsoup4 module is used to obtain the HTML data from HTML and XML files and extract relevant data (Richardson, 2018). Thus, obtaining the desired data from a specific HTML tag. There are four different features implemented in Covid Live.

The provision of a download option was the first feature so that users could do anything with the scraped file, such as sharing, tweeting, or posting it somewhere or on any other social media. More functionalities like sharing the output had to be added to the user module to differentiate Covid Live from the other web scraping tools. Sharing functionalities will be more valuable for those who want to share a live update of COVID-19 cases and make people more aware via any social media platform.

The second feature is storing the scraped data. If data is not stored, then it will have to be collected again for an indefinite amount of time. The stored data is in either a text or CSV file. The file is retrieved in the desired format by clicking a button. Specifically, structured data in the CSV format is preferred as it is easy to maintain and track. Also, there are many packages in different languages and software to deal with them.

As far as the third feature is concerned, apart from the file storage, a text-to-speech feature is also included, facilitating the users more and leading to a better user experience. To implement this feature, a python library, gTTS - Google Text-to-Speech is used. The gTTS library helps convert text into speech and is used to interact with the user by providing the scraped data as voice output.

Finally, feature four deals with the data analysis to highlight the countries that are more vulnerable according to the cases and deaths and the ones which are performing much better in terms of recovery rate. A representation of the same, using bar plots and pie charts, gives a more detailed view and is more straightforward to interpret.

With Covid Live, the user can choose any of the three features or all three features together and get the final desired end output. Moreover, being a progressive web application, Covid Live runs as a web application that can be installed on any device irrespective of the Operating System and run natively.

BACKGROUND STUDY

COVID-19 – Data Set Report for Analysis

This work analyzes the research activities concerning COVID-19 and performs the scraping of information. It shows data wrangling for performing python web scraping and pre-processing using pandas. The analysis does not contain any case information or other reports of the effect of COVID-19. Furthermore, the research contains static data and not real-time data (Santos et al., 2020).

Sentiment Analysis – Social Life Impact of Coronavirus

Mrityunjay Singh and Amit performed sentiment analysis on the impact of the coronavirus but did not include the scraping of any data. They used a pre-processed dataset for sentiment analysis (Singh, Jakhar, & Pandey, 2021).

Applications of Web Scrapping

This research paper gives various insights on the various applications of web scraping, its pros and cons, and the means of web scraping syntactic, semantic, and computer view. It also discusses the various avenues where web scraping can be applied (Singrodia, Mitra, & Paul, 2019).

There are many scraping works for all kinds of data. Also, there are related works for scraping live COVID-19 data. Covid Live outperforms other related works with more features' implementation for the best user experience, and also, the scalable nature opens the scope for future enhancements. Most related works lack in providing the data faster. This drawback is overcome by using multi-threading for scraping the data but still does not provide additional features for providing the data in different formats and other functionalities for the user to explore. One of the existing works is the automatic retrieval of COVID-19 data from the web. Building a web page and collecting data from six websites is displayed on a web page with no other functionalities. Still, storing the scraped data is done in the PostgreSQL database. Thus, from knowing the related works, Covid Live is improved and improvised to get it to the hands of people everywhere.

FUNCTIONAL WORKFLOW AND IMPLEMENTATION

Covid Live provides live COVID-19 data of several countries by scraping the relevant data from https://www.worldometers.info/coronavirus/. This website was selected due to its genuine content and active data checks. One of the options is scraping preferred countries' data. This option lets the user choose the countries. The user can choose any country, and only the data from the selected countries are scraped. Multi-threading plays a significant role in scraping data. It fastens up the process many times.

At the initial comparative analysis of run time for execution with multi-threaded scraping and without multi-threaded scraping, multi-threaded scraping turned out to be more efficient and faster than without multi-threaded scraping. For scraping, the program sends an HTTP request to the URL and then starts to scrape the data from the particular page. Once the scraping process is complete, we need to get the desired data from the entire content. At first, junk data is scraped from the HTML code. Next, Beautiful Soup is used to filter the HTML code from the junk code. After getting the pure HTML code, searching for the desired tag is done. In his case, the content needed is present in specific div tags. So, only the data of the div tag is filtered out from the whole HTML code. However, the catch is that there are multiple tags with the same class, so the *find_all* method is used to get all the values and iterate them over. Next, data is stored in a text file and a CSV file on the server-side.

One additional feature is, listening to the audio of the generated file and downloading the corresponding audio file. The other feature is downloading the scraped file for further sharing of data or reference, according to the user's needs. The audio feature is a text-to-speech implementation where the bot will convert the scraped data into audio data so that the user can listen. The easy-to-use interface provides an option to download the audio file as well. It was implemented using a python library called gTTS, a text-to-speech conversion library available in Python. Next, the download feature provides a download

Figure 1. Web application workflow and implementation of Covid Live

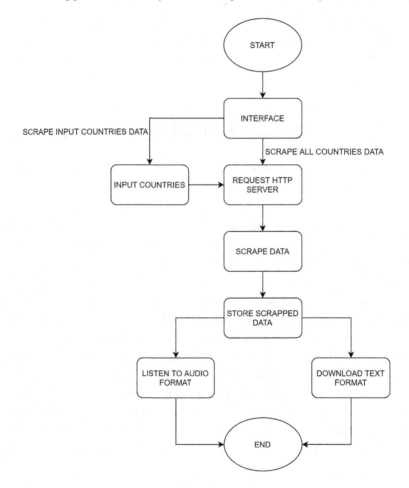

option for the scraped file so that users may either save it for reference or perform research and analysis on it. Users may also send the downloaded file to anyone or publicly post it on any social media platform according to their choice and convenience. The next option is scraping all countries' COVID-19 data. Covid Live works similarly to scraping preferred countries' data but scrapes all the data at once.

The entire implementation of Covid Live as a web application can be represented by a workflow diagram as in Figure 1.

It starts initially from the application interface and the choice of two options, the scraping of preferred country data or all country data. Next is the implementation of features takes place. The mobile application implementation of Covid Live depicted in Figure 2 starts with the user interface, allowing the

Figure 2. Mobile application workflow and implementation of Covid Live

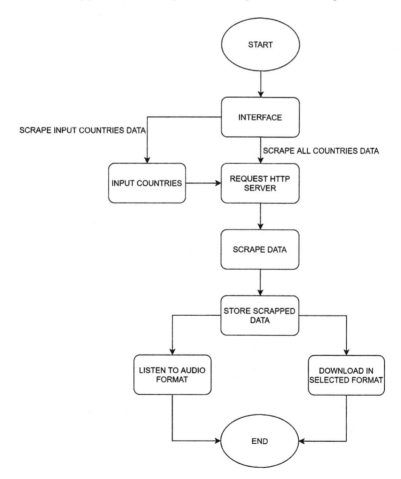

user to interact with the features provided. Here, storing scraped data in the file is different because an additional functionality to choose different formats of files like pdf and excel is added. Next, data will be stored on the server-side once scraping has finished.

CORE COMPONENTS

Several modules are in Covid Live for performing the desired functionalities, namely, Flask, requests, Beautiful Soup, thread, and gTTS.

Flask

Flask is a micro web framework python module that eases the development of web applications. It enables many features like page routing and rendering output from a template-based file using the *render_template* function and the templating engine, Jinja2. It also supports the use of request objects and response function.

Requests

The request module sends HTTP requests to the URL. The website's URL is the input and the request module will get the data that the user is requesting. Figure 3 shows an HTTP request for client-server interaction.

Figure 3. HTTP request for client-server interaction

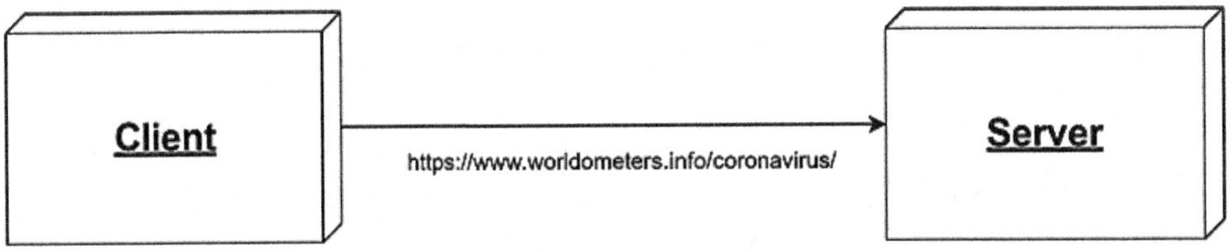

The URL is provided as input to the server from the client as a request. Data is scraped if the server returns true without any exception error. However, suppose the server acknowledges a false case when the user provides an invalid input, that is, where an invalid country name or a spelling error occurs. Data cannot be scraped from the request URL, and an error message is displayed.

Beautiful Soup

Beautiful Soup is a python library for pulling out data from HTML and XML files. It works with the parser to provide some idiomatic ways for navigating or traversing, searching, and modifying/editing the parse tree. It saves time and is a very programmer-friendly library used for scraping data. It extracts the data in a proper hierarchical manner, on which it is easy to perform further operations. Beautiful Soup presents the data in a better format and more readable manner, as can be seen in Figure 4.

Figure 4. Beautiful Soup provides an idiomatic way of performing operations.

Thread

The *Thread* is the main module of the entire application. This module helps users create, control, and manage threads in python and increases the overall speed. Covid Live uses this module for scraping the data from the specified URL according to the input provided. Multi-threading, which uses multiple threads within the same process as depicted in Figure 5, helps us scrape multiple country data simultaneously to give the user a very efficient and faster application speed for scraping the data.

Figure 5. Multiple threads enable faster process execution.

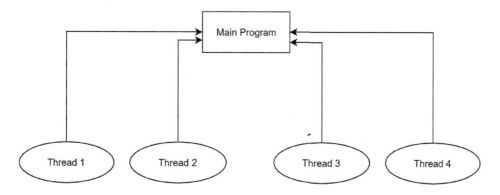

gTTS

It is a python module and CLI tool that interfaces with Google Translate text-to-speech API. It converts the text into a speech format and then generates the audio out of the data.

Interface

The Home Screen of Covid Live

The home screen of Covid Live provides a brief description of the scraper as a whole and its functionalities, as shown in Figure 6.

Figure 6. Web interface for the home screen of Covid Live

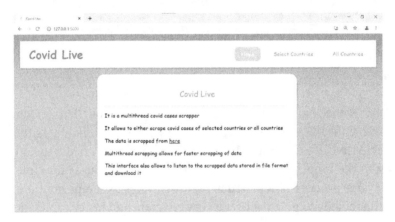

Preferred Countries' COVID-19 Data

Here, the data of only preferred countries is scraped. As the user preferred only the five countries, US, India, Singapore, Turkey, and Brazil, the application will only be scraping the data for these five countries.

Multi-threading helps to scrape the data faster. The output is seen on the output page once the data is scraped. The time taken to complete the scraping process is displayed on the output page. Next, there is an option for hearing the audio and downloading the file. Figure 7 depicts a screenshot of the application.

Once the scrape button is clicked, the output page is displayed, which shows the number of cases, deaths, and recovered cases in the respective countries,

Figure 7. Web interface for selected countries' input page.

Figure 8. Web interface for selected countries' output page.

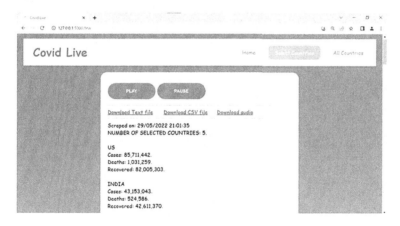

Figure 9. Web interface for selected countries' output page.

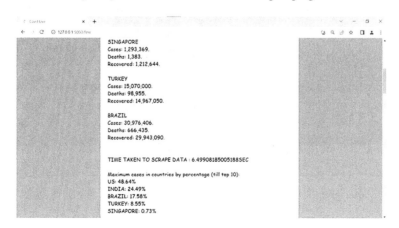

Figure 10. Countries with maximum cases – bar chart.

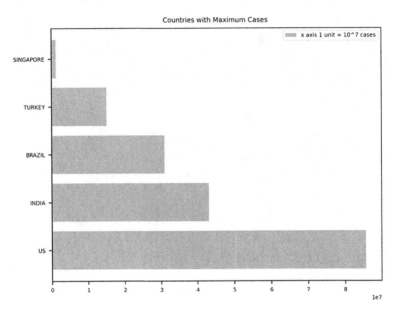

Figure 11. Countries with maximum cases – pie chart.

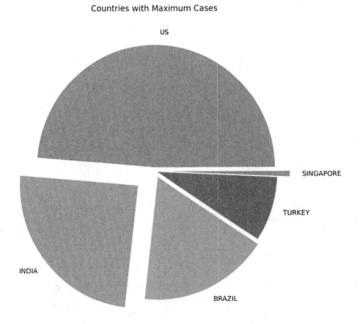

Figure 12. Countries with maximum deaths – bar graph.

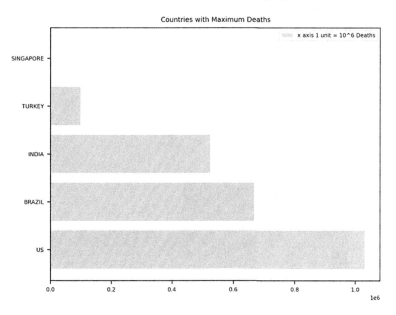

Figure 13. Countries with minimum deaths – pie chart.

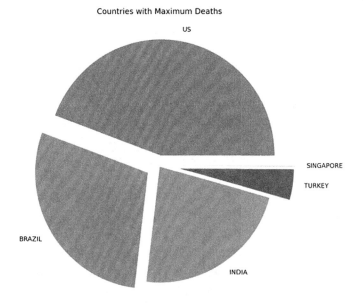

Figure 14. Countries with maximum recovered – bar graph.

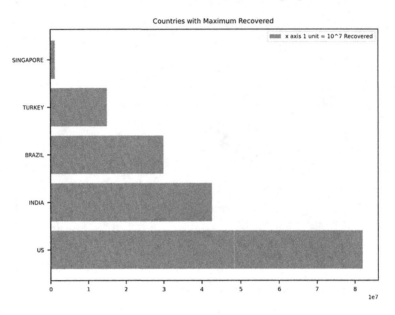

Figure 15. Countries with maximum recovered – pie chart.

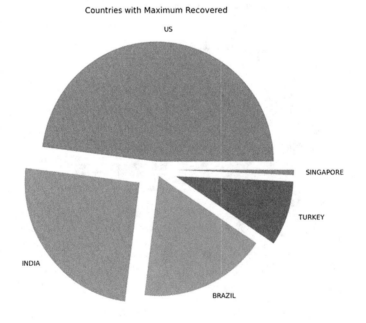

along with the time of scraping, percentage of cases for the maximum number of cases in respective countries along with the time required to scrape the data.

We represent the number of Covid cases, deaths, and recovered cases in bar plots and pie charts. Figure 8, Figure 9, Figure 10, Figure 11, Figure 12, Figure 13, Figure 14, and Figure 15 show the output page after the scraping process and the graphs generated on the output page.

The output text file holds the COVID-19 details for selected countries and can be downloaded using the Downloaded file button. This is the file in which the scraped data is stored in the backend.

All Countries' COVID-19 Data

Scraping COVID-19 data for all countries is similar to the previous implementation. Data is scraped for all the countries and will take a longer time than the previous implementation but is still faster since it is scraping all the countries' COVID-19 data, which is relatively extensive. This page involves only a Scrape button which triggers the scraping process once clicked, as shown in Figure 16.

Figure 16. Web interface for all countries input page.

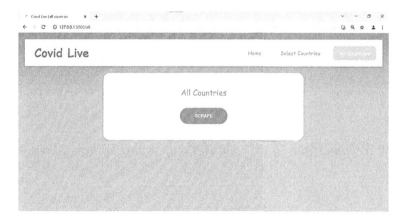

The scraped data is displayed on the output page with options to listen to the audio or download the audio and the scraped data. Figure 17, Figure 18, Figure 19, Figure 20, Figure 21, Figure 22, Figure 23, Figure 24, Figure 25, Figure 26, Figure 27 and Figure 28 display the number of Covid cases, deaths, and recovered cases in bar graphs and pie charts.

Figure 17. Web interface for all countries output page of Covid Live

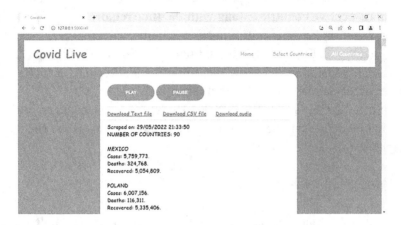

Figure 18. Web interface for all countries output page of Covid Live

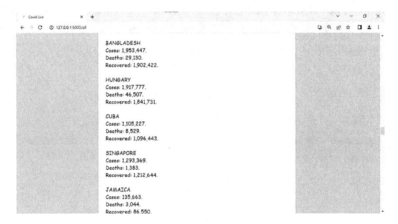

Figure 19. Web interface for all countries output page of Covid Live

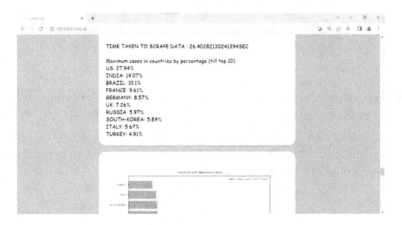

Figure 20. Countries with maximum cases – bar graph

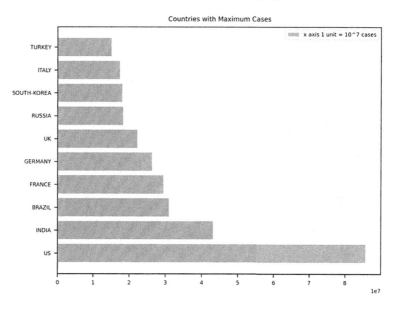

Figure 21. Countries with maximum cases – pie chart

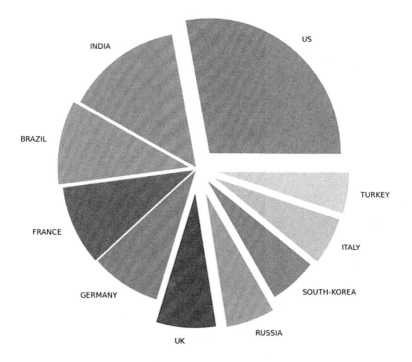

Figure 22. Countries with minimum cases – bar graph

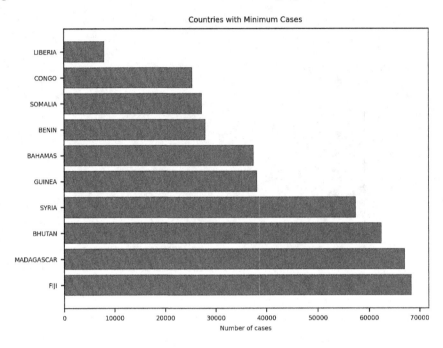

Figure 23. Countries with maximum deaths – bar graph

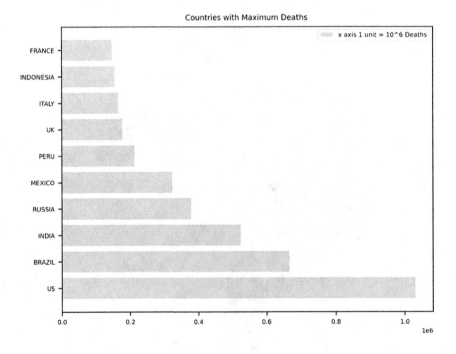

Figure 24. Countries with maximum deaths – pie chart

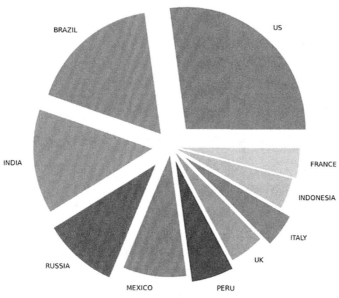

Figure 25. Countries with minimum deaths – bar graph

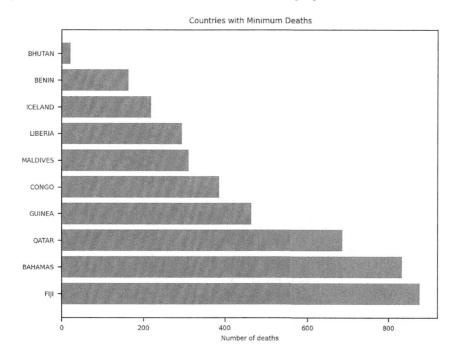

Figure 26. Countries with maximum recovered – bar graph

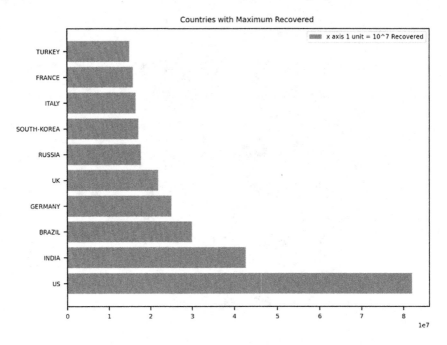

Figure 27. Countries with maximum recovered – pie chart

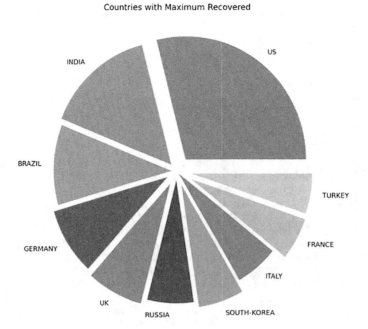

Figure 28. Countries with minimum recovered – bar graph

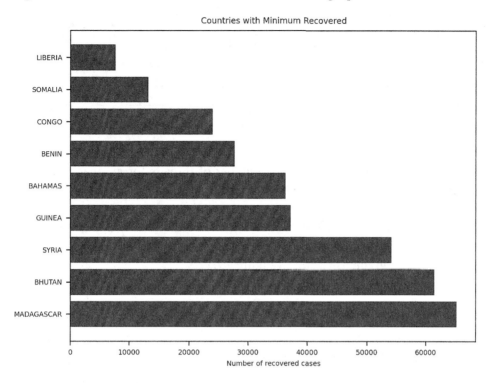

Use the Download file option to include a text file with additional information for all countries with data scraped. The text file contains the total number of Covid cases, deaths and recovered cases along with top ten percentage of cases.

The statistics that informs about the countries with highest cases, deaths and recovered people, and the countries with lowest cases can be interpreted from these graphs.

EVALUATIONS AND INFERENCES

Varying the number of threads for the program also varies the time take to scrape the data. Table 1 shows the performance of the scraper against the time taken for different number of threads.

Table 1. Number of threads vs time taken to scrape

Number of Threads Used	Time Taken to Scrape All Countries' Data in Seconds
4	28.25
8	26.40
12	27.34
16	30.12

It is observed that increasing the number of threads for an operation does not always decrease the execution time of the program. While increasing the threads, a point of maximum speed, or reduced time taken is obtained. Beyond this point, increasing the number of threads will lead to reducing the efficieny of the application by taking more time. The same pattern can also be observed in the form of a graph as shown in Figure 29.

Figure 29. Number of threads vs execution time for scraper

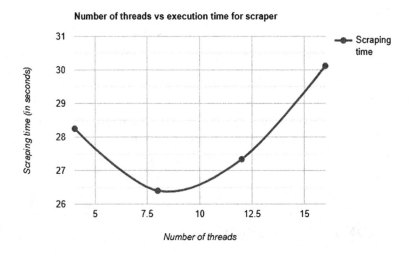

FUTURE RESEARCH DIRECTIONS

In the future, we will increase the number of functionalities. We will allow users to share with friends on all platforms and applications like Facebook and Twitter. More features, such as user location and alert notifications if the number of Covid cases has increased in the user country. Another plan is to include the automatic deletion of temporary files in the backend after a fixed time and save storage space. Also, make the app mobile responsive and enhanced by including push notifications and alarm alerts to make it more interactive and provide an engaging experience. Figure 30 and Figure 31 show the mobile responsive form of Covid Live.

Figure 30. Mobile responsive – selecting all countries

Figure 31. Mobile responsive – selecting all countries

CONCLUSION

Covid Live helps to provide relevant COVID-19-related information for many countries and additional features for performing more operations on the data. Scraping live COVID-19 data using the defined modules and implementing additional functionalities as text-to-speech and download options for further sharing or reference with the graphical analysis on it opens up the scope for this work in the technology-related field. Covid Live used multi-threading as a core feature. Multi-threading fastens up the run time of scraping data for preferred countries and all countries. After scraping, listening to audio and download features were implemented using the related modules and finally graphically displayed and interpreted for better inference.

FUNDING

This research received no specific grant from any funding agency in the public, commercial, or not-for-profit sectors.

REFERENCES

1Point3Acres. (2021). *Global COVID-19 Tracker & Interactive Charts.* 1Point3Acres. https://coronavirus.1point3acres.com/

Angwin, J., & Stecklow, S. (2010). 'Scrapers' dig deep for data on Web. *The Wall Street Journal.* https://www.wsj.com/articles/SB10001424052748703358504575544381288117888

Atalan, A. (2020). Is the lockdown important to prevent the COVID-19 pandemic? Effects on psychology, environment and economy-perspective. *Annals of Medicine and Surgery (London)*, *56*, 38–42. doi:10.1016/j.amsu.2020.06.010

Breton, R., Clews, G., Metcalfe, L., Milliken, N., Payne, C., Winton, J., & Woods, A. (2015). *Research indices using web scraped data.* Office for National Statistics.

CDC. (2021). *COVID Data Tracker.* CDC. https://covid.cdc.gov/COVID-data-tracker

Chen, T., Peng, L., Yin, X., Rong, J., Yang, J., & Cong, G. (2020). Analysis of user satisfaction with online education platforms in China during the COVID-19 pandemic. *Health Care.* doi:10 doi:.3390/healthcare8030200

Dong, E., Du, H., & Gardner, L. (2020). An interactive web-based dashboard to track COVID-19 in real time. *The Lancet Infectious Diseases*, *20*, 533–534. doi:10.1016/S1473-3099(20)30120-1

Ihm, H., Jang, K., Lee, K., Jang, G., Seo, M.-G., Han, K., & Myaeng, S.-H. (2017). Multi-source food hazard event extraction for public health. *2017 IEEE International Conference on Big Data and Smart Computing (BigComp)*, (pp. 414-417). doi:10.1109/BIGCOMP.2017.7881747

Jarmul, K., & Lawson, R. (2017). *Python Web Scraping* (2nd ed.). Packt Publishing.

La, V.-P., Pham, T.-H., Ho, M.-T., Nguyen, M.-H., Nguyen, K.-L. P., Vuong, T.-T., & Vuong, Q.-H. (2020). Policy response social media and science journalism for the sustainability of the public health system amid the COVID-19 outbreak: The Vietnam lessons. *Sustainability*, *12*. doi:10.3390u12072931

Majumder, M. S., Santillana, M., Mekaru, S. R., McGinnis, D. P., Khan, K., & Brownstein, J. S. (2016). Utilizing nontraditional data sources for near real-time estimation of transmission dynamics during the 2015–2016 Colombian Zika virus disease outbreak. *JMIR Public Health and Surveillance, 2.* doi:10.2196/publichealth.5814

Mitchell, R. (2018). *Web Scraping with Python* (2nd ed.). O'Reilly Media, Inc.

Pawar, N., Rajeswari, K., & Joshi, A. (2016). Implementation of an efficient Web crawler to search medicinal plants and relevant diseases. *International Conference on Computing Communication Control and automation (ICCUBEA),* (pp. 1-4). doi:10.1109/ICCUBEA.2016.7860006

Persson, E. (2019). *Evaluating tools and techniques for web scraping.* [M.S. Thesis, Kth Royal Institute Of Technology, Sweden].

Pollett, S., Althouse, B. M., Forshey, B., Rutherford, G. W., & Jarman, R. G. (2017). Internet-based biosurveillance methods for vector-borne diseases: Are they novel public health tools or just novelties? *PLoS Neglected Tropical Diseases, 11.* doi:10.1371/journal.pntd.0005871

Rennie, S., Buchbinder, M., Juengst, E., Brinkley-Rubinstein, L., Blue, C., & Rosen, D. L. (2020). Scraping the Web for public health gains: Ethical considerations from a 'big data' research project on HIV and incarceration. *Public Health Ethics, 13,* 111–121. doi:10.1093/phe/phaa006

Richardson, L. (2018). Beautiful Soup Documentation. *Crummy.* https://www.crummy.com/software/BeautifulSoup/bs4/doc/

RVest. (n.d.). *Easily harvest (scrape) web pages.* Tidyverse. https://rvest.tidyverse.org

Santos, B. S., Silva, I., Ribeiro-Dantas, M. d., Alves, G., Endo, P. T., & Lima, L. (2020). COVID-19: A scholarly production dataset report for research analysis. *Data in Brief, 32.* doi:10.1016/j.dib.2020.106178

Saurkar, A. V., Pathare, K. G., & Gode, S. A. (2018). An Overview on Web Scraping Techniques and Tools. *International Journal on Future Revolution in Computer Science & Communication Engineering, 4,* 363–367.

Sha, D., Liu, Y., Liu, Q., Li, Y., Tian, Y., Beaini, F., & Yang, C. (2021). A spatiotemporal data collection of viral cases for COVID-19 rapid response. *Big Earth Data, 5,* 90–111. doi:10.1080/20964471.2020.1844934

Shaiket, H. A., Anisuzzaman, D. M., & Saif, A. S. (2019). Data analysis and visualization of continental cancer situation by Twitter scraping. *International Journal of Modern Education and Computer Science, 11*, 23–31. doi:10.5815/ijmecs.2019.07.03

Singh, M., Jakhar, A. K., & Pandey, S. (2021). Sentiment analysis on the impact of coronavirus in social life using the BERT model. *Social Network Analysis and Mining, 11*. doi:10.100713278-021-00737-z

Singrodia, V., Mitra, A., & Paul, S. (2019). A Review on Web Scrapping and its Applications. *International Conference on Computer Communication and Informatics (ICCCI)*, (pp. 1-6). doi:10.1109/ICCCI.2019.8821809

Sirisuriya, D. S. (2015). A Comparative Study on Web Scraping. *Proceedings of 8th International Research Conference.*

Vargiu, E., & Urru, M. (2013). Exploiting web scraping in a collaborative filtering- based approach to web advertising. *Artificial Intelligence Review, 2*, 44–54. doi:10.5430/air.v2n1p44

Weng, Y., Wang, X., Hua, J., Wang, H., Kang, M., & Wang, F.-Y. (2019). Forecasting horticultural products price using ARIMA model and neural network based on a large-scale data set collected by Web crawler. *IEEE Transactions on Computational Social Systems, 6*, 547–553. doi:10.1109/TCSS.2019.2914499

Xu, Q., Shen, Z., Shah, N., Cuomo, R., Cai, M., Brown, M., ... Mackey, T. (2020). Characterizing Weibo social media posts from Wuhan China during the early stages of the COVID-19 pandemic: Qualitative content analysis. *JMIR Public Health and Surveillance, 6*. doi:10.2196/24125

Yang, C., Sha, D., Liu, Q., Li, Y., Lan, H., Guan, W. W., & Ding, A. (2020). Taking the pulse of COVID-19: A spatiotemporal perspective. *International Journal of Digital Earth, 13*, 1186–1211. doi:10.1080/17538947.2020.1809723

KEY TERMS AND DEFINITIONS

Beautiful Soup: Beautiful Soup is a package in python that parses the HTML and XML documents to extract relevant information.

HTTP Request: HTTP Requests are requests for an action to be performed sent by the client to the server. Some examples of HTTP Requests are GET, POST, PUT, etc.

Multithreading: Running multiple threads concurrently is multithreading. It is within the same process and shares the process resources, but executes independently.

Parse Tree: A parse tree is a set of the terminal and non-terminal symbols arranged in a hierarchical tree-like structure that symbolizes the syntactic structure of a sequence of symbols based on some context-free grammar.

Parsing: It is the analysis and processing of a sequence of symbols in any language or data structure, be it computer-based or human interpretable, that follows formal grammar rules for that language or data-structure.

Progressive Web Application: Also called as PWAs are web-delivered applications that can be downloaded on mobile devices to act like a native application without specifically and separately writing code for that mobile device operating system.

Thread: A thread is a sequential control flow or instructions (programmed) which is also called a lightweight process and can be managed by a scheduler independently, within an Operating System.

Web Scraping: Web scraping is the extraction of desired information from web pages for processing or any use.

Chapter 3
Fragment Assembly Based Fast and Optimal DNA Sequencing

Raja G.
Koneru Lakshmaiah Education Foundation, India

Srinivasulu Reddy U.
ⓘD https://orcid.org/0000-0002-6478-3839
National Institute of Technology Tiruchirappalli, India

ABSTRACT

Growth of healthcare systems has resulted in growth of personalized medicine. Genome sequencing is one of the major players that can enable personalized medicine. The huge computational requirement of this process has made this facility costly and unaffordable for many. DNA sequencing methods that can be performed at computationally low cost and with better performance are sought. The first model presents particle swarm optimization (PSO) and cuckoo search (CS) based models and analyzes their performance levels on sequencing DNA. The sequence assembly is performed using particle swarm optimization (PSO) and cuckoo search (CS). The work then analyzes the pros and cons of using PSO and CS to determine the most effective model. The second method presents the approximate matching model for DNA sequence assembly. The third technique proposes a MapReduce based highest exact matches which successfully exploits and maps between DNA sequences using parallel index method.

DOI: 10.4018/978-1-6684-6523-3.ch003

INTRODUCTION

Advanced technologies for leveraging data have resulted in generation of huge amounts of data, in which biological data also plays a major role. The sheer size of biological data being generated has made the processing abilities of the traditional data processing systems null and void. They require huge amount of processing and since processing and time are directly proportional to the cost, the cost of processing biological data is very large. Bioinformatics is an interdisciplinary field that works based on methods and software tools helpful for understanding biological data. This is an interdisciplinary field of science, which combines computer science, mathematics, statistics and engineering to study and process biological data.

The field of bioinformatics pursues to provide tools and analyses that facilitate better understanding of the molecular structures, by analyzing and correlating genomic and proteomic information. As increasingly large amounts of genomic information, including both genome sequences and expressed gene sequences, becomes available, more efficient, sensitive, and specific analyses become critical. Specifically, the area of bioinformatics includes Next Generation Sequencing (NGS), Virtual Screening, Genotyping, SNP (Single Nucleotide Polymorphism) discovery, Gene expression and Proteomics. Hence computationally, the following functionalities such as, Sequence mapping, Sequence analysis, Peak caller for CHIP-sequencing data, Identification of epistatic interactions of SNPs and Drug discovery can be carried out.

The field of bioinformatics has shown huge growth, and with it the sequencing techniques. The parallel sequencing technologies are known as the Next-Generation Sequencing (NGS). NGS techniques produce high-throughput genome fragments from the input DNA. These sequences are usually of short lengths. Ordering of the nucleic acid molecules in DNA can be used to uncover vital information that can effectively depict a person's hereditary properties. Measuring these sequences can aid in effective identification of anomalies contained in DNA and curing disease. Genome Sequencing is act of determining the nucleotide sequence of given DNA molecules from a short segment of a single molecule, such as a regulatory region or a gene, up to collections of entire genomes.

Although substantial reduction of cost could be observed in the genome sequencing domain, the costs are still considerable and beyond the reach of a common man. Variations in the genome sequencing costs are shown in Figure 1. Reducing these costs is of great interest, as they impact the scope and scale of genomic projects (Chial, 2008). Lowered costs can also lead to more genome sequences that can be used to further improve the scope of experiments in this domain. Accurate determination of the sequencing cost is not possible. Several parameters and nuances are to be considered.

Figure 1. Genome Sequencing Cost

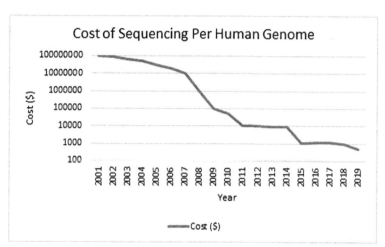

Fragment assembly is the process of arranging genome fragments obtained from the sequencing machines such that the entire genome structure is obtained (Elloumi et al., 1999). Fragment assembly can be done based on a reference genome or can be without a reference genome. The reference genome contains the entire genome sequence. This is usually a sample genome corresponding to an organism like the current organism in study.

Genomes and Genome Sequencing

Genomes are composed of DNA, the vital components of a cell. DNA is the basic building block of a cell. They are composed of four chemical components which are the building blocks of a DNA. They are the Adenine (A), Cytosine (C), Guanine (G) and Thymine (T), which are usually represented as A, C, G and T (Figure 2). Bases are pair complemented, i.e. A is complementary to T and G is complementary to C. Hence, a genome encoded as AAGTTC can also be encoded as TTCAAG, which is known as the complementary encoding. DNA is double stranded. Hence, if one of the strands contains the first encoding, the other strand will contain the complementary encoding.

Figure 2. A sample of Human Genome

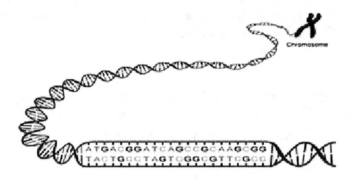

The order in which these bases are arranged reveals the biological information encoded within DNA. The genome of the bacterium E. coli has ~5 million bases, while that of a fruit fly is ~123 million bases, and that of a human is ~3,000 million bases (or ~3 billion bases). A single human genome has ~3 billion bases, as it is diploid in nature, the actual size of the genome is ~6 billion bases.

LITERATURE REVIEW

Computational Approaches to Genome Sequencing

The past decade experimental characterization of features was very expensive, time consuming, and difficult to genome assembly (Pazos et al. 2006). This resulted in the development of computational techniques such as BLAST (Altschul et al. 1997) and FASTA (Pearson et al. 1988), which are based on sequence similarity. Initially these methods were promising; however, subsequent studies have revealed significant limitations, as mentioned in many past studies (Devos et al. 2001; Gerlt et al. 2000; Rost et al. 2003; Sasson et al. 2006).

Hybrid Genetic Algorithm (HGA) where the whole evolutionary process is run on the GPU and only the random number generation is done in CPU (Wong et al. 2006). Each GA individual is set to each GPU and each one selects probabilistically an individual in its neighborhood to mate with (Wong et al. 2005).

Metaheuristic Based Sequencing Models

(Huang et al., 2015) was proposed PSO based DNA fragment assembly. This method helps an overlap consensus-based model to find the mapping sequence to carry out the DNA fragment assembly process. (Schatz, 2009) was proposed cloud burst DNA fragment tools. Cloud burst model was not suitable for scoring algorithm in paired read quality values and do not use a hash table, but BWT based short read aligners can be used to execute parallelization and *Hadoop Distributed File System (*HDFS).

(Abouelhoda et al., 2014) was proposed DNA sequence matching technique used for long fragment sequence mapping. This model failed in addressing the variants of the maximal exact match extraction problem and its performance was low.

(Bou et al., 2014) was proposed Firefly optimization techniques used to huge DNA fragment mapping used in several meta-heuristic-based solutions. (Allaoui et al., 2018) was proposed hybrid crow search algorithm for solving the DNA fragment assembly problem.

Problem Definition

The process of genome assembly is modeled as an optimization problem. The major aim is to identify the most optimal sequence for the input DNA fragments.

Let F={x1, x2, x3,...xn}be the unordered fragment set obtained from the process of Shotgun sequencing. Consider that every fragment is composed on multiple bases xi={b1,b2,...bm} where m > 0 and m ϵ Z. The requirement for a sequencing model is to identify fragment pairs xi and xj, where i and j overlap fragments arc between 1 to n, where n is the total number of fragments and i ^{1} j that contains maximum overlapping bases on the suffix of xi and the prefix of xj, such that xi and xj can be arranged in a sequence, and the overlap level between xi and xj is defined as Oij. The main aim of the sequence assembly process is to identify a sequence that includes all the fragments in F and provides the highest overlap levels.

Motivation

Computational biological problems existing in DNA sequencing are challenging ones because the difficulty of genome sequencing assembly process. The important limitation is to find high identical sequence that is composed of maximum number of valid overlap sequences.

Genome assembly process helps into several aspects of human life and in the process of curing a disease. This serves as the major motivation for the proposed work.

METAHEURISTIC ALGORITHM FOR GENOME SUBSEQUENCE ASSEMBLY

The major acquired for this field is a better and more precise DNA subsequencing assembly mechanism. The DNA sequencing assembly process very hard due to the vast scope of DNA fragments. In the proposed model presents a meta-heuristic-based solution for sequencing DNA effectively. The proposed model utilizes Particle Swarm Optimization SO) and Cuckoo Search (CS) to implement DNA fragment assembly problem. The contribution analyzes the pros and cons of using meta-heuristic models analysis the process of genome sequencing. This is followed by the identification of best matches using the fitness of the subsequence and the consensus match identification.

Need for Metaheuristic Based Models in Sequence Assembly

Bioinformatics is in the verge of becoming a part of everyday life due to the research carried out in the perspective of genomes. DNA sequencing is on the path to become an everyday tool in medicine, by which personalized medicine becomes possible, visualization of dynamic movements such as heartbeats becomes possible etc. But computing has now become the bottleneck in bioinformatics. Computing, not sequencing, is now the slower and more costly aspect of genomics research.

Major problems faced by the computational technologies concerning biological processing are the size and speed. Biological data are in general huge (in terms of GBs for a single DNA), hence the storage requirements are way beyond single systems. This also leads to a cascaded problem namely fast retrieval of the stored data. Employing appropriate algorithms for retrieving the stored data is required.

Computational techniques that provide effective, faster, and cheaper results have become mandatory. This can be in terms of better algorithms, renewed focus on data storage and manipulation techniques, and especially on "big data" approaches in managing and processing data.

Big Data Analytics perfectly suits the requirements of bioinformatics; hence Big Data Analytic techniques can be effectively used to combat the issues in bioinformatics. This contribution uses Hadoop based optimization models to solve the problem of DNA sequence assembly.

Genome Fragment Assembly

Fragment assembly is the process of arranging genome fragments obtained from the sequencing machines such that the entire genome structure is obtained (Elloumi et al. 1999). Fragment assembly can be done based on a reference genome or can be without a reference genome. This work is based on using a reference genome for effective fragment assembly. The reference genome contains the entire genome sequence. This is usually a sample genome corresponding to an organism like the current organism in study. The fragments obtained from the fragment generators are taken and matched with the reference genome to identify the exact position where the fragment could fit into the genome sequence as depicted in Figure 3.

Figure 3. Reference Genome based Fragment Assembly

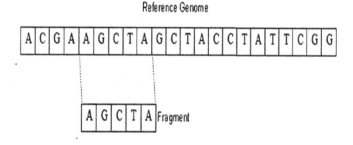

DNA Subsequence Assembly Using PSO

The PSO is a metaheuristic optimization model developed by (Kennedy, 1995; and Eberhart, 1998). It is a search space-based optimization model that aims to identify the best solution from the existing search space. The model operates on intelligent agents known as particles. These particles travel through the search position to identify the better solution and the model converges on the best solution. Further, the model is also based on two values: *pbest* and the *gbest*. Every particle has a *pbest*, which contains the best value obtained by the particle until the current time. The value of *gbest* is global and is shared by all the particles. The movement of particles is determined by these values. The sequence of steps involved in the proposed PSO based fragment assembly is depicted in Figure 4.

Figure 4. PSO based Fragment Assembly

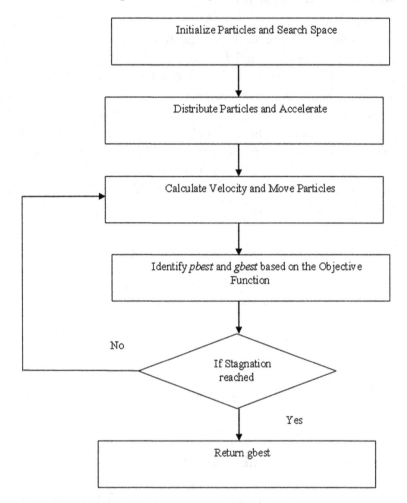

The search space is constructed using the permuted fragments, and particles are distributed in the search space, in random. The initial velocity is computed using the equation given below

$$v_i \sim \cup\left(-\left|b_{up} - b_{lo}\right|, \left|b_{up} - b_{lo}\right|\right) \tag{1}$$

where Vi is the velocity, bup and blo are the upper and lower bounds of the search space respectively.

The particle best (pbest) and global best (gbest) values are calculated. Particle acceleration is triggered using the velocity details obtained from equation (6.1). The acceleration aims to move the particle from the current solution to a better solution. The new position of the particle is represented by Xi,d. After movement, the new pbest and gbest values are determined by the below equation

$$v_{i,d} \leftarrow \omega v_{i,d} + \varphi_p r_p \left(p_{i,d} - x_{i,d} \right) + \varphi_p r_p \left(g_d - x_{i,d} \right) \tag{2}$$

where Pi,d and gd are the parameter best and the global best values, rp and rgare the random numbers, Xi,dis the value of current particle position and the parameters ω, φp, and φg are selected by the user.

However, the fragment assembly process is discrete in nature. Hence the solutions are discretized using the following function,

$$P' = \min \left(\sum_{j=1}^{n} \left[\sum_{k=1}^{d} \sqrt{\left(P_{ik} - N_{jk} \right)^2} \right] \forall i = 1 \, to \, p \right) \tag{3}$$

where Pik refers to the particle i's current location corresponding to dimension k, Njk refers to the kth dimension of node Ni.

The next phase is the identification of new velocity values for the particles. This is obtained using the following equation

$$V_{i,d} \leftarrow \omega V_{i,d} + \varphi_p r_p \left(P_{i,d} - X_{i,d} \right) + \varphi_p r_p \left(g_d - X_{i,d} \right) \tag{4}$$

where rp and rg are the random numbers, Pi,d and gd are the parameter best and the global best values, Xi,d is the value current particle position, and the parameters ω, φp, and φg are selected by the practitioner. This is followed by identifying the pbest and the gbest solutions.

The process of best solution identification and acceleration is continued until particle convergence is achieved and the search space is stagnated. After stagnation, the gbest value is considered as the best solution. The fitness function is used to identify the best solution. The fitness function used for the sub sequence reconstruction problem is based on the shortest position value (SPV) rule. Fitness is defined by the number of fragments matches from the reference genome to the current genome under analysis. Higher fitness values represent better solutions.

Algorithm for Fragment Assembly using PSO:

1. Search space construction using aligned fragments
2. Search space boundary identification
3. For each particle i=1...p
    a. Initialize the location of the particle in-random
    b. Initialize *pbest*, *gbest* and velocity
4. For each particle i=1...p
    a. Identify *pbest* and gbest
    b. Randomly generate rp and rg
    c. Particle velocity identification using Eq.
    d. Update the particle's position
    e. If *pbest* < current fitness
        i. Assign current fitness to be the *pbest*
    f. If *gbest* < *pbest*
        i. Assign *pbest* as the current *gbest*
5. Repeat step 4 until convergence
6. *gbest* contains the best-found solution

DNA Subsequence Assembly Using Cuckoo Search

Cuckoo search (Deb et al., 2010) is used as an alternative technique to solve the fragment assembly problem. CS is a population-based model that aims to solve NP-Hard problems. The DNA subsequences form the input. These subsequences are used as the search space and are used to determine the final solution. DNA subsequence assembly is rebuilt for each of the nests. The fitness of each combination determines the fitness of the fragment. The major aim of the model is to identify a not-so-good

solution to be replaced with a better-quality solution. The steps involved in the proposed CS based Fragment Assembly are depicted in Figure 5.

Figure 5. CS based Fragment Assembly

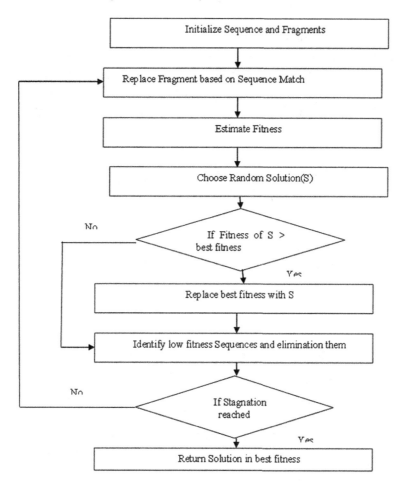

Fitness Subsequence Match Identification

The identical function, G(I), identifies the overlap value for fragments. This helps in ordering the fragments to arrive at a final solution. Fitness function is calculated by mapping of DNA fragments.

$$G(I) = \sum_{i=0}^{n} w\big(G[i], G[i+1]\big) \qquad (5)$$

where, i - individual fragment; n - total number of fragments; w(G[i]), w(G[i+1])- pair wise overlap fragments.

EXPERIMENTS AND RESULTS

In the experiment was conducted using the fasta and fastq data of Echinopstelfairi, Biomphalariaglabrata and Sarcophilusharrisi. Analysis was performed using the fastq files containing the genome fragments and the reference genome.

A tabulated view of the coverage levels of APSO, CPSO, PSO and CS are shown in Table 1. It could be observed that the CS based model exhibits high coverage levels compared to the PSO based models.

$$Coverage = \frac{\sum_{f=1}^{n} length\ of\ the\ fragment\ f}{Total\ length\ of\ the\ target\ DNA} \qquad (6)$$

where,

n - total number of fragments;
f - fragment number.

Table 1. Coverage Sequence Analysis.

Dataset	Total Base Counts (Total Length of Fragments)	Coverage (Bases= Fragment Length)			
		APSO	CPSO	PSO	CS
Echinopstelfairi	16549	14603	14669	15364	15531
Biomphalariaglabrata	13670	12703	12669	13565	13605
Sarcophilusharrisii	1606	1426	1491	1598	1601

DNA SUBSEQUENCE MAPPING FROM APPROXIMATE MATCHING TECHNIQUES

DNA Fragment assembly is a mapping the total base counts of an unknown sequences of genome. The reconstruct of genome sequence providing a strands of the DNA. During the process of sequencing, the only information available is the similarity of fragments and their level of overlap. The major limitations in genome subsequence assembly includes DNA fragment repeats, misperceptions between similar fragments originating from the same parent sequence and fragments that share the same repeat pattern and finally the intrinsic errors occurring during the sequencing process.

Figure 6 depicts the steps involved in approximate matching based genome sequencing process.

Figure 6. Approximate Matching based Genome Sequencing

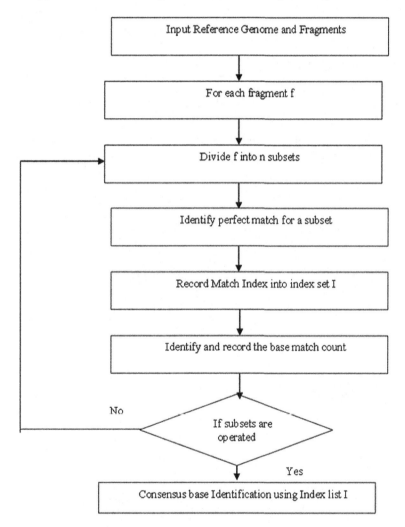

Similarity Assessment Using Hamming Distance

In this method to identify the positions where a perfect match found between the genome subsequence and the genome reference including the matches through least hamming distance location. However, minimizing the hamming distance was carried out for the entire genome. Genome subsequence match from reference genome and the intersecting region of query sequences.

Experiments and Results

A comparison of the coverage levels was shown in Figure 7. It could be observed that the approximate matching model showed better coverage levels on Biomphalariaglabrata and Sarcophilusharrisii and slightly reduced levels on Echinopstelfairi. Table 2 presents the results obtained with the proposed approach.

Table 2. Base Count based Performance Analysis

Dataset	Base Count	Coverage (Bases)	Gap	Mapping (Bases)	Contiguous	Hamming Distance
Echinopstelfairi	16540	16364	185	15317	27	373
Sarcophilusharrisii	1602	1577	3	1407	1	18
Biomphalariagla brata	13677	13656	4	13665	2	5

Figure 7. Comparison of Coverage % with Approximate Matching Technique

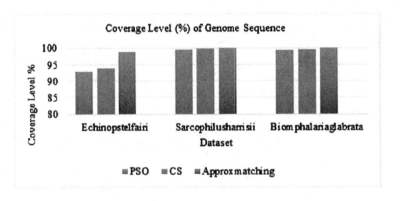

Exact Matches for DNA Fragment Assembly

The proposed method MapReduce based Maximum identical which effectively exploits the finding and mapping between genome fragments using parallel index structure. This method employs by reconstruct fragments according to the genome reference. A DNA fragment is initially matched with the sequence reference to find the possible matching positions. These identified positions are then analyzed for complete DNA fragments.

In this, model reconstruct to DNA fragments too genome reference sequence from the absolute matching in the index structure. Finally, assembly function produces the common identity regions for both sequences. The reduce task rebuilds the intermediate results and produces new maximum exact match read sequences.

Algorithm for MapReduce –Exact Matches DNA Fragment Assembly

```
Input:  (i) Fragment sequence (F)
          (ii) Genome reference (G).
Output: Assembly sequence.
Mapping:
Divide G in to g1, g2, -- - - -, g_m;
Divide F in to f1, f2, -- - -, f_n;
Intermediate:
Mapping output from the input as intermediate phase (key-
pair) sequence pairs
<G id, Suffix-prefix > pairs and intermediate value as <G id,
Exact Match > pairs
Take intermediate value pairs and find the complete set of
high similarity position
<Gid, Exact Match> pairs
Reducing:
Reduce function value as <Gid, Exact Match> pairs and
generates reconstructed
Sequence as a result
```

The result was performed of the gap levels and coverage levels subset mapping of the DNA fragment. Table 3 shows the performance of genome mapping analysis and the results obtained from the proposed approach. In the proposed

Exact Mapping offers better coverage level for chrXh, chr2h and E.colik12 datasets respectively.

Table 3. Performance of Genome Analysis

Genome	Total Base Counts (Total Length of Fragments)	Coverage%	Exact Match%	Coverage%	Exact Match%
		Greedy	MR-MEM	Greedy	MR-MEM
chrXh	16549	92.8	93.6	92.8	93.6
Chr2h	16067	99.5	99.7	99.5	99.7
E. colik12	13670	99.2	99.5	99.2	99.5

Genome Subsequence Assembly Using Hybridized Catfish PSO

This model proposes a hybridized Catfish PSO model for the process of DNA fragment assembly problem. PSO algorithm is enhanced by incorporating the Catfish particles to enable the model to get out of the local optimal solutions. Further, the local search process has been hybridized to incorporate Simulated Annealing (SA), such that the model performs faster selection of solutions. The proposed DNA subsequence assembly problem using the proposed Hybridized Catfish PSO technique enhances time effective and better results.

Genome subsequence aligning problem can be converted into Travelling Salesman Problem (TSP) (Lawler et al., 1985). Every DNA fragment was considered as node and of the graph. The Genome subsequence assembly problem is a maximization problem, where the track with the maximum identical level is to be determined. Hence, the objective function is of the form:

$$z = \sum_{i=1}^{n} \sum_{j=i+1}^{n} O_{ij} \tag{7}$$

where,

z is the total maximization of overlap;
n is the number of fragments;
Oij is the overlap level of fragments i and j.

This technique helps to finding the subsequence of genome that are to be searching to obtain the best possible of overlap level in genome. Consensus assembly is the process of reconstruct the final outcome with the maximum overlap levels in shotgun sequences. The steps involved in the process of search

Figure 8. Hybridized Catfish PSO

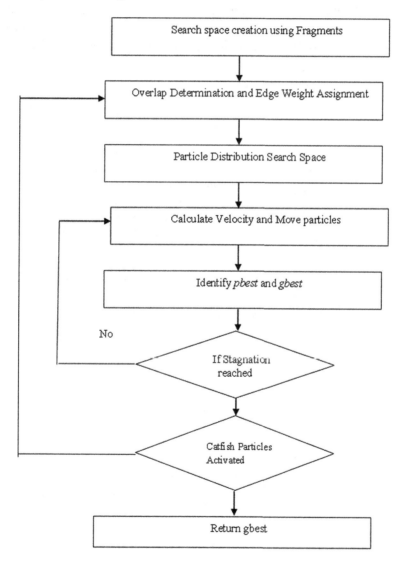

space creation with fragments by the proposed Hybridized Catfish PSO are depicted in Figure 8.

Experiments and Results

The result was carried with the CSA-P2M*Fit (Allaoui et al 2018), PPSO+DE, QEGA (Mallén-Fullerton et al., 2013), SA (Firoz et al., 2012) and PALS (Minetti G et al., 2010) models. A genome performance (overlap levels) comparison of the obtained results was shown in Table 4. The overlap value was a region of high similarity between two or more fragments. Figure 9 exhibits the hybrid Catfish PSO technique it shows the lower time requirements compared to that of the CSA-P2M*Fit model. The proposed model exhibits reduced time requirements compared to the CSA-P2M*Fit model.

Table 4. Performance Comparison (Overlap Levels)

Datasets	Hybrid catfishPSO	CSA-P2M*Fit	PPSO+DE	SA	PALS	QEGA
X60189_6	18301	18301	18301	18301	18301	18266
X60189_5	14161	14161	13642	14027	14021	14027
X60189_4	11478	11478	11478	11478	11478	11476
m15421_5	38746	38746	38686	38578	38583	38526
M15421_6	48052	48052	47669	47882	48048	48048
J02459_7	116700	116700	114381	116222	116252	115320

Figure 9. Time Comparison in Genome mapping

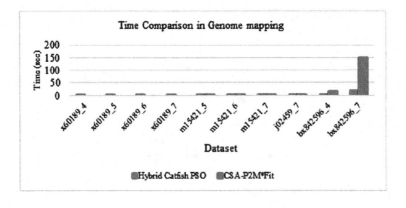

CONCLUSION

This work presents DNA fragment assembly problem. Three contributions operate on DNA fragments and arrange them based on the reference genome. The final contribution performs assembly based on the overlaps alone and without the reference genome. The initial contribution was based on metaheuristic-based models. The second and third contribution was based on an appropriate and exact matching rule-based algorithm. Pros and cons of the approaches were analysed, and the final contribution was based on a Hybridized Catfish PSO algorithm that overcomes the issues contained in both the sequencing mechanisms. The final contribution performed assembly based on the overlaps alone and without the reference genome, hence making the model more generic. The proposed model was able to achieve effective sequencing by eliminating the issues in the PSO model scalability was achieved by utilizing a meta heuristic model and by the process of hybridization, which enabled faster selection of optimal DNA sequences.

REFERENCES

Abouelhoda, M. (2014). Extracting Maximal Exact Matches on GPU. *IEEE 28th International Parallel & Distributed Processing Symposium Workshops*, pp. 1417–1426. IEEE.

Allaoui, M., Ahiod, B., & El Yafrani, M. (2018). A hybrid crow search algorithm for solving the DNA fragment assembly problem. *Expert Systems with Applications*, *102*, 44–56. doi:10.1016/j.eswa.2018.02.018

Altschul, S. F., Madden, T. L., Schäffer, A. A., Zhang, J., Zhang, Z., Miller, W., Allaoui, M., Ahiod, B., & El Yafrani, M. (2018). A hybrid crow search algorithm for solving the DNA fragment assembly problem. *Expert Systems with Applications*, *102*, 44–56. doi:10.1016/j.eswa.2018.02.018

Bou Ezzeddine, A. (2014). Applying the Firefly Approach to the DNA Fragments Assembly Problem. *Annales Univ. Sci. Budapest. Sect. Comp.*, *42*, 69–81.

Chang, Y., & Sahinidis, N. V. (2011). An integer programming approach to DNA sequence assembly. *Computational Biology and Chemistry*, *35*(4), 251–258. doi:10.1016/j.compbiolchem.2011.06.001 PMID:21864794

Chial, H. (2008). DNA sequencing technologies key to the Human Genome Project. *Nature Education*, *1*(1), 219.

Deb, S., & Yang, X.-S. (2010). Engineering optimization by Cuckoo search. *International Journal of Mathematical Modeling and Numerical Optimization*, *1*(4), 330–343. doi:10.1504/IJMMNO.2010.035430

Devos, D., & Valencia, A. (2000). Practical limits of function prediction. *Proteins*, *41*(1), 98–107. doi:10.1002/1097-0134(20001001)41:1<98::AID-PROT120>3.0.CO;2-S PMID:10944397

Elloumi, M., & Kaabi, S. (1999). Exact and approximation algorithms for the DNA sequence assembly problem. *SCI in Biology and Medicine*, *8*, 24.

Firoz, J. S., Rahman, M. S., & Saha, T. K. (2012). Bee algorithms for solving DNA fragment assembly problem with noisy and noiseless data. *In Proceedings of the 14th annual conference on Genetic and evolutionary computation*, (pp. 201-208). ACM. 10.1145/2330163.2330192

Gerlt, J. A., & Babbitt, P. C., (2000). Can sequence determine function?. *Genome Biology*, *1*(5).

Huang, K. W., Chen, J. L., Yang, C.-S., & Tsai, C.-W. (2015). A memetic particle swarm optimization algorithm for solving the DNA fragment assembly problem. *Neural Computing & Applications*, *26*(3), 495–506. doi:10.100700521-014-1659-0

Hunkapiller, T., Kaiser, R., & Hood, L. (1991). Large-scale DNA sequencing. *Current Opinion in Biotechnology*, *2*(1), 92–101. doi:10.1016/0958-1669(91)90066-E PMID:1367715

Indumathy, R., & Maheswari, S. U. M. a, & Subashini, G. (2015). Nature-inspired novel Cuckoo Search Algorithm. *Springer India*, *40*, 1–14.

King, R. D., Karwath, A., Clare, A., & Dehaspe, L. (2000). Accurate prediction of protein functional class from sequence in the Mycobacterium tuberculosis and Escherichia coli genomes using data mining. *Yeast (Chichester, England)*, *17*(4), 283–293. doi:10.1155/2000/107461 PMID:11119305

King, R. D., Karwath, A., Clare, A., & Dehaspe, L. (2001). The utility of different representations of protein sequence for predicting functional class. *Bioinformatics (Oxford, England)*, *17*(5), 445–454. doi:10.1093/bioinformatics/17.5.445 PMID:11331239

Lawler, E., Rinnooy-Kan, A., & Shmoys, D. (1985). The Travelling Salesman Problem, p. 463. John Wiley and Sons.

Mallén-Fullerton, G. M., & Fernandez-Anaya, G. (2013). DNA fragment assembly using optimization. *In 2013 IEEE Congress on Evolutionary Computation*, pp. 1570-1577. IEEE. 10.1109/CEC.2013.6557749

Minetti, G., & Alba, E. (2010). Metaheuristic assemblers of DNA strands: Noiseless and noisy cases. *In IEEE Congress on Evolutionary Computation*, pp. 1-8. IEEE. 10.1109/CEC.2010.5586524

Minetti, G., & Alba, E. (2010). Metaheuristic assemblers of DNA strands: Noiseless and noisy cases. *In IEEE Congress on Evolutionary Computation*, pp. 1-8. IEEE. 10.1109/CEC.2010.5586524

Pazos, F., & Bang, J. W. (2006). Computational prediction of functionally important regions in proteins. *Current Bioinformatics*, *1*(1), 15–23. doi:10.2174/157489306775330633

Pearson, J., & Havill, D. C. (1988). The effect of hypoxia and sulphide on culture-grown wetland and non-wetland plants: II. Metabolic and physiological changes. *Journal of Experimental Botany*, *39*(4), 431–439. doi:10.1093/jxb/39.4.431

Pospichal, P., & Jaros, J., (2009). *GPU-based acceleration of the genetic algorithm*. GECCO competition.

Rost, B., Liu, J., Nair, R., Wrzeszczynski, K. O., & Ofran, Y. (2003). Automatic prediction of protein function. *Cellular and Molecular Life Sciences CMLS*, *60*(12), 2637–2650. doi:10.100700018-003-3114-8 PMID:14685688

Sasson, S. (2006). Expression of interleukin (IL)-2 and IL-7 receptors discriminates between human regulatory and activated T cells. *The Journal of Experimental Medicine*, *203*(7), 1693–1700. doi:10.1084/jem.20060468 PMID:16818676

Schatz, M. C. (2009). Cloudburst: Highly sensitive read mapping with mapreduce. *Bioinformatics (Oxford, England)*, *25*(11), 1363–1369. doi:10.1093/bioinformatics/btp236 PMID:19357099

Setubal, J., & Meidanis, J. (1999). *Introduction to Computational Molecular Biology*. International Thomson Publishing.

Shi, Y., & Eberhart, R. (1998). A modified particle swarm optimizer. In Evolutionary *Computation Proceedings, IEEE World Congress on Computational Intelligence*, pp. 69-73. IEEE.

Wong, H. L., Bendayan, R., Rauth, A. M., Xue, H. Y., Babakhanian, K., & Wu, X. Y. (2006). A mechanistic study of enhanced doxorubicin uptake and retention in multidrug resistant breast cancer cells using a polymer-lipid hybrid nanoparticle system. *The Journal of Pharmacology and Experimental Therapeutics, 317*(3), 1372–1381. doi:10.1124/jpet.106.101154 PMID:16547167

Wong, S. L., Rual, J. F., Venkatesan, K., Hao, T., Hirozane-Kishikawa, T., Dricot, A., Li, N., & Klitgord, N. (2005). Towards a proteome-scale map of the human protein–protein interaction network. *Nature, 437*(7062), 1173–1178. doi:10.1038/nature04209 PMID:16189514

Chapter 4
Gait Analysis Using Principal Component Analysis and Long Short Term Memory Models

Maheswari R.
Vellore Institute of Technology, India

Pattabiraman Venkatasubbu
ⓘ https://orcid.org/0000-0001-8734-2203
Vellore Institute of Technology University, India

A. Saleem Raja
University of Technology and Applied Sciences Shinas, Oman

ABSTRACT

Human analysis and diagnosis have become attractive technology in many fields. Gait defines the style of movement and gait analysis is a study of human activity to inspect the style of movement and related factors used in the field of biometrics, observation, diagnosis of gait disease, treatment, rehabilitation, etc. This work aims in providing the benefit of analysis of gait with different sensors, ML models, and also LSTM recurrent neural network, using the latest trends. Placing the sensors at the proper location and measuring the values using 3D axes for these sensors provides very appropriate results. With proper fine-tuning of ML models and the LSTM recurrent neural network, it has been observed that every model has an accuracy of greater than 90%, concluding that LSTM performance is observed to be slightly higher than machine learning models. The models helped in diagnosing the disease in the foot (if there is injury in the foot) with high efficiency and accuracy. The key features are proven to be available and extracted to fit the LSTM RNN model and have a positive outcome.

DOI: 10.4018/978-1-6684-6523-3.ch004

INTRODUCTION

When we look at the way a person is walking or running, we can detect the subtle movements of individuals, determine normal walking patterns, detect and diagnose problems causing pain, as well as applied and examine treatments to correct abnormalities. Human analysis and diagnosis have become attractive technology in many fields. In digital imaging, a person can be analyzed by his or her unique facial features, iris, hair, a particular region of the eyes, gait, smell, finger, and palm. Gait defines the style of movement. Gait analysis is a study of human activity to inspect the style of movement and related factors used in the field of biometrics, observation, diagnosis of gait disease, treatment, and rehabilitation, etc. Gait recognition can be done through involvement and inefficiency-personal involvement in the recognition process. In the case of personal involvement, the person is directly contacted in the recognition system with the help of a separate sensor, accelerometer, Gyroscope, or monitoring devices. The exclusion method uses the remote camera to identify a person's identity with or without their knowledge based on its performance. Gait analysis is more common than other features because the features can be removed from the low resolution and without the involvement of any person. The biggest restriction and limitation with advancement in gait analysis technology is not the ability to produce high-quality data but to know how to use the data in the best way for the benefit of patients suffering from abnormalities or any injuries. Clinical studies investigate the movement pattern using one of two given ways: movement analysis or visual perception. Gait analysis is best for treating any kind of disorder faced by the person which leads him/her to walk properly. Whenever a person faces any problem in moving then through this analysis one can know about the injury before it can lead to permanent injury or issue. Using this analysis one can get cured from any time of difficulty faced while moving the body. The movement of the foot section in a particular direction while walking is something that no one probably doesn't think about too much. As it is just a basic way of walking or moving on a surface, but if a person is not able to walk properly then this can lead to a drastic change in one's life. And so it can affect one's freedom and create serious health issues. Most people can continue surviving with unusual gait patterns for years and years without symptoms. On the other hand, whenever one experiences injury or pain in one's body, normal gait patterns can be disrupted, leading to abnormal gait patterns thus leading to serious health problems. This is why Gait analysis is so important.

RELATED WORKS

The main purpose of writing the research was to use machine learning algorithms using temporal parameters for gait assessment whereas its main objective is to validate the classification using a probability modeling approach for different gaits taken into account. Features from the data were extracted using different models such as Hidden Markov Models and Support Vector Machine was used for getting information on signals in time and also frequency domain. The goal was to assess gait in day-to-day life and also detect gait to check whether the artificial intelligence algorithm used in gait analysis can help and verify the support in the medical evaluating section (Mannini et al., 2016). In medical practices, the common methods used in assessing gait patterns were too expensive and also complicated. Therefore various inertial Sensors and Artificial Algorithms were used. Submitted papers are analyzed for their data acquisition and processing methods for specific questions (Caldas et al., 2017) . Still, further improvement and evaluation are needed in the patient's performance using Artificial Intelligence in support of Gait analysis. New Deep Learning approach that has used input as Raw Inertial data. Various studies involved such as information acquired from multiple sensors from the sample. The challenging part was to use the OU-ISIR dataset which was considered the largest dataset available till then. The approach was successful in taking State of art results. The accuracy was identified and improved from 83.8% to 94.8% whereas the error was solved from 5.6 to 1.1. It also helps in showing that the number of sensors helps in improving the results achieved (Delgado et al., 2018). The main purpose of this paper uses a machine-learning approach to detect the disease using Gait analysis. In order to prove the approach, feasibility classification was done where identification of the disease was taken into account. And thus for classification different parameters were selected. The various algorithms which were used in this research include (RF) Random forest, MLP, and support vector machine for classification purposes. The accuracy was achieved at 100% for the random forest, SVM, and also for MLP whereas 96.4% accuracy was obtained for boosting (Joyseeree et al., 2015). Depth study of deep learning for Gait analysis. For collecting the gait data many sensing technologies were used such as floor sensors and wearable sensors along with Video Sequences. The Deep Learning methods used in this study are LSTM and neural network (NN) and also a deep learning algorithm was used to know about the features includes in the gait dataset (Alharthi et al., 2019). Reported that accelerometer and gyroscope sensor when placed at points of interest to analyze the running gait is the most effective, accurate, and also provided the best results. The parameters which were identified during this review helped in research and training with the best performance. Accelerometer and gyroscope together are used successfully in the construction of focused boundaries for research, including different parameters and different gait patterns. Therefore these sensors are used in achieving reliable and accurate results in measuring gait (Norri et al., 2014). Reported about inertial measurement unit sensors which were helpful in detecting the different gait variables by extracting various features of gait . The dataset was obtained using a self-developed application (Anwar et al., 2018). The accuracy was obtained for different age groups (old and children). The estimated accuracy of children was found to be 97.73% and 98.82% for both legs whereas the accuracy obtained for old people was 88.71% and 89.88%. The purpose also revealed that wearable devices were really helpful in identifying the symmetry of gait without the requirement of any laboratory setup. Thus served as a tool for assessing individual mobility disorders and also open up opportunities for home-based asymmetry testing. Use a different variety of accelerometer sensors in estimating the movement of humans. In this study body, mounted sensors were used to evaluate a three-dimensional kinematic system. So basically a comparison was done between a measurement with a 3D gyroscope and also a 3D accelerometer and on the other hand measurement of video analysis, which used a six-camera system for tracking the positions of the marker. It was found that there was a correlation in the result obtained from both methods. Collecting walking acceleration from Smartphone for identifying and authenticating gait. The methods used were LSTM and Recurrent Neural Network. These methods helped in feature extraction more perfectly and in a better way than conventional methods (Watanabe et al., 2020). The main purpose of the study was to bring out the difference of gait variables in spacio-temporal of people with disease both in the case of analyzing gait in the laboratory or using the wearable accelerometer in a clinical setup (Staab et al., 2014). The outcome of the study suggested that the result were more accurate when the assessment of gait was done in similar conditions avoiding any errors (Kececi et al., 2020).

Machine Learning-Based Gait Analysis

The advantage of using gait as a biometric is that it may be used to identify the subject at a distance. The system built by the author accomplishes the same concept where the action of the leg and the length of the stride are taken into account (Hnatiuc et al., 2021). In this system, Inertial Measurement Unit (IMU) sensors in smartphones and an Arduino's resistive flex sensor are used to capture human walk patterns. Diverse classifiers, including tree classifiers, rule-based classifiers, Support Vector Machines, K Nearest Neighbors, and Naive Bayes, were employed to recognize the subject. Data collected from a wide range of subjects was used to train the models.

In this work, a patient's gait is examined using ANNs and SVMs in order to diagnose muscular Parkinson's disease (Pau et al., 2018). During the training of the models, the kinetic, kinematic, and spatiotemporal factors are taken into consideration. The researchers also investigate the use of intra-group and inter-group normalization, two independent preprocessing strategies. The results of the models reveal that the intra-group normalized spatiotemporal parameter combination delivers good performance for both neural networks and support vector machines.

The research focus on wearable sensors and machine-learning algorithms in the field of human gait analysis is listed in a great manner (Saboor et al., 2021). This study discusses two key technological improvements that have been made in the field of human gait analysis. Wearables provide a useful, efficient, and cost-effective technique for collecting data, and Machine Learning Methods (MLMs) help in retrieving gait data for evaluation. This work examines the most recent developments in step evaluation using wearable sensors and MLMs. From the outset, an outline of step examination and wearable sensors is introduced. This study focuses on the most recent developments in step analysis, concentrating on the utilization of wearable sensors and MLMs. An overview of step examination, as well as the use of wearable sensors, is also presented here. The crucial step boundaries, wearables, and the materialist aspects of stride evaluation will be the primary concern. The accuracy of the SVM classification is at its maximum when the step boundaries are acquired by employing Principal Component Analysis (PCA), which eliminates the repeating stride data. These results have an accuracy of 87% which is superior to those obtained by employing a 101-layered step architecture in which PCA is not applied.

Deep Learning and Wearables in Gait Analysis

The usage of the CASIA Gait Database and the state-of-the-art in gait classification using image data were investigated. However, it was observed that innovative gait classifiers classify data from a range of sensors. The objective of the study is to enhance the performance of deep learning models in the field of human gait analysis (Khan et al., 2021). The feature selection has been highlighted as an effort to improve the performance of CNN models in gait analysis. To prevent the loss of any features the Kernel Extreme Learning Machine (KELM) was employed which achieves the highest recognition accuracy for the CASIA dataset. The system ensures substantial improvement over the previous system with an increase in accuracy as well as its execution time with 96.50% and 96.90%.

This research makes use of information obtained from inertial sensors that are integrated into smartphones (Zou et al., 2020). Owing to the extensive use of smartphones, data collection is practical, unconstrained, and cost-effective. CNN and RNN are utilized to abstract the features that are then represented by a hybrid Deep Neural Network in order to learn and model the data pertaining to the user's gait. Different datasets are obtained for identification and authentication using smartphone sensors. The recognition and verification accuracy rates of the users were 93.5% and 93.7%, respectively.

Figure 1. Gait Cycle

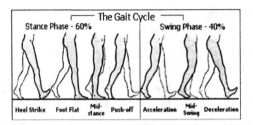

GAIT CYCLE

"Gait cycle" is known as an interval that starts from the heel contact of a foot to the heel contact of the same respective foot. When a person starts walking which is considered to be the best way in order to cover short distances then their flexibility in joints is. When the body is moving in a forward direction then there is the support of the appendage. Gait analysis can be known as part of functional assessment. When gait analysis is done then it is wise to look at the patient from the front, the back, and the side. The Gait cycle is divided into two phases as shown in Figure 1.

A detailed explanation is given below:

i. Stance Phase

This phase starts when there is a touch of the foot with the surface of the ground and ends when the same foot leaves the contact from the ground.60% of the total gait cycle composes of the "stance phase". Let us define the events that make up this phase. The first event is the initial contact and it marks the beginning of the total gait cycle. The main goal of this event is to the foot contact with the ground. The foot flat at 8% is an event where the full plantar surface of the foot contacts the ground. Mid stance at 30% is when the femur is directly over the standing foot. Heel off at 40% marks a period when the heel lifts off the ground and so off at 60% is a period when the toe leaves contact with the ground.

ii. Swing Phase

This phase of the gait cycle starts when the foot is off the ground and advancing forward, and body weight is supported by the contralateral limb ending the phase soon after the same foot comes in contact with the surface of the ground. 40% of the total gait cycle composes of the Swing phase. Now let's take a look at this phase's events. We have three main events acceleration at 75% mid-swing at 85% and deceleration at 100 completing the gait cycle.

Finally, let's take at the ranges of motion at initial contact the ankle is in a neutral position as the foot lowers to the ground the ankle moves into 5 degrees of plunder flexion. As the body moves over the foot the ankle dorsiflexes to about 10 degrees. In the last two stances phases, the ankle undergoes plantar flexion at the heel of the ankle is in neutral and the toe of the ankle is maximally plantarflexed to about 20 degrees. At the initial contact, the knee starts off neutral just like the ankle. Then for purposes of shock absorption and energy conservation, it moves to about 15 degrees of flexion. At mid-stance, the knee doesn't quite fully reach the locked-out position once again for purposes of energy conservation. It stays about 5 degrees of flexion. The heel of the knee is back to a neutral position and then slowly undergoes flexion to about 30 degrees to prepare for the acceleration phase of the gait. The hip is flexed to 20 degrees at initial contact.

Noticed that it moves from a let position to an extended position through the stance phase and from an extended to a flex position in the swing phase. At the foot flat, the hip is flexed to about 15 degrees and neutral at midstance. At heel of the hip is in 15 degrees of extension and reaches a peak extension range of motion at toe-off. Now let's take a look at the swing phase range of motion from acceleration to deceleration. Ankle dorsiflexes to clear the ground. The range of motion changes from 10 degrees of plantar flexion to zero degrees of neutral. The knee moves from a maximally flexed position of 60 degrees at acceleration to full extension at deceleration and the hip keeps moving into a maximally flexed position at 30 degrees at deceleration as shown in figure 2.

SENSOR-BASED METHOD

Firstly video-enabled devices were used in the gait analysis but slowly and gradually technologies involving sensors were used in the analysis of the gait. So in these techniques, two sensors are used. One is Body Mounted Sensors and the other one is a sensor using force. Accelerometers, inertial measurement units, or inertial measurement units in combination with the global positioning system are called body-mounted wearable devices. These wearable devices are thus used for calculating the movement of humans. Electronic devices which are small and consist of sensors and which also have the potential of computing are called wearable devices. These play a very crucial role in all fields and especially the health sector for analyzing and monitoring.

Figure 2. Percentage of Gait cycle

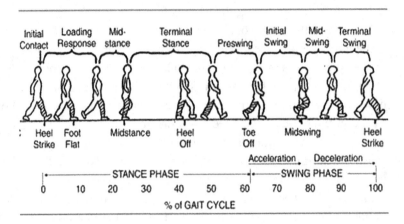

Inertial Sensors

IMUs or inertial measurement units are small invasive electronic devices with multiple sensors. These sensors usually include an accelerometer, a gyroscope, and/or a magnetometer. One can attach these units to specific body segments and then they can measure acceleration, angular rate, and orientation of the body at the specific body segments. So let's just take a closer look at these sensors used in IMUs as each sensor has different capabilities and uses so if we take a look at the accelerometer, then they can detect the change in speed. A gyroscope detects changes in the orientation of the angular velocity whereas the magnetometer measures the magnetic field of a location. In addition, these sensors are attractive and used for the analysis of the gait. Inertial sensors help in providing results for analyzing movement.

Further, these technologies are useful in measuring spatial factors such as angular rotation, velocity, stride length at the time of external motion tracking, and foot type. In addition, when IMUs are placed on parts of the body the measurement of special and temporal variables can take place perfectly and correctly. Working includes IMUs sensors involving the detection of acceleration linearly by the use of one or more wearable devices.

Researchers and investigators have always tried many combinations of inertial measurement units by placing them on different human body parts. These are installed on the foot and various other parts of the body for gait analysis. The data obtained from these devices are further used for research purposes. Researchers and investigators have always tried many combinations of inertial measurement units by placing them on different human body parts. These are installed on the foot and various other parts of the body for gait analysis. The data obtained from these devices are further used for research purposes.

Wearable Sensors for Gait Analysis

a) Accelerometer Sensor

These sensors detect changes in speed in one, two, or three axes. Let's focus on the three-axis or tri-axial accelerometer and what they are. So they can detect changes in three dimensions and these axes are known as the X, Y, and Z. axis. They relate to moving forward and backward, up and down as well as left and right, and are used in measuring the speed along the critical axis. The principle behind the common operation of accelerometers is totally dependent on a sensing element comprising of attachment of mass to a system, relative to a reference frame. These sensors are used in determining and monitoring the position of the object. The data thus obtained is used for analysis. Hence, these types of accelerometers are very suitable for the measurement of the state of movement on a human scale. These accelerometers are attached to different parts of the body (such as feet) to analyze and determine the performance of analysis of the gait.

b) Gyroscope Sensor

These sensors are very useful in knowing about angular velocity. The concept on which the gyroscope is based includes power measurement that is the same power/force equal to the angular circular rate in the circulatory reference frame. This sensor can be useful in finding out the posture of the body during the analysis of the gait. The angular velocity can be known by placing a gyroscope at the point of interest including a person's feet or leg. Various rearrangements of stages of movement can be determined easily. During the analysis of gait patterns mostly the gyroscope and accelerometer are combined together to form a sensory system.

PROPOSED METHOD

This section includes a description of the architecture for the diagnosis of gait disorder. Here, our methodology consists of 5 essential steps: data description, data pre-processing, features engineering, Classification, training estimators, and finally prediction is shown in Figure 3.

A study of the relationship identified in the gait sequence is made using these methods. The LSTM approach can be used for the prediction of time series data very

Figure 3. Proposed Architecture for Gait Analysis

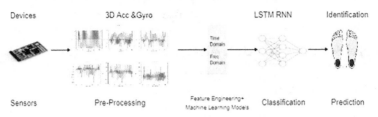

accurately. The output activation function is used by LSTM whereas it is not used by GRU. RNN method calculates the activation function by retaining the majority of previously hidden layers in the internal memory. However, during the actual calculation, it tends to investigate the most recently used hidden layers. By adding dynamic loops to the network, signals in an RNN can traverse both backward and forward directions. LSTMs constitute a form of RNN that allows the recurrent unit in adaptation of varied time scale dependencies. Figure 4 presents the various layers of the deep gait recognition system using RNN.

Using RNN, this system produced optimized outcome for the given subject's gait activity. This model is made up of numerous layers of LSTM cells and dense output layers utilized for user recognition. This proposed neural network was examined in a variety of circumstances for verification and proof of its effectiveness. Even when new subject information is exposed to the system, the proposed technique offers a better gait recognition with good generalization properties. The proposed neural network outperformed when accomplished with the subject walking pattern than when trained with other actions such as running and leaping.

Figure 4. Gait Recognition System using RNN

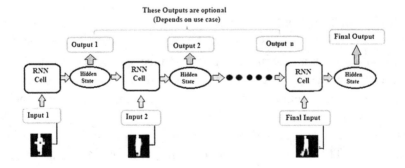

Data Description

This research is primarily based on a dataset acquired from wearable devices (accelerometer and gyroscope sensors).The dataset includes nine columns such voltage1, voltage 2 which are represented as force, accelerometer_x, accelerometer_y, accelerometer_z, gyroscope_x, gyroscope_y, gyroscope_z, time. The dataset contains four categories such as inward, outward, tandem, and normal (foot direction). Through wearable devices Real-time datasets were collected from 35 subjects and 16 important features were collected for measurement of the accurate gait signals, the dataset size collected from these subjects are approximated to 36,710.

Data Pre-processing

This step involves the conversion of raw data into a meaningful and understandable way for the project to move forward. Whenever data is obtained from another source where it is likely that the data may be erased and thus loses some important information. This step, therefore, helps to provide useful information. A few steps are involved the following:

First, all the important libraries are imported, and then start working on the database first i.e. all the pre-set data is imported. After this, if any values are not considered. Additional data classification was performed on training data and test data. The accelerometer signal and gyroscope signal were pre-processed. Noise filters were applied during pre-processing of these signals by applying noise filters. All the data was loaded into a specific format. The timeline for the trials was changed so that it becomes a continuous timeline.

A. Data Combiner

In order to combine two or more datasets the data combiner process is used. When you have so much data stored in many files and it wants to analyze all in one go then this process is used more often. Assume all trials have the same fields; each trial is stored as a panda's data frame trials are managed by the following format in a dictionary.

B. Augmentation of Data

A technique that is used to expand the training dataset size artificially is data augmentation. It expands the size by taking into account the existing dataset to create the modified data. Data augmentation is very useful in preventing the overfitting of data and is also considered a good practice if the initial dataset is too small for training or even if we need better performance from the model. It becomes crucial when we have a large dataset to work with and so the performance of both machine learning and LSTM Recurrent Neural Network might get affected hence data augmentation is done to avoid this problem. Therefore data augmentation is considered to be good for increasing the performance of models used in this work.

Features Engineering

It means that in order to obtain the features from the data provided a deep study is required. Whenever we need to obtain the feature then many learning algorithms are used in order to obtain the output from the given input. The data which is in input format consists of some features and these features are placed in the column. Two main goals are possessed, one is the proper preparation of data which is used as input it fulfills the requirement of the learning models used and the other goal is to the improvement of ML algorithms.

All of the features in the dataset are generated from the raw 3-axis Gyroscope and accelerometer signals.

Methodology Used

Dimension Reduction-Principal Component Analysis (PCA)

When we classification of any problem using ML then it is very important to keep in mind the factors from which the classification can take place. The important factors are only the features. If there are more amounts of data for training then it becomes quite difficult to work and visualize. It happens most of the time that the features are interrelated and also redundancy is found. So at this stage, we need to reduce the dimension. It basically helps to reduce the randomly occurring variables. The variables which are obtained can be further split into "extraction of the feature" and "selection of feature". Many methods can be used to reduce the dimension. It helps in compressing the data and thus reduces the space required for storage and also reduces the calculation time.

Now ML in a general way wonderfully works when provided a set of data is large and is also more informative. Usually, it is said that when there is a huge amount of data then it helps you in building a better model which is predictive because a huge amount of data helps in training the machine in the best way. But on the other hand, there are some downfalls in using a large dataset. The large pitfall is due to the dimension of data. To get rid of this cause we have come up with the process which is known as "dimensionality reduction". The dimensionality reduction process is used so that filtration can be done to only less number of features that are needed and used in training of the model or predicted model or machine learning model. And this is exactly where Principal Component analysis comes into the picture. The principal component analysis is a technique used for dimension reduction that helps in enabling to identify patterns and correlations in a dataset in order to transform it into another dataset of lower dimension and it also makes sure that we are not losing much information while transferring the data from high dimension to low dimension. The key idea of PCA is to look out for patterns and correlations within features that are different in the datasets. The reason for finding highly correlated features because highly correlated dependent features usually cause an output that is very biased and if two features within the dataset are very much correlated, then there will problem of output produced which will be going to be very much biased. These features are considered to be redundant because they don't account for the final output obtained. So we need to make sure that we remove all inconsistencies in the data after removing redundant data. So that's how dimensionality reduction is done in the most basic way possible. We remove data that is not essential keeping the most significant data for predicting the output.PCA is implemented in the majority of machine learning algorithms because machine learning has a limitation that it cannot process or it cannot handle data of high dimension.

Frequency Feature-FFT

Frequency domain analysis also helps visualize the effect of filtering and various other window and filtering techniques. Since the sampling frequency in this study falls at a range of 40-51 kHz, performing a domain time analysis has been shown to be challenging due to the size of the data included which is why frequent domain analysis works to understand process features. Signal strength also contains relevant information about the source of signal processing. Typically, the (FFT) was used to determine the power spectra. In stochastic systems, performing FFT will not help to differentiate the noise embedded in the signal produced, as the frequency of interest can be eliminated by lateral lobes created by high-frequency content. Therefore some measurements need to be made to increase the S / N ratio and make all the embedded waves visible.

Training Estimators

The models are trained for testing with ML algorithms which includes Logistic Regression, (SVM) Support Vector Machine with Platt scaling, Gradient Boosted Tree, and finally LSTM Recurrent neural network so that we can evaluate and compare the accuracy and performance of the model in order for diagnosing the gait disorder.

Table 1. Comparison of Accuracy with various models.

Model	Accuracy
Logistic Regression	91.18
SVM	97
GBT	97.72
LSTM-RNN	98.25

Predicting the Result

Particular foot pattern is predicted by using a test dataset on the trained model which contributes to knowing about gait disorder or abnormality in the foot section with high accuracy result. The below table shows the accuracy achieved by the models used in the project for the predicted probability of categories. The ML model such as logistic regression, SVM, and Gradient boosted Tree prediction was more than 90%. For predicting the probability of different categories involved in the dataset. After good extraction of key features to be available and then extracted to fit the LSTM Recurrent Neural Network model whose predicted probability was much higher to 98.25% as shown in Table 1.

The graphical representation of the accuracy analysis tabulated is presented in figure 5 across the various models. The analysis infers that the LSTM-RNN model outperforms with the other model for the gait analysis.

RESULTS AND DISCUSSION

FFT

Representation of signal is done using the function named FFT. In order to obtain information about the signal in the frequency domain, the FFT was performed on the up-sampled values. These findings were utilized to determine which frequencies in the signal were most important. Finally, the FFT results as shown in Figure 6 were utilized to estimate the mathematical expression for the signal in question using a reduced form of the Fourier series. In the below diagram, we can see the result obtained after analyzing the data used in this work.

Figure 5. Accuracy Analysis with various Models

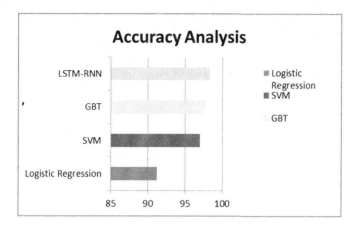

Histogram Analysis and PCA

The feature distribution in our project is done using a Histogram which helps in understanding what kind of feature we are working on, and the values we expect this feature to possess. We generally find as a result of the values are scattered or centered. Why is distribution important? Distribution is done because machine learning models as well as LSTM-RNN models learn from data. If the data provided is incorrect, then it will lead to incorrect learning. A deep learning model results therefore totally dependent on the data we feed it. Here the comparison of two PCA of all test data is done using a Histogram gives the following visualization is shown in Figure 7 and Figure 8.

After feature engineering, we train the SVM model, logistic regression model, and GBT model which takes around 68 seconds, 1 second and 58 seconds respectively to get trained using the training dataset of tandem, inward, outward, and normal foot

Figure 6. FFT Result Analysis

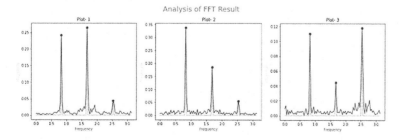

patterns. Once the model was trained, the sample test data of the outward pattern was tested which gave the predicted probability against all the categories.

Figure 7. Visualization of Voltage using PCA

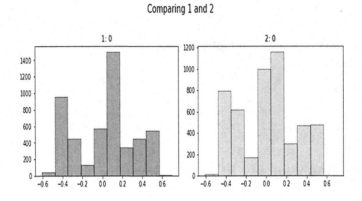

Figure 8. Visualization of Accelerometer, Gyroscope using PCA

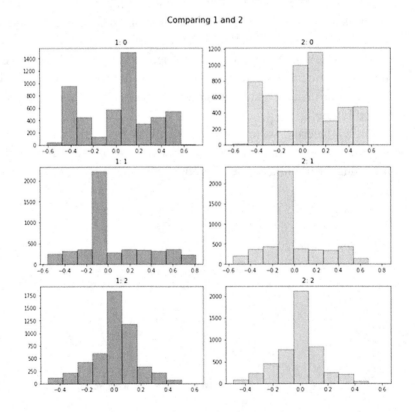

Figure 9. Accuracy of LSTM Recurrent neural network

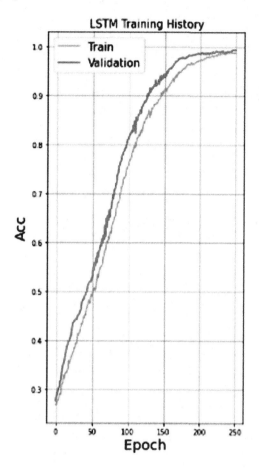

In order to check whether the model which is trained is working well with a high percentage of accuracy result then it's very important to do the validation. The data which is obtained for carrying out the project is split into a set of data for training and validating. The output of the Training history of the LSTM Recurrent neural network shown in Figure 9, that the validation accuracy obtained is perfect after the data set is trained.

CONCLUSION

In this work, various pre-data processing techniques especially the performance of sensor data were examined. Machine learning models such as Logistic Regression and SVM Platt Scaling, Gradient boosted tree and LSTM Recurrent Neural Network models to compare and evaluate their performance given the complexity of sensory data. With proper fine-tuning of machine learning models and the LSTM Recurrent Neural Network, we found that every model has an accuracy obtained greater than 90% with LSTM slightly higher than machine learning models. The models helped in diagnosing the disease in the foot (such as if there is any injury in the foot section) with high efficiency and accuracy. Machine Learning Models, key features are proven to be available and extracted to fit the LSTM Recurrent Neural Network model and have a positive outcome.

REFERENCES

Alharthi, A. S., Yunas, S. U., & Ozanyan, K. B. (2019). Deep learning for monitoring of human gait: A review. *IEEE Sensors Journal*, *19*(21), 9575–9591. doi:10.1109/JSEN.2019.2928777

Anwar, A. R., Yu, H., & Vassallo, M. 2018. An automatic gait feature extraction method for identifying gait asymmetry using wearable sensors. *Sensors, 18*(2), 676.

Caldas, R., Mundt, M., Potthast, W., Buarque de Lima Neto, F., & Markert, B. (2017). A systematic review of gait analysis methods based on inertial sensors and adaptive algorithms. *Gait & Posture*, *57*, 204–210. doi:10.1016/j.gaitpost.2017.06.019 PMID:28666178

Delgado-Escano, R., Castro, F. M., Cózar, J. R., Marín-Jiménez, M. J., & Guil, N. (2018). An end-to-end multi-task and fusion CNN for inertial-based gait recognition. *IEEE Access: Practical Innovations, Open Solutions*, *7*, 1897–1908. doi:10.1109/ACCESS.2018.2886899

Hnatiuc, M., Geman, O., Avram, A. G., Gupta, D., & Shankar, K. (2021). Human signature identification using IoT technology and gait recognition. *Electronics (Basel)*, *10*(7), 852. doi:10.3390/electronics10070852

Joyseeree, R., Abou Sabha, R., & Mueller, H. (2015). Applying machine learning to gait analysis data for disease identification. In *Digital Healthcare Empowering Europeans* (pp. 850–854). IOS Press.

Kececi, A., Yildirak, A., Ozyazici, K., Ayluctarhan, G., Agbulut, O., & Zincir, I. (2020). Implementation of machine learning algorithms for gait recognition. *Engineering Science and Technology, an International Journal, 23*(4), 931-937.

Khan, M. A., Kadry, S., Parwekar, P., Damaševičius, R., Mehmood, A., Khan, J. A., & Naqvi, S. R. (2021). *Human gait analysis for osteoarthritis prediction: A framework of deep learning and kernel extreme learning machine*. Complex & Intelligent Systems.

Mannini, A., Trojaniello, D., Cereatti, A., & Sabatini, A. M.. (2016). A machine learning framework for gait classification using inertial sensors: Application to elderly, post-stroke and Huntington's disease patients. *Sensors, 16*(1), 134.

Norris, M., Anderson, R., & Kenny, I. C. (2014). Method analysis of accelerometers and gyroscopes in running gait: A systematic review. *Proceedings of the Institution of Mechanical Engineers. Part P, Journal of Sports Engineering and Technology, 228*(1), 1, 3–15. doi:10.1177/1754337113502472

Pau, M., Corona, F., Pili, R., Casula, C., Guicciardi, M., Cossu, G., & Murgia, M. (2018). Quantitative assessment of gait parameters in people with Parkinson's disease in the laboratory and clinical setting: Are the measures interchangeable. *Neurology International, 10*(2), 69–73. doi:10.4081/ni.2018.7729 PMID:30069292

Saboor, T. Kask, A. Kuusik, M. M. Alam, Y. Le Moullec, I. K. Niazi, A. Zoha and R. Ahmad. (2021). Latest research trends in gait analysis using wearable sensors and machine learning: A systematic review. *IEEE Access: Practical Innovations, Open Solutions, 8*, 167830–167864.

Staab, W., Hottowitz, R., Sohns, C., Sohns, J. M., Gilbert, F., Menke, J., & Lotz, J. (2014). Accelerometer and gyroscope-based gait analysis using spectral analysis of patients with osteoarthritis of the knee. *Journal of Physical Therapy Science, 26*(7), 997–1002. doi:10.1589/jpts.26.997 PMID:25140082

Tahir, N. M., & Manap, H. H. (2012). Parkinson disease gait classification based on machine learning approach. *Journal of Applied Sciences, 12*(2), 180–185. doi:10.3923/jas.2012.180.185

Watanabe, Y., & Kimura, M. (2020). Gait identification and authentication using LSTM based on 3-axis accelerations of the smartphone. *Procedia Computer Science, 176*, 3873–3880. doi:10.1016/j.procs.2020.09.001

Zou, Q., Wang, Y., Wang, Q., Zhao, Y., & Li, Q. (2020). Deep learning-based gait recognition using smartphones in the wild. *IEEE Transactions on Information Forensics and Security, 15*, 3197–3212.

Chapter 5
Hybrid Deep Learning Models for Effective COVID –19 Diagnosis with Chest X–Rays

Maheswari R.
Vellore Institute of Technology, India

Prasanna Sundar Rao
Shri Sankarlal Sundarbai Shasun Jain College, India

Azath H.
Vellore Institute of Technology, Bhopal, India

Vijanth S. Asirvadam
Universiti Teknologi Petronas, Malatysia

ABSTRACT

The survey on COVID-19 test kits RT-PCR (reverse transcription-polymerase chain reaction) concludes the hit rate of diagnosis and detection is degrading. Manufacturing these RT-PCR kits is very expensive and time-consuming. This work proposed an efficient way for COVID detection using a hybrid convolutional neural network (HCNN) through chest x-rays image analysis. It aids to differentiate non-COVID patient and COVID patients. It makes the medical practitioner to take appropriate treatment and measures. The results outperformed the custom blood and saliva-based RT-PCR test results. A few examinations were carried out over chest X-ray images utilizing ConvNets that produce better accuracy for the recognition of COVID-19. When considering the number of images in the database and the COVID discovery season (testing time = 0.03 s/image), the design reduced the computational expenditure. With mean ROC AUC scores 96.51 & 96.33%, the CNN with minimised convolutional and fully connected layers detects COVID-19 images inside the two-class COVID/Normal and COVID/Pneumonia orders.

DOI: 10.4018/978-1-6684-6523-3.ch005

INTRODUCTION

With the proceeded with development of the COVID-19 pandemic, researchers overall are attempting to understand better and minimize its spread. Key areas of examination incorporate concentrating on COVID-19 transmission, working with its location, creating potential immunizations and medicines, and understanding the financial effects of the pandemic. In this, the model examines how Artificial Intelligence (AI) can add to these objectives by upgrading continuous exploration endeavors, working on the effectiveness and speed of existing methodologies, and proposing unique lines of examination. According to a sub-atomic point of view, AI can be utilized to assess the construction of SARS-CoV-2-related proteins, distinguish existing medications that might be reused to treat the infection, propose new mixtures that might be promising for drug advancement, recognize potential immunization targets, further develop determination, and better grasp infection infectivity and seriousness (Minaee et al., 2020). According to a clinical point of view, artificial intelligence can uphold COVID-19 findings from clinical imaging, give elective ways of following infection development utilizing painless gadgets, and produce forecasts of patient results in light of various information inputs, including electronic health records. According to a cultural viewpoint, AI has been applied in a few areas of epidemiological examination that include demonstrating experimental information, including computing the number of cases given different public arrangement decisions. other works use AI to recognize likenesses and contrasts in the development of the pandemic across areas (Boudrioua et al., 2020). Computer-based intelligence can likewise assist with researching the scale and spread of the information to address the propagation of misinformation and disinformation, as well as the rise of hate speech (Narin et al., 2020). Likewise, the survey is performed over open-source datasets and assets that are accessible to work with the advancement of AI arrangements. Sharing and facilitating information and models, whether they be clinical, atomic, or cultural, is basic to speed up the turn of events and operationalization of AI to help the reaction to the COVID-19 pandemic (Groves et al., 2016). The reason for this review isn't to assess the effect of the portrayed methods, nor to suggest their utilization, but to show the per user the degree of existing applications and to give an underlying picture and guide of how Artificial Intelligence could help the worldwide reaction to the COVID-19 pandemic (Ozturk et at., 2020). In view of the review of the literature, it closes with a progression of perceptions and suggestions. To begin with, will note that while there is an expansive scope of possible uses of AI covering clinical and cultural difficulties made by the COVID-19 pandemic, not many of them are right now mature to the point of showing functional effect (Shi et al., 2020).

Coronavirus

The coronavirus disease 2019 (COVID-19) establishes a public health crisis worldwide. The number of infected individuals and deaths is multiplying each day, which is putting high pressure on our social and medical care framework. Quick detection of COVID-19 cases is a huge advance in the battle against this infection as well as releasing pressure off the medical care system. The COVID-19 pandemic has uncovered the weakness of medical services administrations around the world, particularly in undeveloped nations. It is evident that new computer-assisted diagnosis tools must be created in order to provide quick and affordable screening in locations where traditional conventional testing is not feasible (Guyon et al., 2003). Lung ultrasound is a versatile, simple to sanitize, minimal expense and painless apparatus that can be utilized to recognize lung illnesses. Computer-assisted analysis of lung ultrasound images is a relatively new technique that has shown remarkable promise for identifying aspiratory diseases, making it a practical choice for screening and identifying COVID-19 (Janosi et al., 1988). The coronavirus has undermined the whole world. For the well-being administrations suppliers, it turned into a test to make quick forward intending to assess the transmission pace of SARS-Cov-2 without prepared admittance to analytic strategies and future arranging in light of the supportability of medical services frameworks to adapt to the flare-up (Zu et al., 2020). Preceding recognition through RT-PCR, no strategy is accessible to evaluate Covid-19 contamination during hatching and after the beginning of side effects (Kanne et al., 2020). Thus, a high transmission rate has been accounted for and should be diminished for viable control. This review will assess the ongoing information on Covid-19 pathogenesis and its appearance to form a simple technique (Celik et al., 2020). To identify and survey the Covid-19 course of contamination and to counter episodes by lessening transmission rates through early detection and taking on suitable measures (Muhammad et al., 2020). Artificial intelligence is now more frequently used in medical image detection as patient medical image data has become more widely available. To identify irregularities and extract textural characteristics of the modified lung parenchyma to be connected with explicit COVID-19 virus marks, machine learning (ML) and deep learning can be used effectively (Mahmud et al., 2020). Convolutional neural networks can be used to enhance feature extraction and obtain detailed information from medical images, both of which are very helpful for clinical diagnosis (Luz et al., 2020). Convolutional neural networks have developed over time, and Liang et al. effectively summarised their uses in clinical picture handling. In order to test 2905 COVID-19 chest x-ray images (including three classifications of COVID-19, ordinary, and viral pneumonia), the DenseNet model was proposed (Rahimzadeh et al., 2020) (Minaee et al., 2020). The accuracy, sensitivity, and specificity of the three grouping test results are, respectively, 98.1%, 97.8%, and 98.2% (Punn et al., 2020) (Khan et al., 2020). Wang and Wong developed a convolutional neural network (COVID-Net) specifically designed to recognise chest COVID-19 cases and built the model using publicly available chest x-ray images. When classifying pneumonia cases, Coronavirus Net has an overall accuracy of 92.4% for COVID-19, common, and non-COVID pneumonia (Wang et al., 2020). Narin et al. used the ResNet50 model for grouping tests and achieved an accuracy rate of up to 98% using the new coronary pneumonia informational index that Joseph Cohen and others had previously shared. For the purpose of discovering COVID-19, Apostolopoulos and Mpesiana developed a deep learning model based on the transfer learning technique (Narin et al., 2020). An experimental data set of 1442 x-ray images were collected from the public medical database, including 504 images taken under normal circumstances, 714 images with pneumonia that was both bacterial and viral confirmed, and 224 images with the COVID-19 disease (Hemdan et al., 2020). Results from experiments indicate that using deep learning models to separate lung x-ray images may extract significant features related to COVID-19 disease. For the two classifications (COVID-19 and normal images), the best accuracy, sensitivity, and specificity were 96.78%, 98.66%, and 96.46%, respectively in order to identify acquired pneumonia (CAP) and other non-pneumonia, Li et al. developed a fully automated deep learning framework (COVNet) for detecting and evaluating COVID-19 based on chest CT images. This framework can distinguish between visual highlights from chest CT images (Apostolopoulos et al., 2020). An informational index of 4356 chest CT images from 3322 patients was compiled prior to the analysis. The awareness and explicitness of recognizing COVID-19 in the autonomous test set are partitioned into 90% and 96%, and the responsiveness and particularity of identifying CAP are 95% and 87%, separately. The trial outcomes demonstrate that the deep learning model can accurately distinguish COVID-19 from CAP and other lung infections. In light of the Xception engineering, Khan et al.17 proposed the CoroNet model, which uses x-ray and CT scans to identify COVID-19 (Horry et al., 2007). According to test results, the CoroNet model's accuracy was 93% for the four-class (viral pneumonia, COVID-19, bacterial pneumonia, and common images) try and 95% for the three-class (typical, COVID-19, and pneumonia images) explore, respectively (Loey et al., 2020). 723 COVID-19 test positive and 413 COVID-19 test-negative CT images made up the informational index they used, and the most recent precision rate was 97.4%. An effective method for detecting COVID-19 pneumonia automatically from high-resolution chest x-ray images was proposed (Kumar et al., 2020).

A U-Net model was used to segment the lungs, and the segmentation accuracy was 98.63%. Then, different models (ResNet18, ResNet50, ResNet101, InceptionV3, DenseNet201, and ChexNet) are used to characterize 3616 COVID-19 lung x-ray images, 8851 normal lung x-ray images, and 6012 non-COVID lung diseases. (Bukhari et al., 2020). With accuracy, sensitivity, and specificity of 96.29%, 96.29%, and 97.27%, respectively, the ChexNet model performed the best. In order to advance to the chest x-ray domain and further improve a model's prediction performance given the limited target domain sample data without overfitting, will plan to use domain-invariant portrayals from a source area (Abbas et al., 2020). Additionally, a system of end-to-end learning will be provided, focusing on the transferrable qualities of dormant portrayals across spaces and tasks using move learning, using a dataset gathered from various locations and times. In contrast, because it is instantly accessible everywhere on Earth, x-ray imaging has a variety of use cases in numerous clinical and epidemiological applications (Islam et al., 2020). Because of its lightweight working rate, lower cost, and usability by radiologists, the chest x-ray is a suitable methodology for inspecting and diagnosing cases in this way (Cohen et al., 2020).

Covid-19 Detection

When it comes to the detection of covid-19 using chest x-ray images conventionally they adopt machine learning to fight the COVID-19 pandemic according to an alternate point of view, including a broad literature review and a bibliometric examination. This study is allegedly the first in-depth analysis of research output focusing on various potential applications of machine learning techniques for reducing the ongoing COVID-19 pandemic's global spread. The accuracy of current models is low, and the rate of misclassification is high. However, the proposed model also incorporates a Hybrid Convolutional Neural Network (HCNN). CNN was used to extract features from the X-ray images while on the other hand, was used to deal with the mathematical data. Basically, the number of hidden layers, number of neurons, epochs, and batch size were tuned to work on the model's exhibition. The number of neurons and hidden layers was initially set at random, but the network search strategy was then used to determine the ideal boundaries. Numerous countries around the world, including India, are presently experiencing COVID-19. The proposed model was joined with the CNN architecture (Rothan et al., 2020). A few countries, including the USA, Germany, Italy, and a few others, are dealing with the disease's localized spread, which demonstrates that one infected person can infect more than 100 people who come in contact with him. In this case, isolating the infected individuals will solve the problem by halting the spread of the infection (Li et al., 2020). When dealing with a large number of cases, the rate of diagnosis is impacted by the time-consuming nature of the current diagnostic procedures to identify the infected person (Hanumanthu et al., 2020). The ideal local detection of positive cases is one of the fundamental steps in controlling the viral spread. Numerous molecular and serologic tests have been developed, approved, and put into use by clinical research facilities to test SARS-CoV-2 nucleic acid.

Reverse Transcriptase-Polymerase Chain Reaction (RT-PCR) is a research lab testing method that combines the amplification of specific DNA targets using the common Polymerase Chain Reaction with reverse transcription of RNA into DNA (known as complementary DNA or cDNA) (PCR). It has been noted that RT-PCR evidence is effective at detecting SARS-CoV-2 infection. However, this approach has drawbacks, such as lengthy delays in obtaining test results, patients with high clinical suspicion testing falsely negative when RT-PCR testing begins frequently requiring multiple tests to approve the result, and a significant amount of other logistical challenges in the lab. Low test responsiveness could be explained by: subpar clinical examination techniques; variations in viral burden; and producer test unit awareness (Ardakani et al., 2020). Dealing with these RT-PCR-negative patients is primarily laborious because this population has a high flood of cases. Laboratories and virology research centers are making strides toward overcoming the ebb and flow constraints of RT-PCR testing in order to empower more precise locations of Covid. Procedural adherence requirements in the lab and a large portion of the testing qualities can be attributed to these groups. Chest imaging assessment is a valuable and practical methodology for identifying clinical symptoms of COVID-19 suspected and recovered cases, as indicated by the World Health Organization recommendations of October 2020 (Alazab et al., 2020).

Hybrid Model Detection

The traditional machine learning and deep learning approaches were used in previously completed projects, but these methods occasionally misclassified images, resulting in lower accuracy scores. Therefore, in order to prevent misclassification, the system introduces a new hybrid neural network that combines both CNN and RNN models. This will help us classify chest images accurately and prevent misclassification of images (Albahli et al., 2020). The limitations of the conventional machine learning model can be overcome by unified machine learning, including Traditional machine learning involves moving all data sources to a single server where the model is built and trained, but this may go against military organization policies, especially if a third party is used to build, train, and maintain the model. However, this may disregard information security when the information is dealt with to create the model. To train the model, the third party should prepare, clean, and restructure the data to be suitable for model training (Albahli et al., 2020). Traditional machine learning models also have some room for error in order to build a model with sufficient accuracy, which could be detrimental to associations, especially recently formed ones. In order to train conventional machine learning models to provide an acceptable level of accuracy, a sizable amount of historical data is also necessary. A secure distributed machine learning methodology that trains clients' data on their servers without violating information security is required. This methodology should also save computational power, solve the virus start problem, and enable clients to receive results right away (Alsharman et al., 2020). The primary impetus for studying the COVID-19 pandemic, which has posed a serious threat to the entire world ever since it first appeared in Wuhan, China. To stop and contain the outbreak, it is essential to know how many COVID-19 cases to expect. In this study, an artificial neural network with a rectifying linear unit-based method is used to predict the number of deaths, recovered cases, and confirmed cases of COVID-19 in Pakistan using historical data from 137 days of COVID-19 cases, from the day on which the first two cases were confirmed on February 25, 2020, to the day on which the case number 10 was confirmed on July 10, 2020 (Altan et al., 2020). To evaluate the effectiveness of the suggested technique, the gathered data were divided into training and test sets. Additionally, the suggested procedure made future predictions while building the model using all available data. The four-class design was created in an effort to determine whether any confusion between COVID-19 and viral pneumonia may have resulted from their shared pathology. The main contribution of this study is the proposal of a deep neural network-based model for extremely accurate COVID-19 infection detection from patient chest X-ray images (Bridge et al., 2020).

Challenges

In addition to having a significant financial impact, the ongoing coronavirus disease 2019 (COVID-19) pandemic has caused a global health and medical care emergency. One of the major challenges in this emergency is quickly and effectively identifying and monitoring COVID-19 patients so that options for their care, observation, and the board can be worked out. During the 2020 Covid pandemic, the limitations and high false-negative rates (30%) of COVID-19 test kits have been an obvious challenge. It takes a lot of resources and time to produce those kits and conduct the tests. A more effective setup and quicker initial monitoring of COVID-19 patients can be provided by radiological images such as chest X-images, according to ongoing research. will use a Hybrid Convolutional Neural Network (HCNN) for mixed data (mathematical/image data) to create a COVID-19 diagnosis model. The model predicts and distinguishes between COVID-19 and non-COVID-19 patients, enabling early diagnosis of the virus and prompt isolation and treatment to halt disease progression. The results demonstrate that overfitting the training dataset and biases in the experimental design can cause deep learning models to misjudge their performance. will use an independent test set for evaluation and will compare the proposed architecture to state-of-the-art techniques, reducing some of the identified bias and overfitting issues. The difficulties in analyzing and interpreting the results of various deep learning algorithms will exist even though the proposed deep learning architecture offers the best performance with the best arrangement. Our experiments suggest that a larger, more comprehensive data set with less inclination is important for creating devices pertinent in actual clinical settings, even though deep learning-based methods using chest imaging data show promise in being useful for clinical administration and emergency care of COVID-19 patients. To lessen the effects of COVID-19 infection, especially in severe cases, quick, accurate, and confident diagnoses are crucial. The development of deep learning techniques to categorize and identify COVID-19 infections from chest radiography images has received a great deal of attention. However, recently, a few concerns have been voiced regarding the clinical applicability and sufficiency of such strategies. The system conducts in-depth analyses on a sizable dataset of COVID-19 chest X-ray images in this work to investigate the challenges associated with developing trustworthy AI solutions from both the data and machine learning points of view. Likewise, it will provide a top-to-the-bottom discussion of the difficulties encountered by some popular deep-learning architectures related to the classification of chest X-rays using the COVID-19 standard.

SYSTEM OUTLINE

It aims to suggest an established information-driven method that could be used as a decision-support tool for global COVID-19 pandemic trend forecasting. The forecasted values will be combined in this method using a stacking strategy to improve accuracy. The system has suggested a method for automatically predicting COVID-19 using chest X-ray images, deep convolution neural networks, and pre-trained transfer models. The system has used the ResNet18 pre-trained model to achieve higher prediction accuracies for three distinct binary datasets, including X-ray images of patients with normal (healthy), COVID-19, bacterial, and viral pneumonia. Since the proposed models have an end-to-end structure without the need for manual feature extraction, selection, or classification, and since the performances of the COVID-19 data across the normal, viral pneumonia, and bacterial pneumonia classes were all higher, the novelty and inventiveness of the proposed models can be summed up as follows. Additionally, it has been thought about with more information than many studies in the writing. However, it has been thought about and evaluated against 5 different CNN models. Moreover, radiologists have been advised to use a high-accuracy decision-supporting network for the automatic diagnosis, detection, and follow-up of patients with suspected COVID-19.

Literature Review

Due to their noteworthy performance in image classification when compared to other methods and human-level analysis, deep learning networks (DNNs) play a significant role in the medical field. The force of the image using CXR was examined and divided into negative and positive cases using a deep learning classification framework that Hemdan et al. introduced. Using 3905 X-ray images and a deep learning-based versatile net framework, Apostolopoulos et al. created a highly accurate method for pulmonary disease diagnosis. Despite the fact that COVID-19 cases were classified using pre-trained models, the training dataset was negatively impacted by this pre-trained model. Image classification, object detection, segmentation, registration, and other deep learning techniques have been preserved, according to Litjens et al. considerations and analysis of various examination papers on deep learning algorithms (Butt et al., 2020).

In order to deal with a small dataset, Afshar et al. proposed the capsule network (CAPS), an elective modeling framework whose architecture was made up of a few cases with a limited number of trainable parameters and convolution layers. To produce CXR images, Waheed et al. developed an auxiliary classifier generative adversarial network (ACGAN). However, it has been difficult to gather a significant number of CXR images in a short amount of time because of the COVID-19 outbreaks (Dey et al., 2020).

CNN performance can be improved by using coronavirus detection. A GAN-based classifier was suggested by Bellemo et al. to create retinal fundus images that work with artificial databases. Five patients who had negative RT-PCR results were examined by Xie et al. The specialist oversaw standard swab examinations for each patient and was ultimately given the COVID-19 diagnosis. Du et al. identified clinical COVID-19 features in both children and adults. They looked at 67 cases from two research centers, including 14 children and 53 adults. The findings showed that kids had serious lung injuries. A COVID-19 detection strategy was promoted by Wang et al. using CXR images, and they also presented an open COVID-Net benchmark dataset made up of 13,975 CXR images from 13,870 patients (Kermany et al., 2018).

Deep learning and machine learning research on COVID-19 was thoroughly examined by Alyasseri et al. They reviewed prior research on COVID-19 and came to the conclusion that CNN primarily employs a deep learning algorithm. a method for examining chest radiographs to analyze COVID-19. It is described as a COVID-DeepNet framework that uses a Butterworth bandpass filter and contrast-limited adaptive histogram equalization (CLAHE) to reduce noise and improve the contrast of CXR images. For the purpose of evaluating the COVID-DeepNet framework, a sizable dataset called COVID-19-vs was created. The main drawback of this approach is that it can separate the input images into COVID-19-infected and healthy categories (Asnaoui et al., 2020).

Agrawal et al. developed an automatic method for COVID-19 identification using COVID-Net that was pre-trained on the ImageNet dataset in response to various examination works. To assess the positive predictive value, the architecture of COVID-Net and the models of VGG-19 and ResNet-50 were compared. Under certain circumstances, it is possible to access the medical dataset for free. The model needs a sizable COVID-19 dataset to train the model, which is a difficult task. The repeated and blurred images could cause the small dataset to collapse simultaneously. To ascertain this, the system suggested an expansion of manufactured data, such as DCGAN, because it can combine high-frequency data and features from the input data where conventional methods are not feasible. Therefore, DCGAN was applied to a discriminator that could distinguish between CXR images along with other crucial features to transfer learning extracts. This improved the generator's ability to identify the true CXR image by allowing the discriminator to distinguish between real CXR images and artificially produced images. Even though COVID-19 is the subject of extensive research, there are still problems with small datasets and ineffective outcomes. This study aims to aid healthcare organizations in efficiently assessing COVID-19 cases (Shi et al., 2020).

Additionally, it can be deduced that the average particularity in CT scan images obtained by the DL method in the case of COVID-19 was higher than 92%, indicating that these images are generally more explicit than earlier texts. In general, the responsiveness of DL strategies was also higher than or on par with that of standard analytic techniques in CT scan images of COVID-19. The diagnosis of these illnesses using unsupervised methods is undoubtedly difficult and complex due to the excessive similarity between the effects of COVID-19 on lung tissue and various types of bacterial and viral pneumonia. Almost all of the studies used the CNN algorithm, though different algorithms were evidently also used in conjunction with the CNN algorithm in various studies, according to the analysis of the algorithms and DL architectures. It is unrealistic to expect to come close to these structures' capacity to recognize and analyze COVID-19 without changing the boundaries of the CNN models used in these studies, each of which has unique image analysis features. The diagnosis of this condition by DL algorithms under the guidance of a radiologist resulted in improved efficacy and decreased diagnostic errors in a variety of cases of pneumonia, particularly COVID-19, according to a review of distributed studies.

Approaches and Methodologies

Following data collection, a few cutting-edge techniques should be used to diagnose COVID-19, and this section illustrates the various approaches used by different papers. First, a description of pre-processing methods along with their characteristics is given. Second, feature extraction methods are thoroughly covered. Following that, segmentation and classification strategies are examined. It's crucial to only train a model with the essential components because adding extra features or image regions degrades the model's performance. Therefore, the better assignment prior to the training phase is to extract the Region of Interest (ROI). As a result, segmentation is useful because it can separate the irrelevant and unnecessary portions of an image. Image segmentation is defined as the process of dividing a digital image into distinct segments based on some pre-defined criteria, where a segment represents a set of pixels in digital image processing and computer vision. By identifying the ROI, such as the lung region, segmentation, like other aspects of medical image processing, improves the efficacy of COVID-19 detection.

Non-Functional Requirements Analysis

- Performance: The performance is completely depending on the model's efficiency so when the model performs well, then the performance is efficient.
- Safety: The system is designed in modules where errors can be detected and fixed easily.
- Reliability: The system runs parallel processing which eases the workload, making the performance better and more reliable.
- Maintainability: After the deployment of the system, any error can be corrected and maintained by the developer.
- Testability: The system will be tested considering all the aspects.
- Usability: The system is accessed through GUI where the output will be generated on the terminal and also the predicted results will be displayed in the form of images.
- Libraries Used: pandas, Keras, TensorFlow, sklearn, torchvision, PIL, matplotlib and Tkinter for creating the GUI.

SYSTEM ARCHITECTURE

Figure 1 describes and shows the model's accuracy and displays the predicted results in the form of images.

Figure 1. Model accuracy to display the predicted results in the form of images.

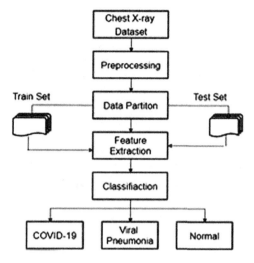

Figure 2. Abstract system design and interaction

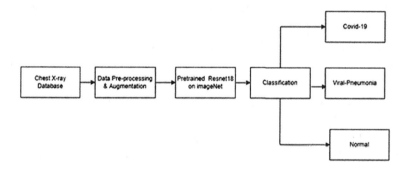

Use Case Diagram

The outline of the use case diagram outline is to describe the interconnection between the actors and its system who take part in the framework. Figure 3. shows the generic use cases and the attributes of the system.

Figure 3. Generic use cases and the attributes of the system.

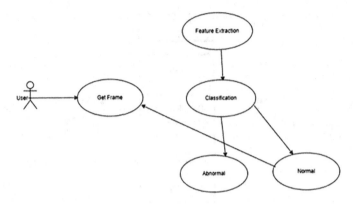

MODULES IMPLEMENTED

Data Collection

By gathering the collection of chest x-rays that were normal, pneumonia-infected, and covid-19-infected, collection of images for the dataset construction, the dataset contains 1125 X-ray images, of which the system used 80% for training and 20% for testing. 500 images of patients who don't experience any effects from COVID-19 pneumonia are mixed in with 625 images of patients with pneumonia and COVID-19. Twenty of the test set's images feature patients with COVID-19 and pneumonia, while the remaining twenty feature patients without either condition. These days, the lockdown phase makes it difficult for scientists and physicians to exchange data. Large COVID-19 data sets are therefore difficult for some scientists to locate. The current COVID-19 automation researches are still in the early stages because a deep learning design requires a sizable number of images to familiarize a model properly and productively. The analysts have, however, proposed and used a few COVID-19 datasets that exhibit unusual results in identifying COVID-19-affected lungs.

Preprocessing

With the aid of OTSU Segmentation, noise information will be removed from the image during pre-processing in order to highlight the affected area of the image and maintain the resolution and clarity of the x-ray images. Because of an increase in the types of interruption, such as those to the imaging and data collection systems, medical images are frequently contaminated by noise information. As a result, it might be extremely challenging to judge them visually. To enhance the information the image generates for the unaided eye or to use it as feedback for algorithms, a few pre-handling techniques can be used. Prior to anything else, the datasets are scaled down to 100100 pixels and converted entirely to grayscale images. After that, every single image is converging into three channels, creating an input shape of 1001003. Furthermore, standardization or Z-normalization is used to normalize the dataset. Standardization. A COVID-19 dataset is likely to contain some unreadable, duplicate, blurry, etc. images that hurt a model's performance. Preprocessing procedures must therefore be carried out on repetitive images. Depending on the issues with the dataset, various preprocessing techniques can be used. Overfitting is one of the serious problems with deep learning.

Data augmentation is utilized during the pre-processing stage to reduce the effects of overfitting. The most common data augmentation techniques include resizing, scaling, editing, flipping, and turning. The following is a discussion of some of these data augmentation techniques:

1. In order to prepare the model, resizing is required because the images are not always within the same estimate. All of the images are resized into a fixed dimension, like 224 224, in order to generalise the data set.
2. To expand the sample size of the data sets, flipping or rotating is done. Flipping is primarily done horizontally and vertically.
3. Scaling or cropping is the second most popular augmentation technique. Not all of the image's components must be used. Therefore, the system has used the cropping method to lessen the redundancy.
4. To increase or decrease the brightness of the images, brightness or intensity adjusting is necessary.

Data Partition

The system will divide the dataset of chest x-ray images into two parts: training and testing. The training portion will contain 80% of the dataset's chest x-ray images. The data splitting ratio used in this dataset of 1125 images for the training, validation, and test sets is 80:10:10. According to the following, the count value of the relevant dataset is Training Dataset: 1125 total images, of which 125, 500, and 500 are the quantities of chest X-ray images that are COVID-19 positive, viral pneumonia-positive, and normal images, respectively. Dataset for testing: In a set of three pictures, one shows viral pneumonia, one shows a normal chest X-ray, and the third shows a COVID-19-positive patient.

Feature Extraction

There are two categories of feature extraction: "Texture Feature Extraction" and "Morphological Feature Extraction." In order to calculate the average, the model will build a matrix to store the input data in an array format based on the image's texture and shape. In computer science, image processing—particularly feature extraction using CNN—is a significant research area. In this proposed work, an experiment was conducted using both scratch and pre-trained CNN models. The results obtained by the scratch model were disagreeable, but the pre-trained model performed well.

Texture Feature Extraction

The Gray-level Co-occurrence Matrix (GLCM), which represents the spatial relationship between pixels in a picture, is used to evaluate the texture features. The frequency with which pixels with intensity value co-occur in a characterized connection with pixels with intensity value is described in each GLCM input picture. The contrast, correlation, mean, entropy, variance, and standard deviation features that make up second-order features were extracted.

Morphological Feature Extraction

The identification of malignant tissues depends heavily on morphological characteristics. Morphological features transform the morphology of a picture into a set of quantitative characteristics that can be used for classification or grouping. The primary goal of the morphological feature extricating technique (MFEM), a nonlinear separating process, is to locate and extract significant information from a picture and modify it morphologically in accordance with the demands of segmentation, etc. The MFEM observes the related components in the clusters with an area greater than a predetermined threshold and accepts binary clusters as input. A picture can be used to extract a number of features, and a region can be determined by counting the number of pixels in the image. The perimeter and area of the image work together to calculate the values of various other morphology features.

Training and Testing

To create the model, data must be trained and tested. The CNN algorithm was used for model training. A convolutional neural network is frequently used in deep learning to analyse visual imagery. Each X-ray image is passed through the Convolution and Max-pooling layers during the model training process, after which the image's data is flattened and fed to the layers of the fully connected neural network. The resulting class is then predicted by the neural network and compared to the actual result. The neural network's weights are then modified using the comparison.

Classification

In order to classify the images, the system will build a model by using hybrid deep learning algorithms. For the analysis of COVID-19 using three different types of X-ray samples, a combined CNN and RNN technique was developed. ResNet18 was used to extract complex features from samples that were 224 x 224 x 3. The RNN classifier used the extracted features to distinguish between COVID-19, pneumonia, and typical cases. The COVID-19 classification by the CNN-RNN network includes these supplementary steps. To extract key features from X-ray images and reshape the component map into the grouping, use various pre-trained CNN models. Finally, use a SoftMax classifier and a multi-layered RNN with the feature map as the input to arranging COVID-19 X-ray images. Rectified Linear Unit (RELU) was used to implement the convolutional layers, and the Dropout layer was used to lessen model overfitting.

Convolutional Neural Networks are essentially used in all of the COVID-19 diagnosis models as feature extractors and softmax or sigmoid as classifiers. A sigmoid layer was also used by some creators to enhance CNN. CNN and the softmax layer were combined by the creators. However, the lack of COVID-19 images makes it difficult to train these models because they require a lot of data. The two main classification methods for COVID-19 images are binary classification and multiclass classification. The creators of the Binary Classification attempted to categorise patients into COVID-19 and non-COVID-19 groups, but this approach is incredibly incorrect because a variety of lung diseases, including viral pneumonia, bacterial pneumonia, community-acquired pneumonia, and viral pneumonia, can be classified as COVID-19. Thus, many authors classify images using a softmax classifier to differentiate between COVID-19, viral pneumonia, bacterial pneumonia, local area-acquired pneumonia, and normal images. Multiclass classifiers outperformed binary classifiers in terms of accurately detecting COVID-19 images. The system will detect and display whether the chest x-ray image is normal, viral pneumonia, or covid-19 infected images, as well as the model performance in the form of accuracy.

DEEP LEARNING MODELS

1. Convolution Neural Network (CNN): CNN is a deep learning model which is mainly used for image recognition, classification and segmentation because of its ability to provide high accuracy.

Figure 4. describes the working of the CNN algorithm

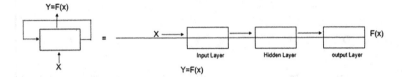

The convolutional layer is the fundamental layer of CNN. This is responsible for deciding the plan characteristics. The input image passes through a channel or filter in this layer. The function map is acquired from the result of similar filters by a convolution operation. CNN's depend for the most part on fully connected layers, which have been demonstrated to be very valuable in computer vision image recognition and classification. Convolution and pooling are the beginning levels of the CNN model, which helps in separating the image into attributes and analyses them separately.

2. Recurrent Neural Network (RNN): An RNN, also known as a sequential model, is a deep learning model with an input layer, a hidden layer, and an output layer that is used for image classification and to predict outcomes in sequential data.

A recurrent neural network (RNN) is a type of artificial neural network in which node associations form a directed or undirected graph along a temporal axis. This enables it to exhibit temporal dynamic behavior. RNNs, which are derived from feedforward neural networks, can deal with variable-length sequences of inputs by utilizing their inner state (memory). As a result, they are suitable for tasks such as unsegmented speech recognition and connected handwriting recognition. Recurrent neural networks are Turing complete in theory and can execute inconsistent programs to process arbitrary sequences of inputs.

3. RESNET18: Residual Networks 18 is a combination of both CNN and RNN models which is 18 layers deep and also mainly used for image classification where it can likewise work on the efficiency of deep neural networks with more neural layers while lessening the percentage of error.

Deeper neural networks are more difficult to train. will present a residual learning structure to aid in the training of networks that are significantly deeper than those previously used. will explicitly rewrite the layers as learning leftover capacities about the layer inputs rather than learning unreferenced functions will provide far-reaching exact proof that these residual networks are easier to improve and can

Figure 5. Working on the RESNET18 algorithm

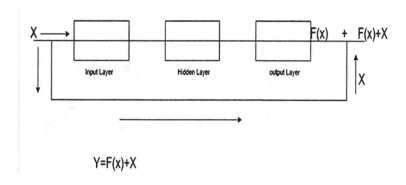

acquire accuracy from greatly increased depth. On the ImageNet dataset, the system evaluate residual nets with depths up to 152 layers greater than VGG nets but with lower complexity. ResNet has emerged as the ground-breaking deep neural network (DNN) model for computer vision tasks. ResNet models with up to 150 layers have addressed this issue by using alternate connections - connections that avoid at least one layer. This allows gradients to pass through without being reduced. In this case, the system used the 18-layer ResNet-18 model as the foundation and fine-tuned it for the classification problem.

The architecture in Figure 5 describes the working of the RESNET18 algorithm that explains the detailed working of Residual Networks -18 by passing the input data through each layer in the model.

RESULTS AND DISCUSSIONS

Figure 6 shows the same x-ray image side by side after applying the OTSU Segmentation to see the highlighted infected area in the image.

Similarly, in Figure 8 the system displays the sample testing data images after starting the model training to check the model performance.

Figure 9 and 10 displays the model accuracy and the training loss of the model after every 20 evaluating steps to notice the model performance.

In Figure 11 the system displays the predicted image by the model to check whether the model predicted the correct image or the incorrect image.

Figure 6. Changes in x-ray images after applying OTSU Segmentation.

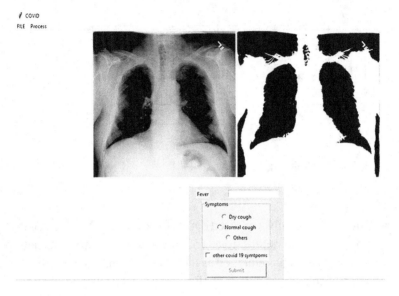

CONCLUSION AND FUTURE WORK

Detection of COVID-19 from chest X-ray images is of essential significance for both doctors and patients to reduce diagnostic time and reduce financial costs. Artificial intelligence and deep learning are equipped for perceiving images for the undertakings instructed. In this, a few examinations were performed for the high-precision recognition of COVID-19 in chest X-ray images utilizing ConvNets. Different groups — COVID-19/Normal, COVID-19/Pneumonia, and COVID-19/

Figure 7. Training data images after the model training.

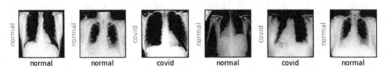

Figure 8. Testing data images after the model training.

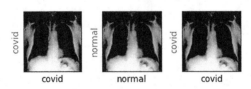

Figure 9. Training loss accuracy after model training

```
>>>
======== RESTART: C:\Users\user\Desktop\Five-2 Code&Dataset\GUI_main.py ========
normal
Found 500normal
Pneumonia
Found 500Pneumonia
covid
Found 22covid
normal
Found 1normal
Pneumonia
Found 1Pneumonia
covid
Found 1covid
Num of training batches 171
Num of test batches 1
```
Squeezed text (122 lines).
```
Starting training..
Starting epoch 1/1
======================
Evaluating at step 0
Val loss: 1.4888, Acc: 0.0000
Accuracy::: 0.0
Evaluating at step 20
Val loss: 1.3869, Acc: 0.3333
Accuracy::: 0.3333333333333333
```

Pneumonia/Normal — were considered for the classification. Different image dimensional aspects, different network designs, cutting-edge pre-trained networks, and machine learning models were used and assessed utilizing images and statistical

Figure 10. Training loss and model accuracy after model training

```
Evaluating at step 40
Val loss: 1.5457, Acc: 0.6667
Accuracy::: 0.6666666666666666
Evaluating at step 60
Val loss: 1.5052, Acc: 0.6667
Accuracy::: 0.6666666666666666
Evaluating at step 80
Val loss: 2.0321, Acc: 0.3333
Accuracy::: 0.3333333333333333
Evaluating at step 100
Val loss: 1.8892, Acc: 0.6667
Accuracy::: 0.6666666666666666
Evaluating at step 120
Val loss: 3.5195, Acc: 0.3333
Accuracy::: 0.3333333333333333
Evaluating at step 140
Val loss: 1.0208, Acc: 0.3333
Accuracy::: 0.3333333333333333
Evaluating at step 160
Val loss: 0.6436, Acc: 0.6667
Accuracy::: 0.6666666666666666
Training loss: 0.0014
Result....
```

Figure 11. Output image predicted by the RESNET18 Model.

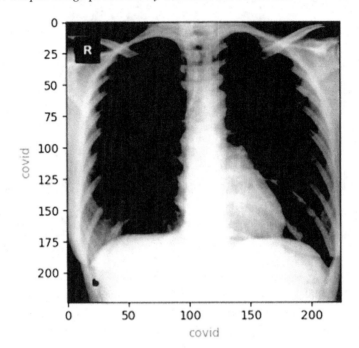

data. Whenever the number of images in the database and the discovery season of COVID-19 (normal testing time = 0.03 s/image) are viewed as utilizing ConvNets, it tends to be proposed that the considered designs decrease the computational expense with elite execution. The outcomes showed that the convolutional neural network with minimized convolutional and fully connected layers is capable of detecting COVID-19 images inside the two-class, COVID-19/Normal and COVID-19/Pneumonia orders, with mean ROC AUC scores of 96.51 and 96.33%, respectively.

Computerized high-accuracy technologies might give significant help to doctors in diagnosing COVID-19. Further examinations, in view of the outcomes acquired in this study, would give more data information about the utilization of CNN designs with COVID-19 chest X-ray images and enhance the results of this review. closer to the outcomes, A sum of 1125 pictures (125 COVID-19 cases, 500 normal and 500 pneumonia cases) have been utilized to examine the performance of the proposed algorithm, where 70% of images of each class are acknowledged for training, 15% are used for validation, and rest is for testing. It is seen that the VGG19 acquires the highest classification accuracy of 88.6%, separately. Especially, DL models need an immense volume of training data with clear labels. In any case, most pictures are physically commented on, which demonstrates a time-consuming procedure that requires expert knowledge .one method for resolving this issue is by empowering clinical image sharing among various research and health centers over the world, which holds incredible guarantees for COVID-19 diagnosis. In view of this, the post-COVID-19 phase might confront more data-sharing between different national and international organizations. In future work, the system could restructure a better solutions by enhancing the efficiency of model performance while predicting the data by implementing some more neural network models for classifying the data collected and could build the model for better prediction using Neural Networks and can definitely expect better results.

REFERENCES

Abbas, M.M. & Abdelsamea, M.M. (2020). *Classification of COVID-19 in chest X-ray images using DeTraC deep convolutional neural network*. Springer.

Alazab, M., Awajan, A., Mesleh, A., Abraham, A., Jatana, V., & Alhyari, S. (2020). COVID-19 prediction and detection using deep learning. *Int J Comput Information Syst Indus Manage Appl, 12*, 168–181. doi:10.1016/j.chaos.2020.110338

Albahli, S. (2020). Efficient GAN-based Chest Radiographs (CXR) augmentation to diagnose coronavirus disease pneumonia. *International Journal of Medical Sciences, 17*, 1439–1448. doi:10.7150/ijms.46684

Albahli, S., & Albattah, W. (2020). Detection of coronavirus disease from X-ray images using deep learning and transfer learning algorithms. *Journal of X-Ray Science and Technology, 28*, 841–850. doi:10.3233/XST-200720

Alsharman, N., & Jawarneh, I. (2020). GoogleNet CNN neural network towards chest CT-coronavirus medical image classification. *Journal of Computational Science, 16*, 620–625. doi:10.3844/jcssp.2020.620.625

Altan, A., & Karasu, S. (2020). Recognition of COVID-19 disease from X-ray images by hybrid model consisting of 2D curvelet transform, chaotic salp swarm algorithm and deep learning technique. *Chaos, Solitons, and Fractals, 140*, 110071. doi:10.1016/j.chaos.2020.110071

Apostolopoulos, I.D. & Mpesiana, T.A. (2020). Covid-19: automatic detection from X-ray images utilizing transfer learning with convolutional neural networks. *Phys. Eng. Sci. Med.* 1–8.

Ardakani, A., Acharya, U. R., Habibollahi, S., & Mohammadi, A. (2020). COVIDiag: A clinical CAD system to diagnose COVID-19 pneumonia based on CT findings. *European Radiology, 31*, 1–10. doi:10.100700330-020-07087-y

Boudrioua M. S. and Boudrioua A. (2020). Predicting the COVID-19 epidemic in Algeria using the SIR model. *medRxiv*.

Bridge, J., Meng, Y., Zhao, Y., Du, Y., Zhao, M., & Sun, R. (2020). Introducing the GEV activation function for highly unbalanced data to develop COVID-19 diagnostic models. *IEEE Journal of Biomedical and Health Informatics, 24,* 1–10. doi:10.1109/JBHI.2020.3012383

Bukhari, S.U.K., Bukhari, S.S.K., Syed, A., & Shah, S. S. H. (2020. The diagnostic evaluation of Convolutional Neural Network (CNN) for the assessment of chest X-ray of patients infected with COVID-19. *MedRxiv*.

Butt, C., Gill, J., Chun, D., & Babu, B. A. (2020). Deep learning system to screen coronavirus disease 2019 pneumonia. *Applied Intelligence, 6,* 1–7. doi:10.100710489-020-01714-3

Celik, Y., Talo, M., Yildirim, O., Karabatak, M., & Acharya, U. R. (2020). Automated invasive ductal carcinoma detection based using deep transfer learning with whole-slide images. *Pattern Recognition Letters, 133,* 232–239. https://doi.org/10.1016/j.patrec.2020.03.011

Cohen, J. P., Morrison, P., & Dao, L. (2020). *COVID-19 Image Data Collection.* https://arxiv.org/abs/2003.11597.

Dey, N., Rajinikanth, V., Fong, S. J., Kaiser, M. S., & Mahmud, M. (2020). Social group optimization-assisted Kapur's entropy and morphological segmentation for automated detection of COVID-19 infection from computed tomography images. *Cognitive Computation, 12,* 1–13. doi:10.20944/preprints202005.0052.v1

El Asnaoui, K., & Chawki, Y. (2020). Using X-ray images and deep learning for automated detection of coronavirus disease. *Journal of Biomolecular Structure & Dynamics,* 1–12. doi:10.1080/07391102.2020.1767212

Groves, P., Kayyali, B., Knott, D., & Kuiken, S. V. (2016). *The big data revolution in healthcare: Accelerating value and innovation.* McKinsey.

Guyon, I., & Elisseeff, A. (2003). An introduction to variable and feature selection. *Journal of Machine Learning Research, 3,* 1157–1182.

Hemdan, E. E.-D., Shouman, M. A., & Karar, M. E. (2020). *COVIDX-Net: A Framework of Deep Learning Classifiers to Diagnose COVID-19 in X-Ray Images.* https://arxiv.org/abs/2003.11055

Horry, M.J., Chakraborty, S., Paul, M., Ulhaq, A., Pradhan, B. (2007). X-Ray Image based COVID-19 Detection using Pre-trained Deep Learning Models.

Islam, M.Z., Islam, M.M., & Asraf, A. (2020). *A Combined Deep CNN-LSTM Network for the Detection of Novel Coronavirus (COVID-19) Us- ing X-ray Images*, 1–20.

Janosi, W. (1988). *Steinbrunn, M. Pfisterer, and R. Detrano, "UCI machine learning repository- heart disease data set*. School Inf. Comput. Sci., Univ.

Kanne, J. P., Little, B. P., Chung, J. H., Elicker, B. M., & Ketai, L. H. (2020). Essentials for radiologists on COVID-19: an update—radiology scientific expert panel. Radiological Society of North America.

Kermany, D., Zhang, K., & Goldbaum, M. (2018). Labeled optical coherence tomography (OCT) and Chest X-Ray images for classification. *Mendeley Data, 2*. doi:10.17632/RSCBJBR9SJ.2

Khan, A.I., Shah, J.L., Bhat, M. (2020). CoroNet: A Deep Neural Network for Detection and Diagnosis of Covid-19 from Chest Xray Images. *Computer Methods and Programs in Biomedicine*.

Kumar, P., & Kumari, S. (2020). Detection of coronavirus Disease (COVID-19) based on Deep Features. Https://Www.Preprints.Org/Manuscript/202003.0300/V1.

Li, L., Qin, L., Xu, Z., Yin, Y., Wang, X., & Kong, B.. (2020). Using artificial intelligence to detect COVID-19 and community-acquired pneumonia based on pulmonary CT: Evaluation of the diagnostic accuracy. *Radiology, 296*, E65–E71. doi:10.1148/radiol.2020200905

Loey, M., Smarandache, F., & Khalifa, N. E. M. (2020). Within the lack of chest COVID-19 X-ray dataset: A novel detection model based on GAN and deep transfer learning. *Symmetry*, 12.

Luz, E., Silva, P. L., Silva, R., Silva, L.., Moreira, G., & Menotti, D. (2020). *Towards an Effective and Efficient Deep Learning Model for COVID-19 Patterns Detection in X-ray Images*, 1–10.

Mahmud, T., Rahman, M. A., & Fattah, S. A. (2020). CovXNet: A multi-dilation convolutional neural network for automatic COVID-19 and other pneumonia detection from chest X-ray images with transferable multi-receptive feature optimization. *Computers in Biology and Medicine, 122*, 103869.

Minaee, S., Kafieh, R., Sonka, M., Yazdani, S., Soufi, G. J. (2020). Deep-COVID: Predicting COVID-19 From Chest X-Ray Images Using Deep Transfer Learning. *Medical Image Analysis*.

Minaee, S., Kafieh, R., Sonka, M., Yazdani, S., & Soufi, G. J. (2020). Deep-covid: Predicting covid-19 from chest x-ray images using deep transfer learning. *arXiv preprint arXiv:2004.09363*.

Muhammad, L. J., Islam, M. M., Usman, S. S., & Ayon, S. I. (2020). Predictive Data Mining Models for Novel Coronavirus (COVID-19) Infected Patients' Recovery, SN. *Computer Science, 1*, 206.

Narin, A. Kaya, C., & Pamuk, Z. (2020). Automatic Detectrion of Coronavirus Disease Using x-ray images and deep convolutional neural networks. ArXiv2003.10849.

Narin, C. K. & Pamuk, Z. (2016). Automatic detection of coronavirus disease (covid-19) using x-ray images and deep convolutional neural networks. *arXiv preprint arXiv:2003.10849*.

Ozturk, T., Talo, M., Yildirim, E. A., Baloglu, U. B., Yildirim, O., & Acharya, U. R. (2020). Automated detection of COVID-19 cases using deep neural networks with X-ray images. Computers in Biology and Medicine, p. 103792.

Punn, N. S., & Agarwal, S. (2020). *Automated diagnosis of COVID-19 with limited posteroanterior chest X-ray images using fine-tuned deep neural networks.* https://arxiv.org/abs/2004.11676

Rahimzadeh, M., Attar, A. (2020). New Modified Deep Convolutional Neural Network for Detecting COVID-19 from X-ray Images. *Informatics in Medicine Unlocked, 19*.

Rekha Hanumanthu, S. (2020). Role of intelligent computing in COVID-19 prognosis: A state-of-the-art review. *Chaos, Solitons, and Fractals, 138*, 109947. doi:10.1016/j.chaos.2020.109947

Rothan, H. A., & Byrareddy, S. N. (2020). The epidemiology and pathogenesis of coronavirus disease (COVID-19) outbreak. *Journal of Autoimmunity, 109*, 102433. doi:10.1016/j.jaut.2020.102433

Shi, F., Wang, J., Shi, J., Wu, Z., Wang, Q., Tang, Z., He, K., Shi, Y., & Shen, D. (2020). Review of artificial intelligence techniques in imaging data acquisition, segmentation and diagnosis for COVID-19. *IEEE Reviews in Biomedical Engineering*.

Shi H., Han X., Jiang N., Cao Y., Alwalid O., Gu J. (2020). Radiological findings from 81 patients with COVID-19 pneumonia in Wuhan, China: a descriptive study. *The Lancet Infectious Diseases*. pmid:32105637

Wang, L., Wong, A. (2020). COVID-Net: A Tailored Deep Convolutional Neural Network Design for Detection of COVID-19 Cases from Chest X-Ray Images. *Scientific Reports*.

Zu, Z. Y., Jiang, M. D., Xu, P. P., Chen, W., Ni, Q. Q., & Lu, G. M. (2020). Coronavirus disease 2019 (COVID-19): a perspective from China. Radiology, p. 200490.

Chapter 6

Machine Learning Approaches Towards Medical Images

Gayathri S. P.
The Gandhigram Rural Institute (Deemed), India

Siva Shankar Ramasamy
International College of Digital Innovation (ICDI), Chiang Mai University, Thailand

Vijayalakshmi S.
Department of Data Science, Christ University (Deemed), India

ABSTRACT

Clinical imaging relies heavily on the current medical services' framework to perform painless demonstrative therapy. It entails creating usable and instructive models of the human body's internal organs and structural systems for use in clinical evaluation. Its various varieties include signal-based techniques such as conventional X-ray, computed tomography (CT), magnetic resonance imaging (MRI), ultrasound (US) imaging, and mammography. Despite these clinical imaging techniques, clinical images are increasingly employed to identify various problems, particularly those that are upsetting the skin. Imaging and processing are the two distinct patterns of clinical imaging. To diagnose diseases, automatic segmentation using deep learning techniques in the field of clinical imaging is becoming vital for identifying evidence and measuring examples in clinical images. The fundamentals of deep learning techniques are discussed in this chapter along with an overview of successful implementations.

DOI: 10.4018/978-1-6684-6523-3.ch006

INTRODUCTION

The creation of biological image processing algorithms has significantly advanced as a result. This has made it possible to create automated algorithms for information extraction through image analysis or evaluation. Segmentation, which splits the image into visually distinct parts with semantic meaning for the given problem, is the fundamental stage in this automated analysis. Each area often has consistent features regarding its color, texture, or grey level. Precise segmentation and discernible sections are crucial for additional research that may require determining the homogeneity levels of texture or layer thickness. There may occasionally be several items of the same class in the image. Instance segmentation is the separation of regions containing items belonging to the same class while disregarding other courses, as opposed to semantic segmentation, in which objects belonging to the same type are not separated, but various categories are. Three categories can be used to categorize all image segmentation approaches manual segmentation (MS), semi-automatic segmentation, and fully automatic segmentation techniques. For MS methods to properly annotate each picture pixel, subject matter experts must first identify the region of interest (ROI) and then draw exact boundaries around the ROI. MS is essential for the advancement of semi-automatic and utterly automatic segmentation algorithms since it gives the tagged ground truth pictures. MS takes a lot of time and is only practical for tiny image datasets. When it comes to high-quality images, the high resolution could mean that the edges are no longer clearly defined. As a result, even little changes in the ROI boundary's pixel selection can cause significant errors. Another problem with manual segmentation is that it is subjective because it depends on the knowledge and experience of the expert, and as a result, there is frequently a lot of variation among and within experts.

A minimal amount of human intervention with automated algorithms is required for semi-automatic segmentation techniques to deliver appropriate segmentation results. The user's input may include choosing an estimated initial ROI that will be used to segment the entire image later on. To reduce segmentation errors, region borders may need to be manually checked and edited. One illustration of a semi-automatic segmentation procedure is the seeded region growing (SRG) calculation, which iteratively blends close-by pixels of a comparable force given a client giving the beginning seed point. Another model is the level-set-based dynamic form model, which begins with introductory limit shapes addressed by forms and iteratively modifies them through a contracting or development activity given the verifiable level of a capability. This strategy enjoys the benefit that it doesn't and 3) limited region-based dynamic form draws near, which enjoys the benefit of overseeing assorted surfaces and using area boundaries to describe the closer view and foundation of the picture utilizing little neighborhood districts.

There is no requirement for human cooperation with the completely programmed division drawing near. The greater part of these techniques, for example, shape models, chart book-based division calculations, irregular backwoods, and profound brain organizations, depend on directed learning procedures that request preparing information. Comparable limitations are forced since both the preparation information and, on account of unaided learning frameworks, the approval information requires labeled pictures created through human division. The significant differences in ROI form, size, texture and some cases, color between patients and the lack of contrast between regions present additional difficulties for the automated segmentation of medical images. Broad changes in the source picture data may also be caused by noise or inconsistent source data capture, which is frequently the case in practical applications. Because of this, most current approaches including those based on clustering techniques, watershed algorithms, and machine learning (ML) have the fundamental issue of not being globally applicable, which restricts their use to a small number of applications. Human feature engineering, which is frequently used in conjunction with machine learning techniques based on support vector machines (SVM) or neural networks (NN), is also time-consuming, unable to handle natural material in its raw form, and frequently incapable of adapting to new information. On the other hand, deep learning algorithms can analyze unprocessed natural data, negating the necessity for manually created features. These techniques have found usage in the segmentation of biological images and the semantic segmentation of photos of nature. Faster central processing units (CPUs) and graphic processing units (GPUs), which have significantly decreased the training and execution times, availability of massive data sets, and improvements in learning algorithms have all contributed to the rising use of deep learning methodologies.

Machine Learning

The classification of the return on original capital investment, such as a sick or sound district, is typically done using an AI-based image division approach. The most crucial step in creating such an application is the pre-handling stage, which can involve using a channel to reduce noise or enhance contrast. Following the pre-handling phase, the image is divided using a division process, such as thresholding, a grouping-based approach, or edge-based division. Highlights from the return on investment are then extracted in light of size, surface, difference, and variety data. Then, using methods like head part investigation (PCA) or measured examination, overwhelming qualities are discovered. The chosen characteristics are subsequently input as information into an SVM- or NN-based ML classifier.

The ML classifier chooses the best limit isolating each class using the information highlight vector and target class markings. After preparing, the ML classifier can be

Figure 1. Comparison of the ML and DLC (Suzuki, K. 2017).

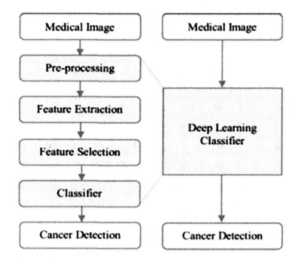

used to arrange fresh, ambiguous data to determine its category. Regular problems include selecting the proper highlights, determining the component vector's length, the classifier's kind, and the crucial pre-handling requirements based on the raw image attributes.

Deep Learning-based Classifier (DLC)

DLC can process raw images directly, hence pre-processing, segmentation, and feature extraction should not be necessary. However, because of the input values restriction, most deep learning methods demand image scaling. While some methods require intensity normalization and contrast enhancement, these steps could be omitted if training uses the data augmentation methods that will be covered later. As a result, DLC has a higher classification accuracy since it can prevent mistakes brought on by inaccurate feature vectors or messy segmentation. In Fig. 1 below, the comparison of the ML and DLC techniques is displayed. Network architecture design for achieving the best results has replaced traditional image processing methods for feature engineering in research using DLC-based approaches. The fact that DLC networks frequently include numerous hidden layers means that, compared to ML-based techniques, more mathematical operations are carried out, making the models for DLC networks more computationally costly.

A contribution of an element vector is used by an AI classifier, as shown in Fig. 1, to deliver the item class. It's interesting to note that a deep learning classifier contributes a picture to offer the item class. It should be noted that theoretically because profound learning includes more layers than traditional fake brain organizations (ANN), it might be seen as an enhancement above ANN. It is thought of as a kind of illustrated learning because each layer diverts the knowledge from the one before into another portrayal at a higher and somewhat more noticeable consideration level. The model can learn both close and between relationships across the entire dataset thanks to a variety of tiered structures.

A deep learning model covers information that arises as a result of a non-straight capability at each tier. The primary layer of representation for a given image is typically used to distinguish between the existence or absence of edges in a particular arrangement and their placement within the picture. To enable the following layers to recognize things using these blends, the third layer links these examples with more complex blends about components of like products. The next layer classifies designs by noticing how edges are placed and ignoring little differences in these placements. Due to its varied levels of highlight representation of learning directly from the information, deep learning has achieved significant progress in several artificial intelligence applications.

Convolutional Neural Network (CNN)

The most widely used deep learning architecture, CNN, shares several traits with conventional NN. Unlike a standard NN, shown in Fig. 2(a), CNN takes an image as input and, as shown in Fig. 2(b) below, has a 3-D structure of neurons that connect with the previous layer only partially.

The CNN is comprised of various layers, including convolutional, pooling, completely associated, and non-straight actuation levels, for example, redressed direct unit layers (ReLU). To deliver volumes of element maps that incorporate highlights extricated by the channel, the convolutional layer plays out a convolution activity between pixels of the info picture and a channel. ReLU is a non-direct initiation layer that supports non-linearity and velocities up preparing by utilizing the capability $f(x) = max(0,x)$ of the info values. Pooling layer calculations are interpretation invariant since they depend on adjoining pixels, and they down-example the info values to bring down the spatial dimensionality of the picture and the computational expense.

Given that all of its neurons are connected to those in the layer before it, the last layer of a CNN is frequently a completely connected layer, comparable to the hidden layers of a standard NN. As mentioned before, CNN is widely used to resolve categorization problems. To use CNN for semantic segmentation, the input image is divided into minuscule patches of the same size. The central pixel of the patch is classified by CNN. The patch then advances, classifying the subsequent center pixel. A loss of spatial information occurs as the overlapping features from the

Figure 2. Neural Network and its layers

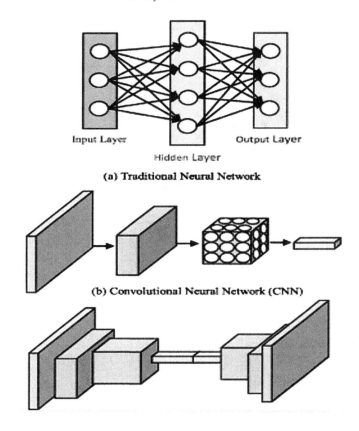

(a) Traditional Neural Network

(b) Convolutional Neural Network (CNN)

sliding patches migrate into the final fully linked network layers, rendering such a strategy worthless.

The convolutional network (FCN), which changes the last completely associated layers of the CNN into rendered convolutional layers, was proposed as a solution for this issue (c). This strategy performs semantic division while applying up-examining to low-goal highlight guides to recuperate the first spatial aspects.

To train deep neural networks, the backpropagation technique is typically combined with an optimization strategy like gradient descent. The optimization procedure must first establish the gradient of a loss function before updating the network weights and minimizing the loss function value.

Figure 3. RBM's Basic architecture (A.I. Wiki, 2020).

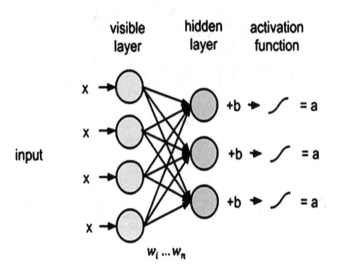

Multiple Inputs

Other Architectures

Restricted Boltzmann Machines (RBMs)

Using the concepts of energy-based models, restricted Boltzmann machines (RBMs) are a type of neural network (EBMs). EBMs encode interdependencies between variables by assigning scalar energy to each unique configuration of the variables. In a fashion that minimizes energy, the values of the observed variables are utilized to infer or forecast the values of the residual variables. Finding an energy function that provides minimal energy for the residual variables' correct values and more energy for their wrong values is how learning is accomplished. The superiority of the energy functions that are readily available during learning is then determined by the minimized loss function. There is no output layer in the RBM; instead, it has one input layer (I1,..., I4), one hidden layer (h1, 2), a bias vector (b1, b2), and a weight vector (w). Fig. 3 depicts the RBM's basic architecture.

The energy function for the RBM with a_i-weighted inputs can be defined as follows using the architecture in Figure 3:

$$E(I,h) = -\sum_i a_i I_i - \sum_j b_j h_j - \sum_{ij} I_i h_j w_{ij}$$

During the preparation of RBMs, the organization boundaries for given inputs limit the energy capability given in Eq (1). RBMs are probabilistic models, thusly the upsides of the info and secret layer neurons demonstrate the state at a particular moment. These numbers display the relevant neuron's active (state 1) or inactive (state 2) status (state 2). (state 0). Each layer in a Deep Belief Network (DBN), a type of RBM created through stacking, communicates with layers above and below it. The lowest two levels are filled with directed connections, whereas the top two layers are filled with undirected connections. Unlike the Deep Boltzmann Machine (DBM), a different kind of RBM network solely includes undirected connections. When inputs are noisy, DBMS is thought to handle uncertainty well.

Deep Learning Architectures Based on Autoencoder

An autoencoder brain network is a solo learning calculation that packs input into an inactive space portrayal utilizing the backpropagation method with target esteems that are indistinguishable from the information sources.

It comprises an encoder piece of the organization, which packs input into a dormant space portrayal communicated by the capability h = f(x), and a decoder part of the organization, which recreates input from the inert space portrayal. The secret layer is compacted by making it more modest in size than the information layer. Such an organization is alluded to as under-complete. Because of the more modest dimensionality of the secret layer, the organization just learns the most striking elements in the preparation set. On the other hand, by principally deactivating the neurons in the covered layer, a sparsity requirement can be utilized to accomplish similar ends.

The input in autoencoder-based deep learning systems is an image that has been downscaled to create a latent representation in smaller dimensions. This enables the autoencoder to be trained and taught using the compressed version of the images. The autoencoder architecture is shown in Fig. 4. One issue with autoencoders is that there are more nodes in the hidden layer than there are input values. A null or identity function, where the input and output are equal, could be learned by the network. Denoising autoencoders, which purposefully corrupt the data by randomly assigned between 30 and 50 percent of the input values as zero, are employed to tackle this problem. The actual values are lowered to zero depending on the network's node count and data size.

The risk of learning a null function is minimized while computing the loss function because the result is compared to the original input. Their uses are somewhat restricted due to discontinuities in the latent space representations that preclude autoencoders from being employed as generative models. To solve this issue, variational autoencoders were developed. Two encoded vectors, one of which

Figure 4. Autoencoder Architecture (Deepak Birla, 2019).

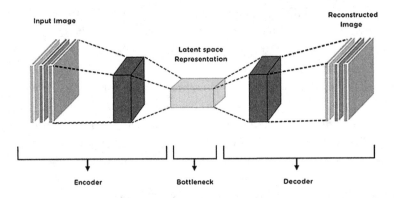

is a vector of means and the other a vector of standard deviations, are the output of the encoder in a variational autoencoder. The random variable that samples the output encoded vector uses these vectors as its inputs. As a result, even with little variations in the same input during training, the decoder can correctly decode the encoded information. Because of the stochastic nature of the autoencoder, random interpolation and sampling are possible because the latent space representation is continuous by design.

Architectures for Deep Learning Based on Sparse Coding

Unsupervised learning techniques known as "sparse coding" select an overcomplete set of basis vectors to represent the input data. An overcomplete representation is one whose dimension is greater than the input. Finding a linear combination of these basis vectors that matches the input is the objective. Additional sparsity restrictions must be implemented to handle any degeneracy due to the overcomplete network. The benefit of sparse coding is that it can identify correlations between related descriptors and record important aspects of images.

Networks of Generative Adversaries (GANs)

The purpose of GANs is to imitate a transform function that receives a random variable as input and, after training, follows the desired distribution. While another network is being trained to function as a discriminator to distinguish between created date and accurate data, While the second network aims to reduce the final classification error between produced and actual data, the first network aims to raise it. As such, the two networks operate as adversaries. As a result, both networks get better after every training cycle.

Recurrent Neural Networks (RNNs)

When it is impossible to forecast the magnitude of the input, RNNs are designed specifically to handle series-type inputs. Since the series input is different from many other inputs in that it influences surrounding values, the network must comprehend this relationship. RNNs are one type of these networks; they learn from past data and base their current output on the input at hand. The previous input data is kept in a hidden state vector and is a network component. This means that depending on the inputs that came before it in the series, the same input could produce a different output. The network becomes recurrent when it is repeatedly altered with different input series values, resulting in different fixed-size output vectors. The secret state is updated with each input. The depth of RNNs can be increased by adding additional hidden state layers, non-linear hidden layers between the input and the hidden state layer, extra layers between the hidden state layer and the output layer, or a combination of all three.

Standard Methods for Putting Deep Learning Architectures Into Practice

Deep learning algorithms have been applied in various ways for image segmentation. The first method involves building and training a neural network from scratch, which takes much time and typically calls for the availability of a sizable labeled dataset. One of the pre-trained CNNs already in use, like AlexNet, which was trained to classify 1.2 million high-resolution photos for the ImageNet Large Scale Visual Recognition Challenge 2010, can be utilized in the second technique. With this approach, the last few network layers are frequently removed and changed out for new, task-specific layers. The low-level properties learned from millions of images in the initial layers are merged with the task-specific features collected in the final layers to deploy the network for the categorization of new images. Since fewer weights need to be determined, this has the benefit of reducing implementation time. Transfer learning, which outperforms random weight initialization, is frequently used with networks trained on ImageNet data.

The third way involves using pre-trained CNNs to extract features from the data, which are then utilized as inputs to train a traditional classifier, such as a support vector machine. This approach eliminates the requirement for manual feature extraction by humans by automatically extracting features for a sizable amount of category data. Two well-known convolutional neural networks are UNet for biomedical image segmentation and V-Net for volumetric medical image segmentation. There are growth and contraction paths in the FCN variant known as U-Net.

The contraction path is composed of the max-pooling layer and subsequent convolutional layers. It is used to extract features while preserving a manageable size for feature maps. In the expansion path, convolutional layers and up-conversion are employed to recover the size of the segmentation map at the expense of the localization data. From the contraction layer to the expansion layer, localization information is transferred through skip connections. Through these parallel connections, signals can travel straight from one network block to another without the need for additional computing complexity. The final convolutional layer before the segmentation output transfers the feature vector to the necessary number of target classes. Similar to U-Net, V-Net comprises two parts: compression and decompression. Each stage of the compression process comprises one to three convolutional layers. Each stage uses convolution operations to learn the residual function from volumetric data made up of voxels. By using convolution like the pooling layer, the compression approach reduces the resolution by half. However, there is no use of the pooling layer to lower memory usage.

A generalization of ReLU, the Parametric Rectified Linear Unit (PReLU), commonly referred to as Leaky ReLU, is utilized as a non-linearity activation function. The network's decompression component increases the spatial coverage of the feature maps to generate enough data for volumetric segmentation. Deconvolution is employed to expand the input size, and the residual function is learned similarly to the network's compression component. Two feature maps with the same size as the input volume are produced by the convolutional layer preceding the output. The projected foreground and background region information can be found on the two feature maps. Skip connections are employed to transmit localization information from the contraction part of the network to the expansion part, like U-Net.

Performance Metrics

By employing accepted criteria, the effectiveness of the picture segmentation system is assessed, allowing for comparison with other methods that have been published in the past. According to the system's functionality, some variables influence the choice of a suitable evaluation metric. These measures could assess accuracy, memory usage, processing speed, and computational complexity, among other things. Many performance indicators can be used to evaluate the segmentation accuracy of deep learning models.

i. Predicted Accuracy

Predicted Accuracy is calculated as the ratio of correctly estimated pixels to all pixels in the image. According to the definition, accuracy is the proportion of correctly identified image pixels. It is sometimes referred to as general pixel precision. Although it is the most fundamental performance statistic, it has the drawback of representing image segmentation performance incorrectly in the event of class imbalance. When one segmentation class outweighs the other, there is a class imbalance. In this situation, the dominating class's superior accuracy will obscure the opposing class's lower accuracy, resulting in skewed results. Therefore, when there is no class imbalance, it is advised to utilize the accuracy measure to assess segmentation performance with images.

An alternative to the preceding definition of accuracy is per-class accuracy, which computes the proportion of correctly categorized pixels for each class and then computes their average. This statistic is useful for images where there is an imbalance in class. In the event of a class imbalance, both the average and the accuracy for each class must be taken into account. The average per-class accuracy is constrained by the decline in confidence measurement of the individual classes. Additionally, fewer instances of a specific class may lead to high variation, affecting the findings' accuracy.

ii. Precision and Recall

Precision is calculated as the ratio of correctly predicted disease pixels to all predicted disease pixels. According to the definition, precision is the percentage of disease pixels that match the actual disease pixels in automatic segmentation results. As it is susceptible to over-segmentation, precision is a valuable indicator of segmentation performance. Low precision scores are the outcome of over-segmentation.

The recall is calculated as the ratio of correctly predicted disease pixels to all actual disease pixels. The percentage of disease pixels in the ground truth that was accurately recognized using artificial segmentation is known as recall, according to the definition given above. It is vulnerable to under-segmentation since low recall scores are the outcome.

iii. F1 Score

Since high values for both imply that the projected segmented zones match the ground truth in terms of both location and level of information, precision and recall can be used jointly for a particular segmentation result. The F1 algorithm, also known as boundary F1, determines the harmonic mean of recall and precision to match contours or boundaries between expected and actual segmentation.

iv. JACCARD and DICE Similarity

The Jaccard Similarity, also known as Intersection-Over-Union (IoU), measures how closely two segmentations match up. Its definition is the ratio of the overlapped and joined areas between the predicted and actual segments.

Because DICE takes into account both false alarms and missed values in each class, it is superior to overall pixel accuracy. In addition to calculating the number of correctly classified pixels, DICE is thought to be superior since it evaluates the accuracy of the segmentation borders. DICE is widely used to evaluate system performance repeatability through cross-validation as well.

Different Biomedical Image Types

The imaging technique determines the kinds of biomedical images that can be produced. The following is a list of some of the most common biomedical imaging modalities. The list below isn't complete because new imaging methods are continually being created to produce quicker and more precise diagnoses.

i. X-Ray

The most popular imaging method for spotting fractures and bone dislocations is X-ray imaging. Two dimensions make up the created image. To develop imaging analysis techniques, the National Institutes of Health (NIH) has made 100,000 chest x-ray images, related data, and diagnoses accessible to the public. To build machine learning models that automatically detect 14 frequent illnesses like pneumonia or punctured lungs, the Massachusetts Institute of Technology (MIT) has also made a dataset available that has a collection of more than 350,000 chest x-rays.

ii. CT Scan

A CT scan is a type of computerized imaging procedure that produces extremely finely detailed cross-sectional images of the internal organs, bones, soft tissue, and blood arteries in the body. Traditionally, the images are captured in the axial or transverse plane perpendicular to the body's long axis. To generate a three-dimensional image, these images—also known as slices—can be reformatted into various planes. It is one of the most prevalent biomedical imaging problems and is often used to find the presence and size of tumors to diagnose cancer. The National Institutes of Health (NIH) have made 32,000 CT pictures, associated data, and diagnoses openly available to improve the accuracy of lesion recognition.

iii. MRI

Strong magnetic fields are utilized in MRI imaging to create images of bodily tissues, organs, and physiological processes. Soft tissues or non-bony body parts are scanned using MRI technology. The primary distinction between it and CT scans is that it employs ionizing radiation from x-rays. Knee and shoulder injuries can be seen more clearly in MRI scans compared to both x-rays and CT images. Grey and white matter in the brain can be distinguished using MRI images, which aids medical professionals in locating tumors and aneurysms. For the benefit of biomedical imaging researchers, the Open Access Series of Imaging Studies (OASIS) project has assembled neuroimaging datasets comprising more than 2000 MRI sessions.

iv. US

The US imaging technique produces visual images of the inside organs, tissues, and blood flow using high-frequency sound waves. It is the approach taken most frequently to monitor the fetus throughout pregnancy. It usually is not used to image bones or tissues that contain air, including lungs; instead, it is mainly employed for abdominal, vascular, and thyroid studies. Utilizing the US has the advantages of being quick and radiation-free.

v. OCT

OCT is a technique that produces two- and three-dimensional micrometer-resolution pictures from inside biological tissue using low-coherence light. Since it provides a cross-sectional image of the retina and allows the doctor to inspect each layer, it is mostly used to diagnose eye disorders. Layer mapping and thickness measurements are made possible as a result, which is beneficial for diagnosis.

vi. Microscopic Images

The microscopic structure of the tissue is examined using microscopic medical imaging. The tissue to be examined is often acquired through biopsy, and small pieces of the tissue are stained and colored to expose cellular characteristics. The images are given color, visibility, and contrast using counterstains. These pictures are frequently used to find cancer. The size, shape, and distribution of the cells in the tissue are among the characteristics that are typically examined.

Data Enhancement

Deep learning neural networks perform best when there is enough data to work with. The issue is that training samples are rarely accessible in sufficient quantities, particularly in medical imaging. To improve the datasets that are currently available but lack reliable data, various data augmentation procedures are employed to generate more training data from the existing dataset.

The data augmentation methods alter the image data while maintaining the class, and they may include:

- flipping images horizontally and vertically by flipping the rows and columns of pixels;
- moving image pixels in a single direction, either horizontally or vertically, without changing the overall image dimensions.
- rotating the image by a specific degree between 0 and 360;
- Alternately zoom in or out of the image at random using either interpolation or the addition of extra border pixels.
- This will train the model to account for such variations in test photos.

The majority of these strategies involve the nearest-neighbor fill, duplication of the boundary pixels, averaging, or interpolation to add new pixels in place of some existing ones. The first four methods covered above are stiff data augmentation methods because the shape itself is not modified. The fifth method maintains the balance between horizontal and vertical augmentation. The first four methods covered above are stiff data augmentation methods because the shape itself is not modified. The fifth method maintains the balance between horizontal and vertical augmentation. The image will stretch more in one direction than the other if it is different. In contrast, the image will be shared if it is just stretched in one direction along the diagonal axis on both ends. Another method, known as elastic deformation, is also an option. It alters the shape of the region of interest in a way that is comparable to stretching under external force. Similar to how solid materials distort when subjected to external tension and can recover if the stress is removed, the shape changes are reversible.

Finally, considering that medical images may have come from several sources, contrast improvements can be used to correct intensity fluctuation in the image. These augmentation methods' main goal is to increase the deep neural network's generalizability while preventing both underfitting and overfitting of the features. Typically, these methods are used automatically while the network is being trained. Additionally, linear transformations are usually sufficient and a safer method to apply. At the same time, significant augmentations may result in unrealistic variances in appearance. The ultimate decision will, once more, be heavily influenced by the characteristics of the target region and the type of medical imaging. The lack of data can be remedied by using data augmentation techniques. However, they do not fully account for all the variances that can exist in actual data.

REVIEW OF ARTICLES ON BIOMEDICAL IMAGE SEGMENTATION USING DEEP LEARNING

A survey of current works involving profound learning methods for biomedical picture division is given in Table 1. The articles picked were every one of those that applied profound learning models to biomedical picture division applications. The table incorporates the reference for the applicable article, the methodology, the approach, and the comments. At last, the exhibition measurements are utilized to assess the calculation.

As found in Table 1, the majority of these procedures depend on CNN-or FCN-based methods. None of these investigations utilize the exchange learning methodology. One of them did, notwithstanding, utilize a profound learning model as a component extraction capability before characterization utilizing an organized help vector machine. Most of these applications utilized CT, MR, or the US, which is where exploration is presently going. One justification for this is the effortlessness with which picture information bases are made open through different contests or from other public sources.

Convolutional layers play the job of totally connected layers, which infers that the info picture can be of any size and that the grouping result will be spatially requested for the whole info picture. Also, it gets rid of the superfluous calculations expected by covering districts in the customary fix-based strategy. To acquire exceptionally thick expectations, the 3D profound oversight technique pulls include maps from the secret layers, upscales them by connecting deconvolutional layers, and uses the SoftMax capability. The SoftMax capability performs standardization on exponentials of information vectors comprising of genuine numbers. It changes over them into a likelihood conveyance to such an extent that the result values are in the span $(0,1)$ with the number of result values equivalent to 1. The grouping mistake of these branch yields contrasted and the ground truth was utilized to change the organization boundaries of the standard organization during preparation.

A voxel-based profound learning model called VoxResNet was proposed by Chen et al.(2018) in light of the remaining organization. Profound learning models regularly construct highlight portrayal in a bit-by-bit design with level changes of low-center high. More data might be advanced as the organization's layer count increments, improving the organization's ability for segregation. Nonetheless, sometimes,

Table 1. Overview of some Deep Learning Techniques

Reference	Modality	Method	Remarks	Performance Metrics and Results
Badea et al. (2016)	Clinical Images	CNN (LeNet and NiN)	LeNet and Network in Network (NiN) models were used for classification of burn images and for performance evaluation by comparing the classification accuracy for Skin vs Burn and Skin vs Light Burn vs Serious Burn.	Accuracy; LeNet was able to achieve an accuracy of 75.91% and 58.01% for classification of Skin vs Burn and Skin vs Light Burn vs Serious Burn, respectively. NiN achieved an accuracy of 55.7% for classification of Skin vs Light Burn vs Serious Burn.
Dhungel et al. (2015)	X-Ray	RBMs and CNN	Deep convolution and deep belief networks which are a type of RBM network are utilized as functions for the conditional random field (CRF), and structured support vector machine (SSVM). The techniques are explored for segmenting breast masses from mammograms.	The Dice index of the proposed approach with all potential functions was 93% using CRF and 95% using SSVM.
Chen et al. (2018)	3D MRI	3D ResNet	A voxel-wise residual network (VoxResNet) built with 25 layers is proposed for segmentation of key brain tissues into white matter (WM), gray matter (GM), and cerebrospinal fluid (CSF).	DICE, the 95th-percentile of the Hausdorff distance (HD), and absolute volume difference (AVD); The DICE score results obtained for the proposed model for GM, WM, and CSF were 86.15%, 89.46%, and 84.25%, respectively when trained on relatively small training data.
Zhou et al. (2018) [7]	CT	CNN	A performance analysis of a proposed segmentation technique was performed for multiple organ detection	The proposed approach achieved a mean JSI value of 79% and 67% for segmentation using 3D- and 2D deep CNN, respectively. Results are averaged for 17 types of organs.
Jia et al. (2017)	Microscopic Images	FCN	An FCN based approach is proposed for the image to image segmentation of histopathology images under deep weak supervision. Additionally, super-pixels instead of pixels were also used which is effective in maintaining intrinsic tissue boundaries.	F1 measure; The proposed algorithm was able to achieve the best F1 measure of 83.6% which was significantly higher than existing weakly supervised algorithms.

execution begins to decline at additional significant layers of the organization, which isn't typically the situation. It has been shown the way that ResNets can take care of the corruption issue since leftover learning simplifies network streamlining. Skip associations are utilized. Subsequently, data can spread forward and in reverse using the whole organization.

VoxResNet, which stretches out from 2D ResNet to 3D ResNet, was proposed to manage volumetric information for mind division from 3D attractive reverberation (MR) examines. The recommended network contains stacked remaining modules, as found in Fig. The info and changed highlights are joined with skip association in the VoxRes module. The size vacillations of 3D physical cerebrum structures are tended to by coordinating staggered logical data with four assistant classifiers (C1-C4). During the preparation stage, loads converged with information from different modalities that offered free data about a similar cerebrum structure in the organization's most memorable layer. Contrasted with results from a solitary methodology, this expanded effectiveness.

Jia et al.(2017) recommended profound frail management as a technique for different occasions of learning. Occurrences are gathered together and alluded to as sacks in the MIL procedure during the classifier preparation. During the preparation, each sack is given a decent or negative name, however, the cases are not given any marks.

The MIL procedure commands that the classifier model lead sack level order notwithstanding occasion level name expectation. Every malignant growth or non-disease picture should be visible according to the point of view of histopathology imaging as a sack, and every pixel inside the picture is an example. Commonly, a classifier predicts names at the pixel level, and afterward, a SoftMax capability or standardized dramatic capability is utilized to assess the expectation at the picture level.

Like Chen et al.(2018) gathered the information for combination, the DWS method exploits various side results from the CNN, frequently after the convolutional layer. An insignificant expectation mistake between the ground truth and each side truth, which prompts better execution, is the point of DWS. The two systems were consolidated to make DWSMIL, another structure.

The worn-out tissue limits that come from regarding pixels as examples are another issue that periodically emerges. This issue was tended to by involving super-pixels as occasions, which decreases the number of cases and thus the computational intricacy.

To section cerebrum growths, Havaei et al.[6] joined included maps from a few levels to inspect different customized CNN structures. A nearby and worldwide pathway was first evolved to evaluate changes in expectation precision brought about by visual subtleties of the region around the pixel and relevantly with regards to the fix's position in the mind. Two Path CNN is the name of the design.

A flowing of two CNNs filled in as the establishment for the subsequent design. A layer of the second CNN was connected with the result layer of the primary CNN. Link happened in three better places in the second CNN: the information layer, the primary secret layer, and the layer straightforwardly before the result layer.

These additional information sources were acquainted with the second CNN to analyze what adjoining marks meant for the division expectation at the end. Compared to the single-way plan, the division was further developed by the two pathways model, aggregate preparation of the two convolutional pathways, and two preparation periods.

Cut-by-cut division of the pictures was finished from the hub view, with the model breaking down each 2D cut. Ngo et al. coordinated a functioning form model with a Deep Belief Network (DBN), a kind of RBM, to expand execution while utilizing less preparation information. Despite their comparative appearance, the recommended approach utilized two autonomous DBNs to section endocardial and epicardial pictures with sensible precision. Because of deficient preparation and testing information, a semi-computerized procedure delivered improved results than a completely programmed one. To make more muddled DBN models, more significant preparation information is fundamental.

The MICCAI 2009 Left Ventricle (LV) Segmentation Challenge utilized a current picture library that incorporates 15 groupings (from cardiovascular cine attractive reverberation) for preparing, testing, and online use. Upon the arrival of the test, the online dataset was at first made accessible for testing the division calculations that the members had submitted. Nonetheless, the total data set and the member results are currently accessible. In a request to characterize consumed photographs, Badea et al.(2016) utilized the LeNet CNN design, which was first evolved in 1998 for written by-hand digit acknowledgment on banknotes. LeNet CNN has seven layers, including one completely associated layer, two pooling layers, and three convolutional layers. Between a block's two huge layers, a multi-facet perceptron recognizes NiN from LeNeT. To work on the organization's ability for reflection, the multi-facet perceptron capabilities as a nonlinear capability approximator. The consumed picture data set had 611 photos at a size of 1664 × 1248 pixels from 53 pediatric patients. To make the last picture size 230 by 240 pixels, the photos were physically edited. As per the outcomes, the clear engineering succeeded at paired arrangement issues, yet execution essentially declined as intricacy rose.

Zhao et al.(2018) told the best way to portion examples of 3D pictures utilizing a profound learning model and a feebly directed way to deal with produce completely explained information. Between a block's two huge layers, a multi-facet perceptron recognizes NiN from LeNeT.

To work on the organization's ability for reflection, the multi-facet perceptron capabilities as a nonlinear capability approximator. The consumer picture information base had 611 photos at a size of 1664 × 1248 pixels from 53 pediatric patients. The photos were physically edited to make the last picture size 230 by 240 pixels. As per the outcomes, the clear design succeeded at parallel arrangement issues, yet execution altogether declined as intricacy rose. Zhao et al. told the best way to portion occurrences of 3D pictures utilizing a profound learning model and a feebly managed way to deal with produce completely explained information.

The inventive part of the proposed strategy is that while it needs a bounding box for each example, it just requires a few full voxel explanations to proceed too, dissimilar to the technique set forth by Chen et al. which needs the whole assortment of voxel comment information. After first identifying all occurrences utilizing 3D bounding box comment, the two-step strategy sections generally identified occasions. To portion 2D cases, cover R-CNN was used. Veil R-CNN can perceive things in an image and give a division cover to each case. Three biomedical datasets were utilized to test the proposed technique: the core of HL60 cells, house-developed microglia cells, and C. elegans creating incipient organisms.

Deep convolutional networks with multiple levels were suggested by Roth et al.(2018) for the segmentation of the pancreas, which has an extremely high degree of anatomical diversity. For diabetic individuals, measuring organ volume requires segmenting the pancreas. The investigation included the ground facts and 82 volumes of abdominal CT that had been augmented with contrast. To obtain more data instances, random non-rigid deformations were also used. To make sure that the warped image had fluctuations like the actual data, the degree of distortion was chosen. Image patches were initially labeled in the bottom-up way that was suggested. An axial, coronal, and sagittal view of the patches was used to create a per-location probability response map for the image patch labeling. The next step was region labeling using a zoom-out method to create super-pixel zones with great sensitivity but low precision at various spatial scales. Each super-pixel was given a chance that contained pancreatic tissue using CNN. Finally, utilizing the probability response map and CT intensity values derived from the superpixel zones, the complete organ was discovered from an abdominal CT scan.

Using CNN and the Hough-based voting technique, Milletari et al.(2017) suggested a patch-wise multi-atlas method for segmenting deep brain areas in MRI and ultrasound images. Even partially visible or artifact-corrupted structures can be locally segmented using this method. Each input is connected to its feature representation that is retrieved from the second-to-last fully connected layer by CNN, which has been trained to distinguish between foreground and background regions in the patches taken from the voxels. Segmentation is carried out using the votes of these neighbors and the related segmentation patches, and the procedure is repeated for all foreground patches. In all parameter settings evaluated, this technique outperformed voxel-wise segmentation of CNNs, used less training data, produced better segmentation outlines, and did not require post-processing.

CONCLUSION

Some critical issues have been brought up in this overview of deep learning methods for biomedical picture segmentation. These studies were founded on empirical findings proving the viability of the suggested strategy for the specified application using small datasets. Why a particular problem responds well to deep learning methodologies must be determined. There is still much to learn about the solution to this problem. To aid in the intuitive comprehension of the feature maps obtained from the hidden layers, many academics are striving to develop unique visual techniques. Additionally, many academics fail to address the issue of the network response's generalizability if the data source alters. That is what a change in data-gathering equipment will mean for the features of an image, such as illumination or color intensity levels.

The performance of the network will suffer because of the lack of generalizability. The requirement for massive image datasets is another issue with DLC-based networks. As a result, there will be a significant need for storage and memory, and the networks will need much time to train. Another area of ongoing research is the reduction of training time and the efficient management of memory and storage needs for enormous amounts of imaging data. A further obstacle to developing DLC-based techniques for biological applications in clinical practice is the lack of suitably big imaging datasets. Even though the healthcare sector holds many imaging data, it is not publicly shared because it either contains protected health information or because the company views it as a proprietary asset. The long-term benefits of data sharing will much surpass any short-term gains obtained by hiding the data. Hence, efforts must be made to make such data publicly available through grand challenge competitions or data donations. Unprecedented performance improvements have been made possible by deep learning techniques in various biomedical applications, from segmenting skin lesions to automatically analyzing CT scans. However, if more tagged photographs are made available to the public, much more can be accomplished. Generating the ground truths still faces a substantial hurdle due to the experts' human labeling of the visual data. Exploring unsupervised learning techniques needs to receive more attention in the absence of ground realities.

REFERENCES

Badea, M. S., Felea, I. I., Florea, L. M., & Vertan, C. (2016). The use of deep learning in image segmentation, classification, and detection. *arXiv preprint arXiv:1605.09612.*

Birla, D. (2019). Basics of Autoencoders. *The Medium.* https://medium.com/@birla.deepak26/autoencoders-76bb49ae6a8f

Chen, H., Dou, Q., Yu, L., Qin, J., & Heng, P. A. (2018). VoxResNet: Deep voxelwise residual networks for brain segmentation from 3D MR images. *NeuroImage, 170,* 446–455. doi:10.1016/j.neuroimage.2017.04.041 PMID:28445774

Havaei, M., Davy, A., Warde-Farley, D., Biard, A., Courville, A., Bengio, Y., Pal, C., Jodoin, P.-M., & Larochelle, H. (2017). Brain tumor segmentation with deep neural networks. *Medical Image Analysis, 35,* 18–31. doi:10.1016/j.media.2016.05.004 PMID:27310171

Jia, Z., Huang, X., Eric, I., Chang, C., & Xu, Y. (2017). Constrained deep weak supervision for histopathology image segmentation. *IEEE Transactions on Medical Imaging, 36*(11), 2376–2388. doi:10.1109/TMI.2017.2724070 PMID:28692971

Milletari, F., Ahmadi, S. A., Kroll, C., Plate, A., Rozanski, V., Maiostre, J., & Navab, N. (2017). Hough-CNN: Deep learning for segmentation of deep brain regions in MRI and ultrasound. *Computer Vision and Image Understanding, 164,* 92–102.

Roth, H. R., Shen, C., Oda, H., Oda, M., Hayashi, Y., Misawa, K., & Mori, K. (2018). Deep learning and its application to medical image segmentation. *Medical Imaging Technology, 36*(2), 63–71.

Suzuki, K. (2017). Overview of deep learning in medical imaging. *Radiological Physics and Technology, 10*(3), 257–273. doi:10.100712194-017-0406-5 PMID:28689314

Wiki, A. I. (2020). A Beginner's Guide to Important Topics in AI, Machine Learning, and Deep Learning. https://wiki.pathmind.com/restricted-boltzmann-machine

Zhou, X., Yamada, K., Kojima, T., Takayama, R., Wang, S., Zhou, X., & Fujita, H. (2018, February). Performance evaluation of 2D and 3D deep learning approaches for automatic segmentation of multiple organs on CT images. In Medical Imaging 2018: Computer-Aided Diagnosis (Vol. 10575, pp. 520-525). Spie.

Chapter 7
Overview of Recent Trends in Medical Image Processing

Chitra P.
Dhanalakshmi Srinivasan University, India

ABSTRACT

The most recent technological progression has been accomplished in clinical imaging throughout the past few years. The medical services framework laid out original strategies to work on clinical information handling. One of the vast areas of exploration development addresses the progression of clinical picture handling through the interdisciplinary field. The fast improvement manages many information handling. The information to be held, from crude information to advanced picture correspondence, might give the total information stream in the cutting-edge clinical imaging framework. These days, these frameworks offer high-goal information in spatial and power aspects, and are likewise quicker in securing times. The cycle can bring about a broad measure of excellent picture information. The handled information assists with achieving precise symptomatic outcomes. Clinical imaging is a pathway to acquire images of the human body parts for clinical purposes to recognize and analyze illnesses.

INTRODUCTION

The deduction of brain network calculations is directed to the new advances in profound realizing, which achieves the strategies of picture characterization or division. The utilizations of flow research included progressed picture examination in the clinical imaging worldview. The requirement for the instrument behind the brain organization and profound learning procedures interface with PC researchers and

DOI: 10.4018/978-1-6684-6523-3.ch007

Figure 1. Medical Image Processing using Deep Learning

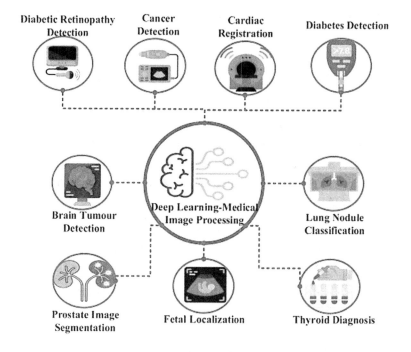

neuro-oncology analysts. The present status of the artistry animates the exhibition and causes the effect of clinical imaging procedures in Deep learning. This study centres around current situations and comments on the progression of the clinical imaging field. By and large, the exploration outlines the turn of events and difficulties behind clinical imaging, which is related to picture includes and associated issues. Additionally, it will examine the challenges to the more far-reaching utilization of these calculations.

Clinical imaging applications secure many lives consistently. The imaging modalities help specialists distinguish and analyze a large number of infections. For instance, it applies to malignant growth treatment, an infected appendix, stroke, and coronary illness. Early sickness identification saves many lives, which assists with expanding logical speculation. Artificial Intelligence (AI) plays a critical part in the clinical imaging industry for productive access and bits of knowledge into patient life-altering events into different sicknesses, wounds, and conditions that might be difficult to distinguish without mechanical mediation.

Images are the most noticeable information source in medical care and, simultaneously, one of the most provoking sources to break down. Clinicians today should depend primarily on clinical picture examination performed by exhausted radiologists and, here and there, explore filters themselves. A clinical master principally makes the understanding of clinical information. As far as picture understanding by a human master, it is restricted given its subjectivity, the intricacy of the picture, the wide varieties that exist across various translators, and weakness.

Regardless of consistent advances in clinical imaging, one out of four patients experiences bogus up-sides on picture readings. This can prompt superfluous obtrusive methods and follow-up filters that add patient expense and stress. And keeping in mind that fake negatives happen now and again, the effect can be disastrous. The shockingly high pace of misleading up-sides is somewhat because of worries among radiologists about missing a finding. Late recognition of sickness essentially drives up therapy costs and lessens endurance rates.

However, this present circumstance is set to change as trailblazers in clinical innovation apply AI to picture examination. The most recent profound learning calculations are now empowering robotized investigation to give exact outcomes conveyed limitlessly quicker than the manual interaction can accomplish. As these computerized frameworks become unavoidable in the medical care industry, they might achieve revolutionary changes in the way radiologists, clinicians, and even patients use imaging innovation to screen therapy and further develop results.

EMERGING TECHNIQUES IN MEDICAL IMAGING

The emerging field of research will focus on the latest techniques to enhance the performance of medical image processing. Numerous applications progressed to improve clinical data processing to achieve better outcomes. The technological-driven application focuses on the medical field, for valuable information has been processed with challenging issues. In the current scenario, many clinical applications are based on deep learning techniques for classifying and diagnosing an abnormality. Many other innovative applications are used to achieve the efficiency of medical image processing. The study will address the current methods and upgrades in medical imaging techniques.

a) Advanced Combination Imaging Procedures

Clinical imaging has an enormous volume of information for handling and transmission. The broad advances in clinical imaging have a few modalities for diagnosing human medical problems. For the most part, the clinical imaging modalities are remembered for a few famous modalities, for example, attractive reverberation imaging (MRI), Ultrasound images, clinical radiation, and angiography and registered tomography (CT). A few checking methods are utilized to envision the human body for demonstrative and treatment purposes. Likewise, these modalities

Figure 2. Medical Imaging Modalities

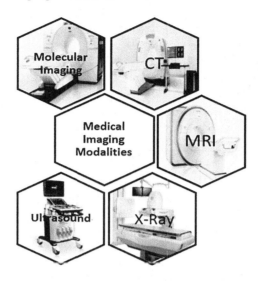

assist with realizing the patient's clinical history regarding the advancement of the sickness state, which has been, as of now, analyzed for therapy plan. The considerable effect is directed to the utilization of X-beams and ultrasound. The clinical imaging modalities are assisted with diagnosing the sickness accurately.

The most widely recognized kinds of analytic radiology tests include:

- Processed tomography (CT), otherwise called a mechanized pivotal tomography (CAT) filter, including CT angiography
- Fluoroscopy – Medical Resonance imaging (MRI) and attractive reverberation angiography (MRA)
- Mammography - Atomic medication, which incorporates such tests as a bone output, thyroid sweep, and thallium heart stress test
- Plain X-Rays, which incorporate chest X-rays
- Positron outflow tomography, additionally called PET imaging, PET output, or PET-CT, when it is joined with CT Ultrasound

b) AI and Neuroimaging

Advancement in Artificial Intelligence (AI) is a trending technique in computer science that deals with machine learning, deep learning and reinforcement learning algorithms. Clinical applications are based on machine learning and deep learning techniques to elevate processing efficiency to overcome risk management issues, radiology for classification, risk assessment, segmentation task, diagnosis, prognosis,

Figure 3. Illustration of (a) Biological Neuron Network and (b) Convolutional Neural Network

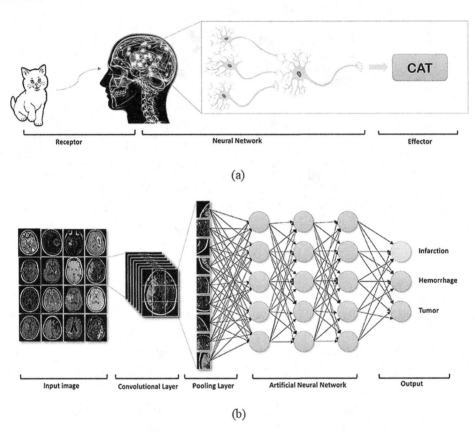

(a)

(b)

and prediction of therapy responses. AI-based techniques are extensively used for brain image analysis to diagnose and classify diseases. In recent techniques, optimization of algorithms is used to improve the computational speed and access the massive amount of data. Deep learning is the right choice to process an enormous amount of data and process the structure of human cognitive functions. Different types of AI-based techniques use neural network concepts like Convolutional neural networks (CNN) and recurrent neural networks (RNN).

Initially, deep learning applications in neuroradiology focused on computer vision techniques for detecting abnormal issues, segmentation of anatomical structures, and detecting lesions. Other innovative applications of AI in various technical aspects of medical imaging. In particular, the techniques applied in the acquisition of images. Various methods are used for image generation and enhancement using deep learning to remove image artefacts and normalize and enhance image quality.

c) Integrated 3-D Imaging

The 3D imaging strategy envelops the high-level perception, handling and examination of 3D picture datasets. The images are obtained from a Magnetic Resonance Imaging (MRI) or Computed Tomography (CT) scanner. Different changes, sifting, picture division and morphological tasks might create the finished clinical picture information during the handling. The handled images quantitatively evaluate simple designs through the silico processes. In 3D picture handling, displaying the designs with high complexity is conceivable. Through this method, the image has made a precise advanced model of the subject testing issues that can be settled in their underlying investigation and recreation.

A Digital model is made utilizing a special output report with the problematic issues which can be tackled through underlying examination and reproduction. The plan of patient-explicit inserts or care plans, streamlining of material designs for target properties, or non-damaging testing of high-esteem parts. The crude information procured from the CT or MRI scanners will be changed over into tomography images from the recreation interaction to decipher and figure out the images. The images are regularly accomplished inside programming upheld by the filtering gadget.

The perception of CT or MRI delivers a 3D bitmap of grayscale forces, comprising a voxel as a 3D pixels framework. Particularly in a CT, examine the grayscale force shifts at a specific voxel connected with the X-beam retention. In MRI machines, the vital sign transmitted by proton particles includes the course of unwinding; post-utilization of solid and attractive fields has various issues centred on there. During the filtering, the picture can show up in different greyscale powers. The recreated picture volume fills in as the standard contribution for 3D picture handling. This interaction means recognizing the districts of interest inside the picture and fabricating a computerized 3D construction model. The interaction is known as division and includes different methodologies relying upon its subject, goals and limit of picture quality. The division cycle focuses on the accompanying vital elements.

- Eliminate or decrease undesirable commotion or antiquities from the images through picture separating and crop or resample information to increment handling simplicity and proficiency.
- Do picture division utilizing different production techniques, including profoundly robotized and client-directed processes.
- Measure or genuinely examine coming about model volumes to evaluate calculations.
- Acquaint CAD parts with model associations with complex picture-based models.

- Product to different configurations for further reproduction and configuration work or added substance.

CHALLENGES AND ISSUES IN MEDICAL IMAGE PROCESSING

Artificial intelligence-based applications for radiology will utilize profound learning calculations and investigation to survey the images for cancer side effects and dubious sores, giving a point-by-point report on their discoveries (Wang, Liang, Chen et al, 2020).

These frameworks are prepared on marked information to distinguish abnormalities. When another picture is presented, the calculation applies its preparation to separate ordinary versus unusual designs (e.g., harmless/threatening). As these devices become more delicate, they will likewise possibly empower prior determination of illness since they will want to distinguish slight differences in a picture that isn't effortlessly spotted by the natural eye. They can likewise be utilized to follow treatment progress, record changes in the size and thickness of growths over the long run that can illuminate treatment, and confirm progress in clinical examinations.

The most recent AI, profound learning, and work process robotization innovation can speed up understanding, develop precision, and diminish reiteration for radiologists and different specialities (Li et al., 2021). Truly most departmental picture filing and correspondence frameworks (PACS) don't give the hidden foundation that empowers these advances to flourish. Deciphering and breaking down images requires simple access and a free progression of imaging to work. Nonetheless, reviews are still frequently covered on CDs, document servers, or numerous hard-to-look through areas, putting them far away from the most recent handling calculations. It's only one reason associations are centred around combining and incorporating imaging into one document — to transform it into an essential resource(Kim et al., 2019).

Ongoing examinations demonstrate how artificial consciousness calculations can assist radiologists with working on the speed and precision of deciphering X-rays, CT scans, and other symptomatic images (Lu et al., 2017). Placing the innovation into regular clinical use directly results from the intricacies of improvement, testing, and getting administrative endorsement.

Radiology calculations centre barely around a solitary tracking down on images from a solitary imaging methodology, for instance, lung knobs on a chest CT filter. While this might help work on symptomatic speed and exactness in specific cases, most importantly, a calculation can address one inquiry simultaneously (Hesamian et al., 2019). Since many kinds of images and a large number of expected discoveries and judgments, each would require a reason constructed analysis. Interestingly, a radiologist considers a heap of inquiries and ends immediately for each imaging test and coincidental discoveries irrelevant to the first justification behind the survey, which is very typical.

In like manner, to ultimately uphold only the analytic piece of radiologists' work, designers would have to make, train, test, look for FDA leeway for, disperse, backing, and update a huge number of calculations. Also, medical services associations and specialists would have to find, assess, buy, and convey various analyses from numerous engineers and then, at that point, integrate them into existing work processes (Singh et al., 2020). Intensifying the test is profound learning models' unquenchable interest for information. Most models have been created in controlled settings utilizing accessible and frequently tight informational collections — and the outcomes that calculations produce are just as hearty as the information used to make them. Computer-based intelligence models can be weak, functioning admirably with input from the climate in which they were grown yet wavering when applied to information produced in different areas with various patient populaces, imaging machines, and strategies (Kim et al., 2018; Liu et al., 2021; Mittal et al., 2020; Raj et al., 2020).

METHODOLOGY USED IN RECENT RESEARCH

While AI commercial centres ought to cultivate far and wide reception of AI in radiology, they likewise can assist with reducing radiologist burnout by enlarging and helping them in two ways (Niyaz & Sambyal, 2018). The first, through the iterative improvement process, is working with the plan of calculations that incorporate flawlessly into radiologists' work processes and work on them. The second is to work on the speed and nature of radiology revealing. These calculations can computerize monotonous undertakings and go about as virtual inhabitants, pre-handling images to feature possibly fundamental discoveries, making estimations and correlations, and consequently adding information and clinical knowledge to the report for the radiologist's audit (Currie et al., 2019).

By assuming control over routine errands, adding quality checks, and upgrading symptomatic exactness, AI calculations can be anticipated to work on clinical results (Fu et al., 2019). For instance, an FDA-cleared model consequently evaluates bosom thickness on computerized mammograms, as thick bosom tissue has been related to an expanded gamble of bosom malignant growth. By taking care of and normalizing that standard yet fundamental errand, the calculation guides their focus toward patient at the most elevated risk. Additionally, AI calculations have demonstrated equivalent to, and now and again better than, a typical radiologist at recognizing bosom disease on screening mammograms (Castiglioni et al., 2021).

As the populace ages, the requirement for symptomatic radiology will, without a doubt, increment. In the meantime, radiology residency programs in the United States have, as of late, switched a long-term decrease in enlistments, raising the phantom of a lack of radiologists as the requirement for them develops (Patibandla et al., 2021). The new rise of AI commercial centres can speed up the reception of AI calculations, assisting with overseeing expanding responsibilities while furnishing specialists with instruments to develop further findings, medicines, and, at last, patient results.

AI and AI innovation are making strides in clinical imaging. For some wellbeing IT pioneers, AI is a welcome device to assist with dealing with the developing volume of computerized images, decrease indicative blunders, and upgrade patient consideration (Klang, 2018; Ma et al., 2021; Yadav & Jadhav, 2019). Notwithstanding its advantages, a few radiologists are worried that this innovation will reduce their job as calculations begin to take a more active part in the picture understanding cycle while ingesting volumes of information a long way past what any human can do.

IMAGE CLASSIFICATION FOR MEDICAL IMAGE ANALYSIS

Image classification, a fundamental computer vision job, is crucial to computer-aided diagnosis. To classify an input image or a sequence of images as either containing one (or a few) of preset disorders or devoid of diseases (i.e., healthy case) is a straightforward application of image classification for medical image analysis (Ting et al., 2017; Wang, Zhang, Yu et al, 2020). Examples of common clinical uses for picture classification tasks include identifying skin illnesses in dermatology and detecting eye diseases in ophthalmology (such as diabetic retinopathy, glaucoma, and corneal diseases). This field also includes the classification of pathological images for many diseases, including breast cancer and brain cancer (Gu et al., 2020; Huang et al., 2017).

The predominant categorization framework for image analysis is the convolutional neural network (CNN) (Ting et al., 2017). The CNN architecture has consistently evolved as deep learning has progressed. A pioneering convolutional neural network, AlexNet (Ting et al., 2017), was made up of recurrent convolutions, each of which was followed by a max pooling operation and ReLU with a stride for downsampling. Convolution kernels and maximum pooling were utilised in the proposed VGGNet (Ting et al., 2017) to streamline AlexNet's structure and demonstrate enhanced performance merely by growing the network's size and depth. The inception network (Gulshan et al., 2016) and its modifications (Bai et al., 2016; Gu et al., 2020) expanded the network's width and adaptability by merging and stacking, as well as convolution kernels and pooling. Skip connections were employed by ResNet

Figure 4. Evaluation Metrics for Deep learning

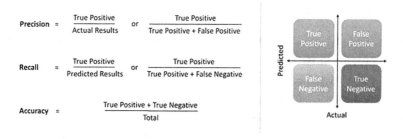

(Huang et al., 2017) and DenseNet (Redmon et al., 2016) to prevent the gradient from vanishing. A squeeze-and-excitation module was suggested by SENet (Hu et al., 2018), allowing the model to focus more on the most informative channel properties. The family of EfficientNet (Lo et al., 1995) utilised compound scaling and AUTOML to uniformly scale the network's width, depth, and resolution in a logical manner, enhancing accuracy and effectiveness. Some of the most popular CNN-based categorization network topologies are shown in Figure 2.

Detection and segmentation are two additional computer vision tasks that CNN-based networks can be used for in addition to image classification. Researchers employ a variety of evaluation metrics to assess image categorization algorithms. The percentage of genuine positives among the detected images is known as precision. The percentage of positive samples in the test set that were correctly identified as positive samples is known as recall. The accuracy rate is used to assess a model's overall accuracy. The score can be thought of as a harmonic average of the model's accuracy and recall, which takes into account both of the classification model's precision and recall. The binary classification model's predictive power is often assessed using the ROC (receiver operating characteristic) curve, and the accuracy of the model in multi-classification tasks is assessed using the kappa coefficient.

Here, we denote TP as true positives, FP as false positives, FN as false negatives, TN as true negatives, and as the number of the testing samples.

OBJECT DETECTION FOR MEDICAL IMAGE ANALYSIS

In general, identification and localization tasks are both included in object detection algorithms. The identification task is determining whether objects from particular classes appear in ROIs, whereas the localization task entails determining the object's location within the image. In medical image analysis, detection frequently aims to find patients first indications of abnormalities. Lung nodule recognition in chest CT or X-ray pictures (Li et al., 2019; Liu et al., 2019), lesion detection on CT images (Liu et al., 2020; Zhang et al., 2020), and mammograms are a few examples of clinical uses of detection tasks.

There are two types of object detection algorithms: anchor-based algorithms and anchor-free algorithms. Anchor-based algorithms can be further subdivided into single-stage algorithms and two- or multistage algorithms. Single-stage algorithms typically require less computing power than two- or multi-stage algorithms, which perform better in terms of detection. The single-shot multibox detector (SSD) and the family of YOLO (Liu et al., 2016; Redmon et al., 2016) are two traditional and popular single-stage detectors with straightforward model topologies. Both architectures are built on feed-forward convolutional networks, as seen in Figures 3(a) and 3(b), and they both produce a fixed number of bounding boxes and the accompanying scores for the existence of object instances of particular classes in the boxes. The last step is a nonmaximum suppression phase, which produces the forecasts. The SSD uses multiscale feature maps as opposed to YOLO, which relies on single-scale feature maps, and as a result offers greater detection performance. Two-stage frameworks produce a group of ROIs and categorise each one using a network. The most widely used two-stage frameworks are Faster-RCNN (Ren et al., 2015) and its offspring Mask-RCNN (Dollár & Girshick, 2017). The Mask-RCNN has an instance segmentation branch, which is the main distinction between it and the Faster-RCNN. An emerging area of research is creating algorithms without anchors. One of the most widely used ones is CornerNet (Fang et al., 2019; Law & Deng, 2018; Ye et al., 2019).

The mean Average Precision (mAP) and the false positive per image (FP/I @ recall) are the two key measures used to assess the effectiveness of detection systems. The average of all average precisions (APs) across all categories is calculated using the mAP formula. The ratio of false positives to missed opportunities, or FP/I @ recall rate, is a measurement of false positives (FP) for each image under a given recall rate.

CONCLUSION

The vast field of medical imaging focuses on deep learning techniques for achieving high-efficiency data for transmitting over the internet. Medical imaging detects early disease prediction, saves many lives, and suggests the appropriate treatment. This chapter presents an overview of medical imaging using deep learning techniques. The highlight of the objective is the defence of knowledge for understanding the related methods and issues. Also, this chapter discusses the challenges in medical imaging. A comprehensive study of medical image processing is given in a concise representation of deep learning techniques.

REFERENCES

Bai, X., Niwas, S. I., Lin, W., Ju, B. F., Kwoh, C. K., Wang, L., ... Chew, P. T. (2016). Learning ECOC code matrix for multiclass classification with application to glaucoma diagnosis. *Journal of Medical Systems*, *40*(4), 1–10.

Castiglioni, I., Rundo, L., Codari, M., Di Leo, G., Salvatore, C., Interlenghi, M., & Sardanelli, F. (2021). AI applications to medical images: From machine learning to deep learning. *Physica Medica*, *83*, 9–24.

Currie, G., Hawk, K. E., Rohren, E., Vial, A., & Klein, R. (2019). Machine learning and deep learning in medical imaging: Intelligent imaging. *Journal of Medical Imaging and Radiation Sciences*, *50*(4), 477–487.

Dollár, K. H. G. G. P., & Girshick, R. (2017, April). Mask r-cnn. In *Proceedings of the IEEE international conference on computer vision* (pp. 2961-2969). IEEE.

Fang, C., Li, G., Pan, C., Li, Y., & Yu, Y. (2019, October). Globally guided progressive fusion network for 3D pancreas segmentation. In *International conference on medical image computing and computer-assisted intervention* (pp. 210-218). Springer.

Fu, G. S., Levin-Schwartz, Y., Lin, Q. H., & Zhang, D. (2019). Machine learning for medical imaging. *Journal of Healthcare Engineering*.

Gu, H., Guo, Y., Gu, L., Wei, A., Xie, S., Ye, Z., ... Hong, J. (2020). Deep learning for identifying corneal diseases from ocular surface slit-lamp photographs. *Scientific Reports*, *10*(1), 1–11.

Gulshan, V., Peng, L., Coram, M., Stumpe, M. C., Wu, D., Narayanaswamy, A., & Webster, D. R. (2016). Development and validation of a deep learning algorithm for detection of diabetic retinopathy in retinal fundus photographs. *Journal of the American Medical Association*, *316*(22), 2402–2410.

Hesamian, M. H., Jia, W., He, X., & Kennedy, P. (2019). Deep learning techniques for medical image segmentation: Achievements and challenges. *Journal of Digital Imaging*, *32*(4), 582–596.

Hu, J., Shen, L., & Sun, G. (2018). Squeeze-and-excitation networks. In *Proceedings of the IEEE conference on computer vision and pattern recognition* (pp. 7132-7141). IEEE.

Huang, G., Liu, Z., Van Der Maaten, L., & Weinberger, K. Q. (2017). Densely connected convolutional networks. In *Proceedings of the IEEE conference on computer vision and pattern recognition* (pp. 4700-4708). IEEE.

Kim, J., Hong, J., & Park, H. (2018). Prospects of deep learning for medical imaging. *Precision and Future Medicine, 2*(2), 37–52.

Kim, M., Yun, J., Cho, Y., Shin, K., Jang, R., Bae, H. J., & Kim, N. (2019). Deep learning in medical imaging. *Neurospine, 16*(4), 657.

Klang, E. (2018). Deep learning and medical imaging. *Journal of Thoracic Disease, 10*(3), 1325.

Law, H., & Deng, J. (2018). Cornernet: Detecting objects as paired keypoints. In *Proceedings of the European conference on computer vision (ECCV)* (pp. 734-750). Academic Press.

Li, Y., Zhao, J., Lv, Z., & Li, J. (2021). Medical image fusion method by deep learning. *International Journal of Cognitive Computing in Engineering, 2*, 21–29.

Li, Z., Zhang, S., Zhang, J., Huang, K., Wang, Y., & Yu, Y. (2019, October). MVP-Net: multi-view FPN with position-aware attention for deep universal lesion detection. In *International Conference on Medical Image Computing and Computer-Assisted Intervention* (pp. 13-21). Springer.

Liu, J., Zhao, G., Fei, Y., Zhang, M., Wang, Y., & Yu, Y. (2019). Align, attend and locate: Chest x-ray diagnosis via contrast induced attention network with limited supervision. In *Proceedings of the IEEE/CVF International Conference on Computer Vision* (pp. 10632-10641). IEEE.

Liu, W., Anguelov, D., Erhan, D., Szegedy, C., Reed, S., Fu, C. Y., & Berg, A. C. (2016, October). Ssd: Single shot multibox detector. In *European conference on computer vision* (pp. 21-37). Springer.

Liu, X., Song, L., Liu, S., & Zhang, Y. (2021). A review of deep-learning-based medical image segmentation methods. *Sustainability, 13*(3), 1224.

Liu, Y., Zhang, F., Zhang, Q., Wang, S., Wang, Y., & Yu, Y. (2020). Cross-view correspondence reasoning based on bipartite graph convolutional network for mammogram mass detection. In *Proceedings of the IEEE/CVF Conference on Computer Vision and Pattern Recognition* (pp. 3812-3822). IEEE.

Lo, S. C., Lou, S. L., Lin, J. S., Freedman, M. T., Chien, M. V., & Mun, S. K. (1995). Artificial convolution neural network techniques and applications for lung nodule detection. *IEEE Transactions on Medical Imaging, 14*(4), 711–718.

Lu, L., Zheng, Y., Carneiro, G., & Yang, L. (2017). Deep learning and convolutional neural networks for medical image computing. *Advances in Computer Vision and Pattern Recognition, 10*, 978-3.

Ma, X., Niu, Y., Gu, L., Wang, Y., Zhao, Y., Bailey, J., & Lu, F. (2021). Understanding adversarial attacks on deep learning based medical image analysis systems. *Pattern Recognition, 110*, 107332.

Mittal, M., Arora, M., Pandey, T., & Goyal, L. M. (2020). Image segmentation using deep learning techniques in medical images. In *Advancement of machine intelligence in interactive medical image analysis* (pp. 41–63). Springer.

Niyaz, U., & Sambyal, A. S. (2018, December). Advances in deep learning techniques for medical image analysis. In *2018 Fifth International Conference on Parallel, Distributed and Grid Computing (PDGC)* (pp. 271-277). IEEE.

Patibandla, R. L., Narayana, V. L., Gopi, Λ. P., & Rao, B. T. (2021). Comparative Study on Analysis of Medical Images Using Deep Learning Techniques. In *Deep Learning for Biomedical Applications* (pp. 329–345). CRC Press.

Raj, R. J. S., Shobana, S. J., Pustokhina, I. V., Pustokhin, D. A., Gupta, D., & Shankar, K. J. I. A. (2020). Optimal feature selection-based medical image classification using deep learning model in internet of medical things. *IEEE Access: Practical Innovations, Open Solutions, 8*, 58006–58017.

Redmon, J., Divvala, S., Girshick, R., & Farhadi, A. (2016). You only look once: Unified, real-time object detection. In *Proceedings of the IEEE conference on computer vision and pattern recognition* (pp. 779-788). IEEE.

Ren, S., He, K., Girshick, R., & Sun, J. (2015). Faster r-cnn: Towards real-time object detection with region proposal networks. *Advances in Neural Information Processing Systems, 28*.

Singh, S. P., Wang, L., Gupta, S., Goli, H., Padmanabhan, P., & Gulyás, B. (2020). 3D deep learning on medical images: A review. *Sensors (Basel), 20*(18), 5097.

Ting, D. S. W., Cheung, C. Y. L., Lim, G., Tan, G. S. W., Quang, N. D., Gan, A., ... Wong, T. Y. (2017). Development and validation of a deep learning system for diabetic retinopathy and related eye diseases using retinal images from multiethnic populations with diabetes. *Journal of the American Medical Association, 318*(22), 2211–2223.

Wang, C. R., Zhang, F., Yu, Y., & Wang, Y. (2020, October). BR-GAN: bilateral residual generating adversarial network for mammogram classification. In *International Conference on Medical Image Computing and Computer-Assisted Intervention* (pp. 657-666). Springer.

Wang, W., Liang, D., Chen, Q., Iwamoto, Y., Han, X. H., Zhang, Q., & Chen, Y. W. (2020). Medical image classification using deep learning. In *Deep learning in healthcare* (pp. 33–51). Springer.

Yadav, S. S., & Jadhav, S. M. (2019). Deep convolutional neural network based medical image classification for disease diagnosis. *Journal of Big Data, 6*(1), 1–18.

Ye, C., Wang, W., Zhang, S., & Wang, K. (2019). Multi-depth fusion network for whole-heart CT image segmentation. *IEEE Access: Practical Innovations, Open Solutions, 7,* 23421–23429.

Zhang, S., Xu, J., Chen, Y. C., Ma, J., Li, Z., Wang, Y., & Yu, Y. (2020, October). Revisiting 3D context modeling with supervised pre-training for universal lesion detection in CT slices. In *International Conference on Medical Image Computing and Computer-Assisted Intervention* (pp. 542-551). Springer.

Chapter 8
Predicting ATP–Binding Cassette Transporters Using Rough Set and Random Forest Model

Rudra Kalyan Nayak
iD https://orcid.org/0000-0003-4447-8391
VIT Bhopal University, India

Ramamani Tripathy
Chitkara University, India

ABSTRACT

In reality, all homosapiens species benefit greatly from the function of ATP-binding cassette (ABC) transporter proteins. Many studies have focused specifically on the drug transporter prediction because to the recent advancements in biology. Machine learning and soft computing with data mining methodologies have been used to identify valid motif sequences from biological datasets in general. In this work, the authors analysed the research on the ABC transporter with the prediction of cellular cholesterol. This research is focused on this new area, as ABC transporters are frequently employed as pharmacological targets. In this instance, the authors have focused on the ABC transporter's legitimate signature motif involving plasma membrane cholesterol. The authors used an unique hybrid model that is rough set with random forest for the prediction of motif structure that has clinical significance for predicting relevant motif sequences.

DOI: 10.4018/978-1-6684-6523-3.ch008

Figure 1. Structural components of Plasma membrane

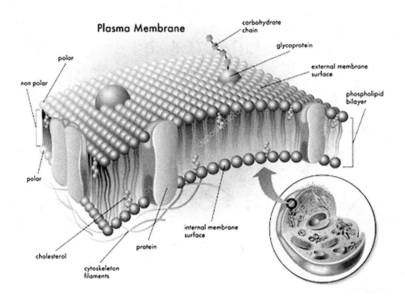

INTRODUCTION

Plasma Membrane

The membrane (Chauhan, 2003) that divides the interior of the cell from the external environment is found in all cells and is referred to as the plasma membrane or cell membrane. A cell wall is affixed to the plasma membrane on the exterior of bacterial and plant cells. A semi-permeable lipid bilayer makes up the plasma membrane. The movement of materials into and out of the cell is controlled by the plasma membrane (Oram, 2002).

Every living thing, including prokaryotic and eukaryotic organisms (Paila et al., 2010), has a plasma membrane that encloses its internal contents and acts as a semi-porous barrier to the outer world. The membrane serves as a barrier, keeping the components of the cell together and preventing the entry of outside chemicals. However, the plasma membrane is permeable to particular molecules, enabling the entry of nutrients and other vital components as well as the exit of waste products from the cell. Small molecules can move freely over the membrane, including oxygen, carbon dioxide, and water, but the movement of bigger molecules, such amino acids and carbohydrates, is strictly controlled.

Prokaryotic and Eukaryotic

The plasma membrane is an inner layer of protection in prokaryotes and plants because a stiff cell wall serves as the outer limit for their cells. Although the pores in the cell wall allow materials to enter and exit the cell, they are not particularly picky about what gets through. The final barrier between the inside of the cell and the outside world is the plasma membrane, which borders the cell wall.

It is generally accepted that eukaryotic animal cells are related to prokaryotes that shed their cell walls. These early organisms would have been able to grow in size and complexity because there would just be the pliable plasma membrane left to confine them. Eukaryotic cells contain membranes that enclose their internal organelles and are typically ten times bigger than prokaryotic cells. These membranes control material flow similarly to the external plasma membrane, enabling the cell to divide its chemical processes into distinct interior compartments.

Transporter

By facilitating the translocation of solutes such as ions, nutrients, neurotransmitters, and a variety of medications across biological membranes, membrane transport proteins perform a crucial job in every live cell. They play a critical part in the success or failure of cancer treatment, and their (mal)function is directly linked to a variety of illnesses, such as autism, epilepsy, migraine, depression, drug misuse, and cystic fibrosis. For target-oriented drug discovery and delivery, they are therefore of primary medical/pharmacological interest. On a regular basis, their activity is investigated in appropriate expression hosts and, if practical, after reconstitution into proteoliposomes. However, to do direct biophysical and structural analyses, including crystallisation, these integral membrane proteins must first be dissolved and purified, as shown in Figures 1 and 2. The absence of a vectorial environment prevents the measurement of transport activity between their extraction from the membrane and restoration. Because of this, studies to determine their role in detergent have been restricted to indirect binding methods, such as protecting substrates from cysteine modification or detecting tryptophan fluorescence changes caused by the substrate. These methods necessitate the fortuitous or engineered localization of cysteines or tryptophans as well as time-consuming development and implementation.

Proteins

Membrane proteins play a crucial role in biology because they help maintain the structural integrity of cells and the passage of material through membranes (Tripathy et al., 2016). Membrane proteins are necessary for the communication inside the cell

Figure 2. Presence of Proteins in Plasma membrane

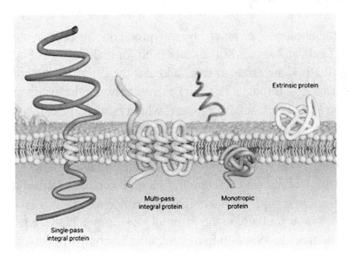

compartment. Without protein, cells cannot respond to external stimuli, communicate with their neighbours, transport nutrients into the cell, or remove waste products from the cell (Tripathy et al., 2015 and Babu et al., 2011). Membrane proteins can be divided into intrinsic or integral and extrinsic or peripheral proteins, respectively (Ahmad, 2005). Peripheral proteins are only momentarily linked to the cell membrane, while integral proteins are permanently bound (Ballesteros et al., 1995).

Integral monotopic proteins are a small subset of integral proteins that only adhere to one side of the membrane. Transmembrane proteins(TM), which frequently traverse the cell membrane, are a different family of integral proteins (Ballesteros et al., 1995, Cherezov et al., 2007 and Zhang et al., 2006). Transmembrane proteins contain three regions: extracellular domain, intercellular domain, and bilayer domain. The TM proteins are always inside the cell when it comes to the intercellular segment, but they are always outside the cell when it comes to the extracellular section. Transmembrane proteins' primary functions include signal transduction, immunology and pathogenicity, bioenergetics, cell-to-cell communication, and enzymatic action (Higgins, 1992, Altschul et al., 1997 and Brooks-Wilson et al., 1997).

Cholesterol

Cholesterol is another crucial part of the plasma membrane. A fat-like substance called cholesterol is essential for a healthy body because it gives body cells their vital power. As an amphipathic molecule with both hydrophilic and hydrophobic sections, cholesterol (Brooks-Wilson et al., 1997) The fluidity of the plasma membrane is impacted by cholesterol, which also contributes to the creation of a strong diffusion barrier. Up the plasma membrane, cholesterol fills in the spaces left by phospholipids to stop water-soluble compounds from diffusing across the membrane. Hormone, vitamin D, and bile synthesis are all significantly influenced by cholesterol.

Figure 3. Chemical structures of cholesterol and ergosterol

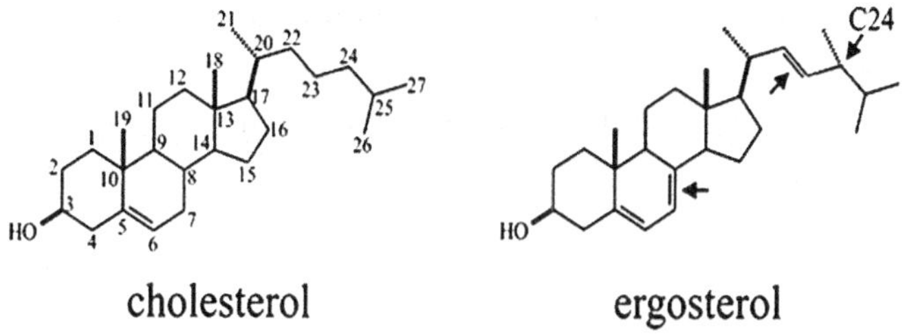

RELATED WORKS

Chandra (2009) developed a prediction model utilising the support vector machine approach to distinguish between P-glycoprotein substrates and nonsubstrates. Seven dissimilar feature types and eight dissimilar threshold values were used in the research conducted by the authors in their paper. These feature types include unweighted, weighted, Euclidian distance, all pair wise centroid distances among substructures in a compound, and all feature combinations. They noticed that the model has a 93% accuracy rate. In addition, Bhavani et al. (2006) suggested using a widely used support vector machine-based classifier framework to predict negative drug effects across various drug classes. The proposed model's prediction accuracy predicted accurate results, but this method produced results that were more accurate when predicting toxicity. Wang et al. (2011) illustrated P-glycoprotein (P-gp), an ABC transporter that is involved in several essential functions, including the transport of lipids and steroids across cell membranes. The authors used a Support vector machine-based model, based on 131 substrates and 81 nonsubstrates P-gp data, to achieve this. The entire study demonstrates that the proposed model offers more significant results in identifying P-gp substrates and nonsubstrates. The above survey directed us to explore the motif sequences which are clinically relevant.

ABC TRANSPORTER

The ubiquitous superfamily of integral membrane proteins known as ATP-binding cassette (ABC) transporters is in charge of the ATP-powered translocation of several substrates across membranes. The nucleotide-dependent motor that propels transport is provided by the extremely conserved ABC domains of ABC transporters. The translocation pathway's transmembrane domains, however, are more erratic. A qualitative molecular foundation for understanding the transport cycle has been offered by recent structural developments with bacterial ABC transporters. Creating quantitative models that explicitly describe the kinetic and molecular mechanisms by which ABC transporters link ATP binding and hydrolysis to substrate translocation is a key objective.

The Human ABC Gene Family

Table 1 below lists the seven subfamilies and 49 ABC genes, from A to G, that make up the human genome. Members of this large and diverse transporter family are essential to numerous cellular functions. For instance, ABC transporters are in charge of cancer cells' multidrug resistance (Ahmad, 2005). Additionally, ABC proteins move a variety of substances across internal membranes as well as the plasma membrane, such as metal ions, peptides, amino acids, carbohydrates, and a sizable number of hydrophobic substances and metabolites. When known, each ABC gene product's function is listed in Table 2's far right column.

Mechanism and Structural Features of ABC Transport

There are three main functional groups for ABC transporters. Importers mediate the uptake of nutrients into the cell in prokaryotes. Ions, amino acids, peptides, sugars, and other compounds, most of which are hydrophilic, are among the substrates that can be transported. The ABC transporter's membrane-spanning section shields hydrophilic substrates from the lipids in the membrane bilayer, creating a passageway through the cell membrane. Exporters move lipids and certain polysaccharides from the cytoplasm to the periplasm in gram-negative bacteria. Importers are absent in eukaryotes. Prokaryotes and eukaryotes both have exporters and effluxers, which act as pumps that extrude toxins and drugs from the cell. The third subgroup of ABC proteins do not function as transporters, but rather are involved in translation and DNA repair processes. ABC transporter's mechanism and structural features are shown below in Figure 4 and 5 respectively.

Table 1. Human ABC gene subfamilies

Subfamily Name	Aliases	Number of Genes	Number of Pseudogenes
ABCA	ABC1	12	5
ABCB	MDR	11	4
ABCC	MRP	13	2
ABCD	ALD	4	4
ABCE	OABP	1	2
ABCF	GGN20	3	2
ABCG	White	5	2
Total		49	21

Role of ABC Transporters in Lipid Transport and Human Disease

It is believed that over half of the 48 human ATP binding cassette (ABC) transporter proteins aid in the ATP-dependent translocation of lipids or substances related to lipids. These substrates include bile acids, phospholipids, sphingolipids, plant sterols, cholesterol, and phytosterols. Many of the 48 human ABC transporters have undergone mutations, and these mutations have been connected to human disease. Indeed, the discovery that aberrant lipid transport and/or homeostasis have been linked to 12

Table 2. Human ABC transporter genes, and their functions, as listed in the HGNC database

Gene	Chromosome Location	Exons	AA	Accession Number	Function
ABCA1	9q31.1	36	2261	NM005502	Cholesterol efflux onto HDL
ABCA2	9q34	27	2436	NM001606	Drug resistance
ABCA3	16p13.3	26	1704	NM001089	Multidrug resistance
ABCA4	1p22	38	2273	NM000350	N-retinylidene-phosphatidylethanolamine (PE) efflux
ABCA5	17q24.3	31	1642	NM018672	Urinary diagnostic marker for prostatic intraepithelial neoplasia (PIN)
ABCA6	17q24.3	35	1617	NM080284	Multidrug resistance
ABCA7	19p13.3	31	2146	NM019112	Cholesterol efflux
ABCA8	17q24	31	1581	NM007168	Transports certain lipophilic drugs
ABCA9	17q24.2	31	1624	NM080283	Might play a role in monocyte differentiation and macrophage lipid homeostasis

Figure 4. Mechanism of ABC transporter

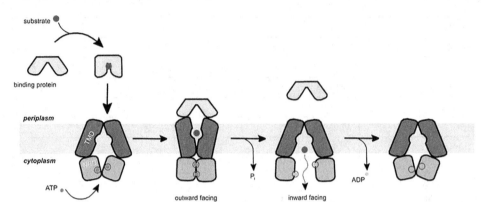

Figure 5. Structural features of ABC transporters

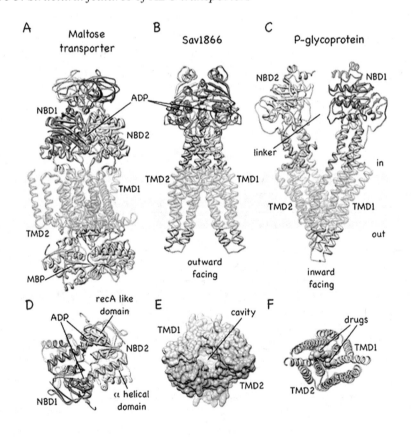

illnesses shows the significance of this family of transporters for cell physiology. In addition to describing ABC transporters' involvement in cellular homeostasis and inherited diseases, this article emphasises how they move and transport lipids.

ATP hydrolysis is used by transmembrane proteins known as ATP binding cassette (ABC) transporters to enable the transportation of a wide range of substrates across membrane bilayers. The ABC superfamily has more than 250 members who, in a crude sense, can be classified as importers or exporters (Brooks-Wilson et al., 1999). Importers are frequently found in bacteria but are not present in eukaryotes; they are typically connected to the uptake of hydrophilic substances into the cell, such as peptides, ions, and sugars. Both eukaryotes and prokaryotes include ABC transporters that are used to export substrates through the plasma membrane and outside of the cell, or out of the cytosol and into an organelle. Figure 7 below illustrates the mechanisms of transbilayer lipid transport and movement.

Based on how their ATP binding cassette is structured, which spans 180 amino acids and comprises three highly conserved motifs: the Walker A/P-loop (12 amino acids), a Signature motif/C-loop (5 amino acids), and the Walker B motif, proteins are categorised as ABC transporters (5 amino acids). Two transmembrane domains (TMD), each generally believed to include six transmembrane -helices, and two ABCs are present in functional ABC transporters (Chauhan, 2003). A further division of ABC transporters is into "full" and "half" transporters. In complete transporters, a single polypeptide encodes the two TMD and two ABCs. The two ABCs interact and hydrolyze ATP to produce energy for substrate transport. The transbilayer lipid's mode of transport is depicted in Figure 6.

METHODOLOGY

Rough Set Theory

Rough set theory introduced by Pawalk is defined as $S = \{U, f \cup A, D, I\}$, where U is the universe of all non-empty set of object, f and A are the non-empty finite set of feature and attributes which satisfy $f \cup A = K$, D refers to the domain of all attributes such that $D = U_{a \in k} D$, where D_a is the set of the value of a, I is the information function for all attributes such that $I = U_{a \in A} I_a$, where I_a is a total function $I_a : \cup \in D_a$. Every subset of attribute $B \subseteq K$ can be associated with an indiscernibility relation $I(B)$ defined as (1) (Rout et al., 2016).

$$I(B) = \{(x, y) \in \cup \times \cup \mid \forall b \in B, I_b(x) = I_b(y)\} \tag{1}$$

Figure 6. Mechanisms of transbilayer lipid transport/movement

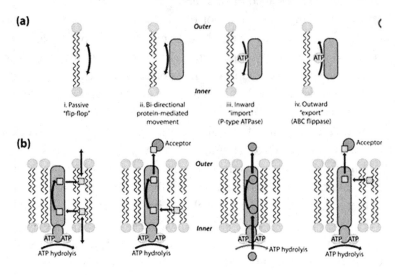

This relationship is transitive, symmetric, reflexive, and equivalent. For an object $x \in \cup$, all objects equivalent to x compose an equivalence class of x, denoted by $x_B = \{y \mid y \in \cup, (x, y) \in I(B)\}$. In rough set theory, all unique equivalence classes based on B form a partition that is caused by B. These equivalence classes are also known as primitive sets. The primary notion of rough set theory is to approximate an ineffable subset X of U by utilising two sets that can be represented by elementary sets. The two sets, which are referred to as the lower and higher approximations of X, respectively, are fundamental ideas in rough set theory.

1.   1. For a subset of objects $X \subseteq \cup$ and a subset of attributes $B \subseteq f$ the lower and upper approximations of X are deðned as (2) and (3), respectively (Pawlak, 1996).

$$\underline{B}(X) = \{x \mid x_B \subseteq X, x \in \cup\}, \tag{2}$$

$$\overline{B}(X) = \{x \mid x_B \cap X \neq \varnothing, x \in \cup\}, \tag{3}$$

The lower approximation set $\underline{B}(X)$ contains all objects which can be certainly classiðed as objects of X based on the set of attributes B. The upper approximation set $\bar{B}(X)$ is the set of objects which can be possibly classiðed as objects of X. The pair $[\underline{B}(X), \bar{B}(X)]$ is referred to as Pawlak's rough set of X with respect to B. The concepts of positive, negative and boundary regions are deðned as (4), (5) and (6), respectively (Midelfart et al., 2002 and Revathy et al., 2015).

$$POS_B(X) = \underline{B}(X), \tag{4}$$

$$NEG_B(X) = \cup - \bar{B}(X), \tag{5}$$

$$BN_B(X) = \bar{B}(X) - \underline{B}(X) \tag{6}$$

The meaning of positive region $POS_B(X)$ is same as the lower approximation set. The negative region $NEG_B(X)$ is the set of all objects which certainly not belong to X based on B. The boundary region is the set of all objects which are difðcult to be classiðed to X or to the complement of X.

Random Forest

A supervised learning approach called random forest is employed for both classification and regression. But it is primarily employed for classification issues. As is common knowledge, a forest is made up of trees, and a forest with more trees will be more sturdy. Similar to this, the random forest algorithm builds decision trees on data samples, obtains predictions from each one, and then uses voting to determine the optimal option. Because it averages the results, the ensemble method—which is superior to a single decision tree—reduces over-fitting (Schwartz et al., 2013, Xiao et al., 2017 and Fu et al., 2017).

Random Forest Algorithm

Random forest is an ensemble classifier, which constructs a group of independent and non-identical decision trees based on the idea of randomization. Random forest can be defined as $\{h(x,\theta_k),\ k=1,...,L)$, in which θ_k is a kind of mutual independent random vector parameter, and x is the input data (Chauhan, 2003). Every decision tree employs a random vector as a parameter, chooses sample features at random, and chooses a subset of the sample dataset at random to serve as the training set.

The following is the random forest creation algorithm. n denotes the number of training samples that each decision tree corresponds to, whereas k denotes the number of decision trees in the random forest. When doing segmentation on a single node of a decision tree, the number of features in a sample, or M, is used., $m<<M$ [2]:

1. Create a k group training set by repeatedly sampling N times from all of the training sample sets (namely bootstrap sampling). Build a decision tree for each training set with samples drawn at random from the k group data out of bag (referred to as OOB);
2. choose m features based on each node of the decision tree and determine the best segmentation characteristics using the m characteristics;
3. let each decision tree grow completely without pruning;
4. combine several decision trees into a random forest model; and
5. use the model to categorise and identify objects. Figure 7 below demonstrates its operation.

EXPERIMENTAL SETUP

Dataset Description

All human gene helices in the ABC super family were retrieved from the Uniprot (UniProt Consortium, 2007) database. We used 49 genes in this study, along with information on their names, protein IDs, helix names, and sequences. Each protein in the ABC family has a maximum of 17 helices, numbered from H1 to H17, but the number of helices varies depending on the gene name.

Experimental Evaluation

There is some biological importance to the challenge of predicting the cholesterol pattern from human ABC transporters to identify a legitimate signature motif (like human diseases). The task of identifying a group of data points as the models for all other data points can be expressed in this way. Rough set works well to characterise the data in order to extract their features. As it manages boundary data, higher approximation, and lower approximation. The motif sequences are then appropriately predicted by the random forest approach. Additionally, rough with random forest

Figure 7. Working of Random Forest Algorithm

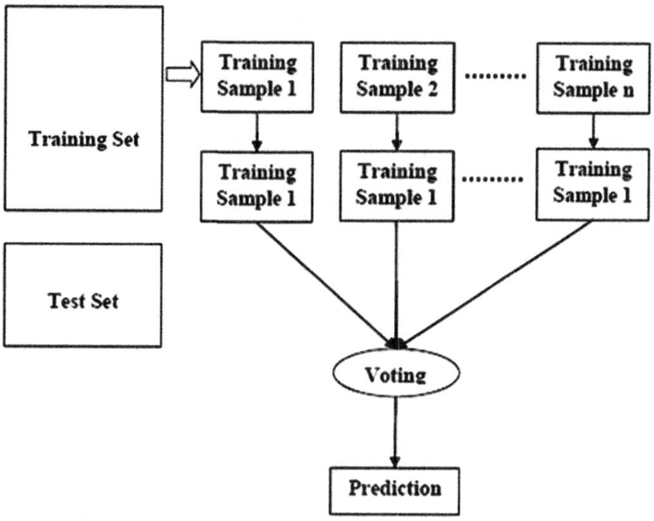

works well on ABC data in terms of temporal complexity. MatLab 10 running on a Windows computer with at least 2GB of RAM is used to conduct the experiment.

The goal of this research is to use both CARC and CRAC motif discovery methods to identify the most relevant motif signatures. A better data mining method is needed to locate the most important motif structures after filtering and looking at the numerous motif sequences that are accessible. For instance, the supplied motif RCYYYAL of length 7 can be categorised under more than one motif type, according to Table 1, including 13, 22, and 31. Therefore, it is necessary to mine this type of information, where data can be a part of several clusters.

The summary of significant cholesterol signature motifs found using the rough set and random forest algorithms is shown in Tables 3(a) and 3(b), along with information on the protein ID, gene name, helix, conserved motif signature, start/ end where the cholesterol motif is present in the ABC protein, and motif type. Based on the family, helix, or location in the membrane leaflet, the results obtained clearly demonstrate that the combinations one may generate from the CRAC or CARC are really constrained and can be further developed as a hallmark motif. When using the hybrid method to find motifs in a cholesterol sequence, considerably more backward motifs than forward motifs were discovered.

Figure 8 depicts the prediction of motif sequences of different length in respective regions by the proposed model.

Table 3(a). Forward signature motifs for ABC derived from L/V-X(1-5)-Y-X(1-5)-R/K

Protein Id	Helix	Sequence	Start / End	Total Motif	Motif Type
ABCA1	15	LIQYRFFIR	end	2	L2Y4R,V3Y4R
ABCA2	6	VPYMYVAIR	end	5	V1Y5R,V3Y3R,L4Y5R,L5Y3R,L5Y4R
ABCA5	15	LLQYYEKK	end	8	L1Y2K,L1Y3K,L2Y1K,L2Y2K,L2Y3K,L3Y1K,L3Y2K
ABCA6	7	LLLALYFDK	end	6	L2Y2K,L3Y2K,L4Y2K,V2Y5K,L3Y5K,V4Y5K
ABCA8	7	LALAIYFEK	end	5	L2Y2K,L4Y2K,V1Y3K,L2Y3K,L3Y3K
ABCA9	7	LVLTLYFDK	end	3	L2Y2K,V3Y2K,L4Y2K
ABCA12	6	VENELSYVLK	end	8	L1Y2K,V5Y2K,V1Y5K,V1Y3K,L3Y3K,L3Y5K,V5Y3K,V5Y5K
ABCB2 (TAP1)	7	LSLFLWYLVR	end	6	L1Y2R,L3Y2R,L5Y2R,L2Y1R,L3Y1R,V4Y1R
ABCB7	2	VLIGYGVSR	start	2	L2Y3R,V3Y3R
ABCB9	3	LFVGIYAMVK	start	2	L4Y3K,V2Y3K
ABCB10	3	VIYGRYLRK	end	5	V1Y1R,V1Y4R,V1Y5K,V4Y1R,V4Y2K
ABCC1	17	LQVTTYLNWLVR	end	2	V2Y5R,L4Y5R
ABCC9	14	LGVAFYFIQK	end	2	V2Y3K,L4Y3K
ABCC10	1	VLSACYLGTPR	end	6	L3Y4R,V4Y4R,L2Y4K,V3Y1K,V4Y4K,L5Y1K
ABCG1	6	LRLIAYFVLRYK	end	4	L2Y5K,L4Y3R,L4Y5K,L2Y3R
ABCG2	1	LVIGAIYFGLK	end	2	V4Y3K,L5Y3K
ABCG4	6	LRLLAYLVLRYR	end	9	L1Y3R,L1Y2K,L1Y5R,V2Y2K,L2Y5R,L4Y5R,L2Y3R,L4Y3R,L3Y2K

Comparison Among Three Methods

Table 4(a) and 4(b) show the comparison among three methods such as rough set with K-nearest neighbour (Arian et al., 2020), rough set with decision tree (Sikandar et al., 2018) and proposed rough set with random forest method with respect to helix name and motif type for both forward with backward region. Rough set method is kept as base for the three classifiers to showcase the ability of it as it is discovered that it plays an essential role in predicting motif sequences (Tripathy et al., 2016). Helix name means it represents the targeted helix name of ABC family. Each time, membrane cholesterol is bound with N-C terminus region of membrane proteins and also with their corresponding helix. Another important part is the motif type which is denoted as forward and backward position. According with the algorithm CRAC and CARC we choose motif type. If motif type is written as 55 means for forward position the formula as: L/V-X5-Y-X5-K/R. Here X5 is any combination of five amino acid which is residing in between L/V and Y and in next part X5 is

Table 3(b). Backward signature motifs for ABC derived from K/R-X(1-5)-Y/F-X(1-5)-L/V

Protein Id	Helix	Sequence	Start /End	Total Motif	Motif Type
ABCA1	9	RKGFFAQIVL	Start		
ABCA1	13	KIPSTAYVVLTSV	Start	13	R3F4L; R3F3V; R2F5L; R2F4V; K2F4L; K2F3V; K1F4V; K1F5L; K5Y5V; K5Y2L; K5Y1V
ABCA2	7	KYFALYEVAGV	Start		
ABCA2	9	RNSKALFSQILL	Start		
ABCA4	1	KRQKIRFVVELV	Start		
ABCA4	7	KDFLAQIVL	Start	14	K5F4V,K5F3L,K5F1V,R4F4V,R4F3L,R4F1V,R4F1V,K2F4V,K2F3L ,K2F1V,K1F4V,K1F5L,R5F4L
ABCA4	11	RKLLIVFPHFCL	Start		
ABCA5	9	KDYVFAAV	Start		
ABCA5	10	KIELYFQAALL	Start	8	K3F2V,K1Y4V,K4F4L,K4F3L,K3Y5L,K3Y4L,K5F5V,K5F1L
ABCA5	12	KFLAVVFCLIGYV	Start		
ABCA7	7	RPTADVFSLAQV	Start	6	R5F4V,R5F1L,R3F4L,R3F3V,R2F4L,R2F3V
ABCA7	9	RRGLFAQIVL	Start		
ABCA8	3	RDSAFWLSWGL	Start		
ABCA8	5	KKSFLTGLVV	Start	9	R3F5L,K3Y1V,K2F5V,K2F4V,K2F3L,K1F3L,K1F4V,K1F5V,R5 F3L,R5F1V
ABCA8	14	RMDVQPFLVFL	Start		
ABCA9	3	RESAFWLSWGL	Start		
ABCA9	5	KKPFLTGLVV	Start	8	R3F5L,R3F1L,K2F5V,K2F4V,K2F3L,K1F3L,K1F4V,K1F5V
ABCA10	7	KMIATFFIL	Start	6	K5F1L,K4F2L,K4F2L,K4F1V,K3F2L,K3F1V
ABCA10	9	KKLNCFPVL	Start		
ABCB2 (TAP1)	5	RRLSLFLVLVVL	start		
ABCB2 (TAP1	8	KKVGKWYQLLEV	end	22	R4F5L,R4F4V,R4F3V,R4F2L,R4F1V,R4F1V,R3F5L,R3F4V,R 3F3V,R3F2L,R3F1V,K5Y4V,K5Y2L,K5Y1L,K4Y4L,K4Y2L, K4Y1L,K1Y1L,K1Y2L,K1Y4V,K4Y5V,K4Y4L
ABCB2 (TAP1	9	KVGILYIGGQLV	start		
ABCB3 (TAP2)	8	RALYLLVRRV	start		
ABCB4	2	RYAYYYSGL	start		
ABCB4	3	KVGMFFQAV	start	12	R4Y2L,R3Y3L,R2Y4L,K4F2V,K3F3V,K5F4V,K5F1V,K4Y5V,K4Y 2V,K4Y1V,K3F4L,K3F1L
ABCB4	7	KTEWPYFVVGTV	start		
ABCB4	8	KCNIFSLIFL	start		
ABCB7	2	RAGAAFFNEV	last		
ABCB7	3	RGISFVLSALV	start	8	R5F2V,R4F3V,R3Y5V,R3F4L,R3F1L,K4F4L,K4F2V,K4F1L
ABCB7	4	KCGAQFALVTL	start		
ABCB9	6	KSMDQFSTAVV	start		
ABCC1	1	KCFQNTVLV	start		
ABCC1	2	KTALGFLLWIV	start		
ABCC1	3	RSRGIFLAPVFL	start	18	K1F3V,K1F4L,K1F5V,K4F4V,K4F1L,R4F5L,R4F3V,R2F5L,R2F 3V,R4Y5L,R4Y4L,R3F5L,R3F1V,K5F4L,,K412L,K4Y1L,K1F4L, K2Y3V,K4F3L
ABCC1	5	RDITFYVYFSLL	start		
ABCC1	6	KVLYKTFGPYFL	start		
ABCC1	12	KAIGLFISFL	start		
ABCC2	2	KQVFVGFLLIL	start	12	K5F3L,K5F1L,K2F4L,K2F3L,K1Y4V,K5F4L,K5F3L,K5F2V,K2Y 3L,K2Y2L,K2Y1V
ABCC2	6	KALFKTFYMVLL	start		
ABCC3	3	RAPAPVFFVTPLV	start		
ABCC3	5	RFTTFYIHFAL	start	9	R5F5V,R5F4L,R5F1V,R4Y3V,R4Y4L,R3F5L,K5F4L,K2F4L,K2F3L
ABCC3	6	KALLATFGSSFL	start		
ABCC4	1	KCYWKSYLVL	start	10	K5Y2L,K5Y1V,K1Y2L,K1Y4L,K1Y5V,R5Y2V,R5Y1L,R4F3V,K 4Y2L,R4F1V
ABCC4	9	RSLLVFYVLV	start		
ABCC6	2	KMVLGFALIVL	start		
ABCC6	5	RHLSTYLCLSL	start		
ABCC6	6	KAIWQVFHSTFLL	start	11	K4F4L,K4F3V,K4F1L,R4Y4L,R4Y2L,K5F5L,K5F4L,K1Y3V,K1Y 4L,R4Y4L,R4Y3L
ABCC6	7	KGYLLAVL	start		
ABCC6	14	RSLLMYAFGLL	start		
ABCC9	2	RWILTFALLFV	start	8	R4F4V,R4F2L,R4F1L,K4Y2L,K1F1L,K1F5L,K4F4L,K4F2L
ABCC9	10	KTFALYTSL	start		
ABCC11	1	RTRLIFDALL	start		
ABCC11	6	RLSVFFVPIAV	end	7	R4F2L,R4F3L,R2F3L,R2F2L,K4F4V,R3Y5V,R3F1V
ABCC12	7	KASGGYLLSL	start		
ABCD1	1	RTFLSVYVARL	end	9	R5Y3L,R1F2V,R1F4V,R5F4L,R5F3L,K4F4L,K4F3L,R1F3L,R1F4L
ABCD1	2	RKDPRAFGWQLL	start		
ABCD3	1	KETGYLVLIAV	start	14	K3Y5V,K3Y2L,K3Y1V,R1Y2V,K5F5L,R5Y1L,R4F5L,K4Y1L,K4Y 1L,R2F4L,R2F3L,K1Y1L,K1F3L,K1F4L
ABCD3	2	KRYLLNFIAAMPL	start		
ABCG1	6	KLYLDFIVL	start	7	K4F2L,K4F1V,R4F1L,R3Y2L,R3Y1V,K1Y4V,K1Y5L
ABCG4	6	KLYMDFLVL	start	7	K4F2L,K4F1V,R3Y2L,R3Y1V,K1Y3L,K1Y4V,K1Y5L
ABCG5	4	RFGYFSAALL	start	4	R3F4L,R3F3L,R2Y5L,R2Y4L

Figure 8. Different Classes of motif sequences in several regions

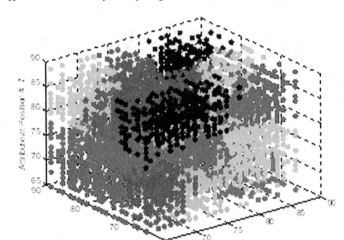

represented as any five amino acid combination reside within Y and K/R. Likewise it is represented for 11,12,--15,21---25,31…35,41…45,51…55 etc. From comparison table (Table 4) we conclude that our proposed model Rough with Random forest target on higher priority motif types such as 55, 52, 53, 51, 31, and 32 in comparison with other methods as follows.

CONCLUSION

The movement of chemicals between organs depends heavily on membrane cholesterol. ABC transporter is a key component of the cell membrane's multi-drug target. Every time an ABC gene is matched with a cholesterol sequence, the cluster points are determined using a rough set-based random forest model, which results in the largest number of potential pattern matching sequences, only some of which may be of biological importance. It was concluded from the current investigation that the transmembrane helices area was significantly modulated by both the forward and backward cholesterol recognition amino acid consensus motifs. Low-density lipoprotein has been identified as a carrier of cholesterol in the circulation and high-density lipoprotein has been treated as a key risk factor of atherosclerosis and myocardial infarction.

The movement of chemicals between organs depends heavily on membrane cholesterol. High-density lipoprotein has been treated as a major risk factor for atherosclerosis and myocardial infarction while low-density lipoprotein has been

Table 4(a). Motif type comparison by different methods

Methods	Helix Name (Forward)	Motif Type (Forward/Backward)
Rough Set with KNN	H3	43,24
	H6	12,21,15
	H2	23,32
	H1	53,35
Rough Set with Decision Tree	H1	35,52,53
	H6	12,15,51
	H7	12,32,21,41
	H14	22,23
Rough Set with Random Forest (Proposed)	H15	24,34,12,13,21,22,23,31,32
	H17	25,45
	H6	25,45,13,33,45,53,12,52,15,25,43,22,23
	H7	22,32,42,25,35,45,13,23
	H1	34,14,24,31,43,53
	H3	43,23,11,14,15,41

Table 4(b). Motif type comparison by different methods

Methods	Helix Name (Forward)	Motif Type (Forward/Backward)
Rough Set with KNN	H5	15,35,44,42
	H12	11,12,31
	H9	51,52,45
	H7	41,54,55
Rough Set with Decision Tree	H3	35,44,31,52
	H8	11,12,14,52
	H9	51,54,42
	H7	54,14,55
Rough Set with Random Forest (Proposed)	H15	-
	H17	-
	H6	52,23,22,21
	H7	54,51,34,33,24,23,42,41,32,31
	H1	54,53,51,24,43,41,21,14,15,44,45,52
	H3	35,31,25,24,23,13,14,15,53,51,55,54,44

discovered as a carrier of cholesterol in the circulation. Only a small number of the potential sequences that match the low consensus cholesterol binding motif (CARC and CRAC) might be biologically significant. Our strategy does, in fact, align with ABC transporters' reports and action. The TM helices of those that were modulated by cholesterol and/or involved in cholesterol transport were found to have a high enrichment of the CRAC/CARC motifs. Due to a lack of cholesterol transport, mutations in these transporters have also been shown to have decreased function. With the use of this research, we were able to forecast the importance of the cholesterol binding motif in ABC transporters with a lot more accuracy.

We draw the conclusion from our work that the significance of membrane cholesterol motif consensus from ABC transporters, which has higher connection with clinical disorders, may be accurately predicted using our novel hybrid Rough set and Random Forest technique.

REFERENCES

Ahmad, N. (2005). The vertical transmission of human immunodeficiency virus type 1: Molecular and biological properties of the virus. *Critical Reviews in Clinical Laboratory Sciences*, *42*(1), 1–34. doi:10.1080/10408360490512520 PMID:15697169

Altschul, S. F., Madden, T. L., Schäffer, A. A., Zhang, J., Zhang, Z., Miller, W., & Lipman, D. J. (1997). Gapped BLAST and PSI-BLAST: A new generation of protein database search programs. *Nucleic Acids Research*, *25*(17), 3389–3402. doi:10.1093/nar/25.17.3389 PMID:9254694

Arian, R., Hariri, A., Mehridehnavi, A., Fassihi, A., & Ghasemi, F. (2020). Protein kinase inhibitors' classification using K-Nearest neighbor algorithm. *Computational Biology and Chemistry*, *86*, 107269. doi:10.1016/j.compbiolchem.2020.107269 PMID:32413830

Babu, M. M., van der Lee, R., de Groot, N. S., & Gsponer, J. (2011). Intrinsically disordered proteins: Regulation and disease. *Current Opinion in Structural Biology*, *21*(3), 432–440. doi:10.1016/j.sbi.2011.03.011 PMID:21514144

Ballesteros, J. A., & Weinstein, H. (1995). Integrated methods for the construction of three-dimensional models and computational probing of structure-function relations in G protein-coupled receptors. In *Methods in neurosciences* (Vol. 25, pp. 366–428). Academic Press.

Bhavani, S., Nagargadde, A., Thawani, A., Sridhar, V., & Chandra, N. (2006). Substructure-based support vector machine classifiers for prediction of adverse effects in diverse classes of drugs. *Journal of Chemical Information and Modeling*, *46*(6), 2478–2486. doi:10.1021/ci060128l PMID:17125188

Brooks-Wilson, A., Marcil, M., Clee, S. M., Zhang, L. H., Roomp, K., van Dam, M., Yu, L., Brewer, C., Collins, J. A., Molhuizen, H. O. F., Loubser, O., Ouelette, B. F. F., Fichter, K., Ashbourne-Excoffon, K. J. D., Sensen, C. W., Scherer, S., Mott, S., Denis, M., Martindale, D., & Hayden, M. R. (1999). Mutations in ABC1 in Tangier disease and familial high-density lipoprotein deficiency. *Nature Genetics*, *22*(4), 336–345. doi:10.1038/11905 PMID:10431236

Chandra, N. (2009). Support Vector Machine Classifier for Predicting Drug Binding to P-glycoprotein, 136.

Chauhan, N. B. (2003). Membrane dynamics, cholesterol homeostasis, and Alzheimer's disease. *Journal of Lipid Research*, *44*(11), 2019–2029. doi:10.1194/jlr.R300010-JLR200 PMID:12951356

Cherezov, V., Rosenbaum, D. M., Hanson, M. A., Rasmussen, S. G., Thian, F. S., Kobilka, T. S., & Stevens, R. C. (2007). High-resolution crystal structure of an engineered human β2-adrenergic G protein–coupled receptor. *science*, *318*(5854), 1258-1265.

Fu, B., Wang, Y., Campbell, A., Li, Y., Zhang, B., Yin, S., Xing, Z., & Jin, X. (2017). Comparison of object-based and pixel-based Random Forest algorithm for wetland vegetation mapping using high spatial resolution GF-1 and SAR data. *Ecological Indicators*, *73*, 105–117. doi:10.1016/j.ecolind.2016.09.029

Higgins, C. F. (1992). ABC transporters: From microorganisms to man. *Annual Review of Cell Biology*, *8*(1), 67–113. doi:10.1146/annurev.cb.08.110192.000435 PMID:1282354

Midelfart, H., Komorowski, J., Nørsett, K., Yadetie, F., Sandovik, A. K., & Lægreid, A. (2002). Learning rough set classifiers from gene expressions and clinical data. *Fundamenta Informaticae*, *53*(2), 155–183.

Oram, J. F. (2002). Molecular basis of cholesterol homeostasis: Lessons from Tangier disease and ABCA1. *Trends in Molecular Medicine*, *8*(4), 168–173. doi:10.1016/S1471-4914(02)02289-X PMID:11927274

Paila, Y. D., & Chattopadhyay, A. (2010). Membrane cholesterol in the function and organization of G-protein coupled receptors. *Cholesterol Binding and Cholesterol Transport Proteins:*, 439-466.

Pawlak, Z. (1996). Rough sets and data analysis, Fuzzy Systems Symposium. *Soft Computing in Intelligent Systems and Information Processing*, 1-6.

Revathy, S., Parvaathavarthini, B., & Rajathi, S. (2015). Futuristic validation method for rough fuzzy clustering. *Indian Journal of Science and Technology*, 8(2), 120–127. doi:10.17485/ijst/2015/v8i2/58943

Rout, S. B., Mishra, S., & Mishra, S. (2016). Fuzzy Applications in Protein Structure Prediction: A New Era to Bioinformatics. *Structure*, 5(4).

Schwartz, M. H., Rozumalski, A., Truong, W., & Novacheck, T. F. (2013). Predicting the outcome of intramuscular psoas lengthening in children with cerebral palsy using preoperative gait data and the random forest algorithm. *Gait & Posture*, 37(4), 473–479. doi:10.1016/j.gaitpost.2012.08.016 PMID:23079586

Sikandar, A., Anwar, W., Bajwa, U. I., Wang, X., Sikandar, M., Yao, L., Jiang, Z. L., & Chunkai, Z. (2018). Decision tree based approaches for detecting protein complex in protein protein interaction network (PPI) via link and sequence analysis. *IEEE Access: Practical Innovations, Open Solutions*, 6, 22108–22120. doi:10.1109/ACCESS.2018.2807811

Tripathy, R., Mishra, D., & Konkimalla, V. B. (2015). A novel fuzzy C-means approach for uncovering cholesterol consensus motif from human G-protein coupled receptors (GPCR). *Karbala International Journal of Modern Science*, 1(4), 212–224. doi:10.1016/j.kijoms.2015.11.006

Tripathy, R., Mishra, D., & Konkimalla, V. B. (2016). A hybridized clustering approach based on rough set and fuzzy c-means to mine cholesterol sequence from ABC family. *Indian Journal of Science and Technology*, 9(22). doi:10.17485/ijst/2016/v9i22/94237

UniProt Consortium. (2007). The universal protein re- source (UniProt). *Nucleic Acids Research*, 36, D190–D195. doi:10.1093/nar/gkm895 PMID:18045787

Wang, Z., Chen, Y., Liang, H., Bender, A., Glen, R. C., & Yan, A. (2011). P-glycoprotein substrate models using support vector machines based on a comprehensive data set. *Journal of Chemical Information and Modeling*, 51(6), 1447–1456. doi:10.1021/ci2001583 PMID:21604677

Xiao, L. H., Chen, P. R., Gou, Z. P., Li, Y. Z., Li, M., Xiang, L. C., & Feng, P. (2017). Prostate cancer prediction using the random forest algorithm that takes into account transrectal ultrasound findings, age, and serum levels of prostate-specific antigen. *Asian Journal of Andrology*, 19(5), 586. doi:10.4103/1008-682X.186884 PMID:27586028

Zhang, Y., DeVries, M. E., & Skolnick, J. (2006). Structure modeling of all identified G protein–coupled receptors in the human genome. *PLoS Computational Biology*, *2*(2), e13. doi:10.1371/journal.pcbi.0020013 PMID:16485037

Chapter 9

Role of Artificial Intelligence and Machine Learning in Drug Discovery and Drug Repurposing

Sameer Quazi

https://orcid.org/0000-0002-1258-4088
GenLab Biosolutions Private Limited, India

Zarish Fatima
University College Lahore, Pakistan

ABSTRACT

Drug designing and repurposing is the most important field in the pharmaceutical industries and biomedical sciences. Because the challenges caused by drug such as low retention time, sensitivity can affect the efficacy of developmental process. As AI or ML has proven to be a potential activity in the health and biomedical sciences and from previous research it has found that AI can learn new data and transform it into the useful knowledge. So, in field of pharmacology, the aim is to design more efficient and novel vaccines using this method which is also cost effective. The underlying fact is to predict the molecular mechanism and structure for increased likelihood of developing new drugs. Clinical, electronic, and high-resolution imaging datasets can be used as inputs to aid the drug development niche. Moreover, the use of comprehensive target activity has been performed for repurposing a drug molecule by extending target profiles of drugs which also include off targets with therapeutic potential providing a new indication.

DOI: 10.4018/978-1-6684-6523-3.ch009

INTRODUCTION

Over the last few years, an immense progress has made in the fields of artificial intelligence, machine learning and bioinformatics and more research is needed for understand the data in biological science and related problems. Bioinformatics is a subdivision of science that involves the analysis of biological data using mathematical principles, statistical tools and certain algorithms in addition to computational approaches (Ezziane, 2006). Artificial intelligence is the ability to solve various problems related to human intelligence and in turn the simulation of these intelligence processes using computer systems or software. It involves machine learning that allows one to perform all of these tasks based on its training (Narayanan et al., 2002). Basic or structural bioinformatics tools use artificial intelligence and machine intelligence for the design of drugs and repurposing various novel compounds against many diseases such as cancer, neural inflammation and others using the silica approach by applying certain tools with principles of artificial intelligence and machine learning. Bioinformatics has been used to analyze data and logical conclusions. The huge amount of data obtained from whole genome sequencing projects and bioinformatics is used for the annotation of biological data in meaningful ways (Nicolas, 2020). Similarly a large collection of problems has been solved by combining the knowledge and abilities of artificial intelligence with bioinformatics approaches for the prediction of genes, studies involving the study of protein interactions, computational systems for drug design, repurposing drugs for better efficiency, next generation sequencing and development of other software. Therefore, both artificial intelligence and machine learning have useful applications in the field of bioinformatics. The proficiency of artificial intelligence can be changed by varying input data. Artificial learning is further classified into generalized and applied branches. Both of them are totally different where applied is involved in the use of machines and algorithms while applied to stimulate the data into expressions similar to the thoughts of humans automatically (Bülow, 2021). Current machine learning has overcome some of the barriers and has predicted a huge amount of data, increased computational power and the revival of neural networks. These algorithms can be trained for exploit further data and thus don't require human labor or programmers for data prediction (Mitra, 2005).

If safety testing has been performed then it will display compatibility of dosage with the new indications. Drug repurposing has been discovered by chance on the basis of random testing and exploration. For example in the market, sildenafil citrate was discovered as a hypertensive drug and then repurposed with Pfizer resulting in the formation of a new drug molecule Viagara for the treatment of erectile dysfunction proved by clinical studies directly from its formulation which in turn provided massive sales in addition to additional health benefits. From the last few years, several computational approaches have been proposed for the repurposing of drug molecules (Kumar et al., 2018). Popular information for this purpose has been acquired from in silico drug repurposing such as electronic records, gene based information, genetic expression response based profiles, mapping of the targeted complex molecules and phenotype- based profile assessment. Drug repurposing hubs and repurpose hub were recently surveyed. There is also some literature on drug design, discovery and optimization of lead during development, leading to the development of a totally novel molecule (Mellit & Kalogirou, 2008).

However, the aim of this review is to use artificial intelligence and machine learning programs that use publicly available data and information. The main point of emphasis is the comprehensive target based activity of the drugs for the discovery of drug molecules and repurposing where existing drug molecules have some target effects over recently identified target effects for the purpose of new indications (Chen et al., 2008). Hence it provides evidence for the further development of drug molecules and their commercialization. This is particularly true for the drugs that are not specific to any target but have the activity for a number of targets showing broad spectrum activity. For example in some cases cancer off target candidates are available which in addition to having anticancer activity also have potential for the production of new drugs. Here the point to consider is that repurposing us not only to cancer related drugs but also advanced to SARC-CoV novel virus which can be readily applied to patients with COVID-19 (Laughton, 1997).

Repurposing was initiated after the phonotypical observation of adventitious drug molecules by polypharmacological activities. For example we observed the most surprising effects of axinitib which is an inhibitor of the endothelial growth receptor, for treating renal cell carcinoma in both chronic and acute cases (Fethi & Pasiouras, 2010). Hence artificial learning is now used for the prediction of personalized drug molecules by analyzing the genomic data of patients using certain computational techniques in addition to its diagnosis (Fethi & Pasiouras, 2010). These algorithms based on training by AI has more efficiency as compared to the software having no AI training. These include logistic regression, k- nearest neighborhood analysis and linear regression in addition to neural networks in the field of bioinformatics for the computational efficiency in field of Pharmacology, immunology and other biological areas etc. as in Fig.01. The improvement of AI and machine learning in the immunoinformatics and pharmacy has led to the development of clinical immunoinformatics or clinical bioinformatics providing the thorough screening which in turn provide more power to computational simulation in bioinformatics. Now the computational methods have the ability to screen about greater than 100,000 influenza virus using different methods for reaching at a logical conclusion (Mellit et al., 2009).

Figure 1. The relationship between data sciences, bioinformatics and biomedical science.

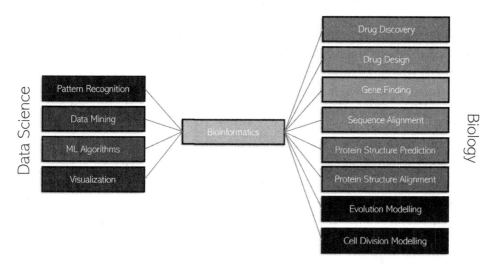

REVOLUTION OF DISCOVERY PROCESS OF DRUG BY ARTIFICIAL INTELLIGENCE

The data which is much huge to be generally analyzed by the commercially available tools or soft wares is referred as the big data. The three main properties of the big data are the volume which shows the quantity of the data generated during an operation, velocity which depicts the rate of generation of the data while the variety shows the variation found to be present in a data set. With the development of a number of the biomedical and sequencing techniques such as reverse transcription PCR RT-PCR, Whole genome sequencing WGS and others, a number of drugs are there which need to be discovered in response to them. In the recent years, next generation sequencing such as whole genome sequencing has been applied for understanding the genetic basis of the diseases (Tripathi & Misra, 2017). Using whole exome sequencing WES, the genetic variants in humans can be identified easily which showed that missense variants are responsible for genetic disease in humans. Not all the variants are associated with genetic variants only deleterious one are involved in Mendalian diseases, cancers etc (Kohli et al., 2019). Identification of these deleterious variants at a time is a much laborious and time consuming procedure due to its complexity. Hence computational methods have been purposed for solving such problems efficiently by using techniques or methods such as sequence evolutionary techniques, sequence homology and structural similarity data. In order to make this more powerful it requires super mount and fastidious techniques which can be later used in an unfrequented way for trained set of data. The field of artificial learning uses the cognitive ability of the physicians and doctors using biomedical and bioinformatics data to produce fruitful results. Artificial intelligence can be broadly classified into almost three categories which include artificial general intelligence, artificial narrow intelligence and super intelligence (Martinez-Romero, 2010). ANI or artificial natural intelligence is still in the process of development and aims to hit the market or research in next decade. It has the ability to develop new data set, analyze them, to find the correlation among them and draw the meaningful or useful conclusions (Yang et al., 2019).

For the discovery of the drug the very first step is the identification of the target which can either be protein or any other component that is involved the pathophysiology of the diseases. Then the step is followed by the discovery of the drug molecule which can react and meddle with these targets in order to vanish the disease in a long run. Here after this, there is need access to the bio, medical data and algorithms to design drugs according to sequences. In the case of the identification of the drug target, a term referred as gene expression is used for the identification of the gene involved in disease along with the mechanism of pathogenicity of disease (Gore & Desai, 2014). In this scenario microarrays and RNA sequencing has generated a huge collection of data for being stored and analysis for gene expression. Some of the most common tools for the expression of gene include NCBI based gene expression omni bus GEO, The cancer genome Atlas represented as TCGA and lastly the arrays are the some of databases which are found to be the great reservoirs for data storage purposes. By analyzing of the gene expression, it is much easier to find out the major reason or mechanism behind any disease or disorder (Singh & Pathak, 2020). As for example in the case of tissue sarcoma or cancer, it is easy to analyze the major biomarkers and rare disease genes found in this via machine learning and artificial intelligence approach. The interrelationship of the genome variants with the specific disease can be found by the Genome wide association studies abbreviated as GWAS (Hoq, 2019). Moreover, it is easy to find out the locus associated to the specific disease in order to find out a specific therapeutic target for that disease. The genes responsible for the risk of disease can be identified by the analysis of various genome and exome specific sequence data. For the storage of the sequencing data, we have public libraries such as NCBI which contain the data obtained from whole gene sequencings. As for example in 2012, li and his colleagues used data for the identification of the locus or target gene responsible for juvenile idiopathic arthritis loci based on the artificial learning and intelligence program. The data was obtained from Gene expression, GWAS, methylation and epigenetics data. Moreover there exist also specific genes the mutation in which can lead to a specific disease are also a promising target (Sharma & Rani, 2020). The most important data sets for the identification of compounds and their synthesis via ChemSpider, ChEMBL, ZINC,

BindingDB, and PubChem during discovery and processing of data. The data thus obtained is then screened for the presence of certain pharmacological properties for discovering of transition forces, discovering and atomic number functionalities. In the case of missense variant identification, almost all of the methods are applied at once being utilized in our studies (Rahmanifard & Plaksina, 2019). Vcards is the computational tool for the identification of genetic variants and has integrated the functional consequences of allele frequencies, computational methodologies and genetic information coded for variants. But it is still difficult to find out the variance in these computational methods because they differ continuously with time (Zhavoronkov, 2020). However a number of studies have compared the missense variation in case of computational methodologies. But they don't employ the use of experimentally obtained datasets. And these studies are based on ROC receiver operating characteristic curves (Quazi & Jangi, 2021; Quazi, 2021). But the other properties must also be taken into account which included accuracy, efficiency, infectivity, absorption and mechanism in AUC which are not yet been considered (Sfetsos & Coonick, 2000). However there also the studies which show that it is used for the prediction of harmful genes in the missense variations. But it us shown that it has to distinguish the pathogenic variants with a high sensitivity using VEST3, REVEL and M-CAP. However a recent method has employed the use of about 23 computational techniques in this field. The data then obtained was then subjected to the process of filtration via certain techniques ADMET, PAINS and toxicity. The filtered data was then subjected to the artificial intelligence techniques such as that of deep learning, neural network and other simulation studies (Sharma & Sarkar, 2013).

Afterwards, the final compound was later visualized for the binding energy and the identification of the active site. Thus the data obtained then was subjected to the prices of validation. But here the quantum mechanics play its central role but these actually does not provide hurdles in the process of drug discovery. These include ab intio, neural activity, deep learning and classification. Quantum mechanics will be more valuable tool in the term of the computational mechanical chemistry. So it will play a directed role in the computation of drug discovery process (Henson et al., 2018).

ARTIFICIAL INTELLIGENCE OR MACHINE LEARNING IN ADDITION TO CONVENTIONAL CHEMISTRY IN DRUG DESIGN

Due to the chemical and classical chemistry problems in drug discovey, the artificial intelligence has been found to be best solution. Due to discovery of the new algorithms and new features the drug designing has been revolution by computer aided drug discovery CADD and National Institute of health NIH has highlighted the fact

Figure 2. General steps for drug discovery using AI and ML

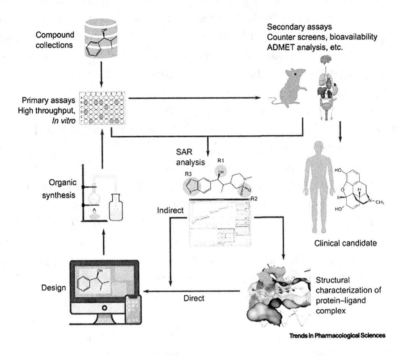

medicine discovery is an emerging strategy for the 'purpose of drug prevention or treatment which also considers the other variations in genetics, libertines and environment. This allows the doctors and physicians to treat and recover diseases more accurately than that of another method employed so far (Lamberti et al., 2019). The most popular pharmaceutical companies are using this deep learning, artificial intelligence and ANI during their development process which aims to identify the unique genetic mutations in a large set of data and thus physicians can use it in various fields of medical science (Jiménez-Luna et al., 2020). As we have already discussed that using this technique we can make drug discovery process more fastidious. The main aim of the scientists now a days is to improve the repurposing and discovery of drug via machine learning programs. This in turn will answer the two main and critical problems of the medicinal chemistry that what will be the next compound to be synthesized and which method is efficient for applying. So the following last two decades has resulted in the invention of a number of new techniques for computer based drug discoveries. These include quantitative structural activity relationship model QSAR and the available free energy techniques (Doniger et al., 2002). In most of the models mentioned, the data appeared to be in the form of the string as compared to linear form and also found to get its input directly as compared to use of any chemical descriptor for the sorting and translation of data or which process language. They have employed the usage of two different types of datasets having Z value is equal to 3 or in the case of whole data set z value will be 3 or 6. Later about 9 different types of the matrices are used for the evolution of the accuracy of data set involved in the study. Similarly the affectivity was predicted by using two QSAR approaches where the authors were found to develop a given QSAR system based on partial least square in the terms of training time and statistical analysis (Daniel et al., 2017). Furthermore for the chemical synthesis of the compounds the scientists were relayed on already present literature. With the advancement in AI and machine learning it is possible to have idea about the difference in the structure of two drug molecules in order to predict the novel compound. Recently Zhang and its colleagues have used different analytical techniques being used in the treatment of COVID-19.Later on these compounds were subjected to analytical methods such as ADME and docking which showed that about 15 compounds were effective against the novel coronavirus (LaValle, 2006).

REPURPOSING OF DRUG

The most deterious effected, lethal and multifactorial diseases are NDDS which are the diseased conditions of nervous system and is associated with a main cause of death throughout the world. These include Addison's disease, Parkinson disease, Amyotrophic sclerosis which can lead to death of neurons in the nervous system in one way or other (Singla et al., 2013). The accumulation of mist toxic, misfolded protein in the major portion of brain is the main cause of disease. Moreover these disorders can lead to a number of cognitive disorders such as loss of memory, slow learning, speaking problems or stiffness of the brain tissues (Singh, 2019). The major problem in the cases of NDDS is the fact that for these diseases no treatment is available which presents 100% efficiency and if present is not suitable to a great extent so there is need to rediscover the drugs. Accurate drug target identification is not only overcome the experimentally mapped DTI based methodology but also have the ability to repurpose the drug molecules by targeting the already available drug molecules which are already approved (Zhavoronkov et al., 2020). There are various in silico based methods available for repurposing of drug molecule using DTI mappings. For instance Mei.et AL proposed a multiple learning method for the repurposing of drug based on already known drug targets. During this process each of the drug molecule is considered as class label and the target protein acts as a learning data for training of I2 logistic based regression model (Weinstein et al., 1994). About 89% correct validation is done by stratified multi-labelled cross validation for one of the drug molecule and proposed framework showed 84.5% accurate DTI predictions as compared to others. The fact shows that proposed framework generally is compatible for large frame drugs and require only the information of drug chemical structure and target identification (Kumar, Sharma, Siddiqui et al, 2017). So this provides the accurate identification of targets and genes responsible for NDDs (Cavalli et al., 2015).

The recently discovered iDrug method integrates DTI and drug repositioning into a new coherent models termed as cross network embedding. It provides the principle way of transferring knowledge across various drugs target relationships and using this it predicts accuracy for both DTI and drug disease relationships. The working of iDrug was tested on various datasets containing data from multiple disease types and hence has become applicable for drug repurposing due to several reasons (Koromina et al., 2019).Similarly it is used for the identification of the inhibitors being employed in the case of NDDS.As for example class 1 and class IIb histone deacetylases inhibitors have been discovered because the enzyme is involved in the PD disease. Similarly some of the scientists employed QSAR enzyme for the finding out of BACEA1 enzyme inhibitor being responsible for the aggregation of beta amyloid in the disease (Fang, 2020).

Molecular transformer drug target interaction MT-DTI is used for getting more accurate results which is pre trained learning based drug targeting model allowed for a number of already present drugs and has been used for the identification of viral proteins effective against SARC-CoV 19.Using this method, atazanavir an antiviral or antiretroviral for HIV treatment and has proved to be the most potent drug having kd value of 94.66 which is comparable to other drugs available for treating SARC-CoV (Bajorath, 2020). Moreover another thing the accuracy of the methods gets decreasing when there are small or insufficient number of ligands available for a drug molecule. Regardless of the limitations, there are number of applications which describe the involvement of AI based tools in molecular docking. For example, thioridazine is an anti-inflammatory compound and has been included in the 1500 FDA approved drugs and also inhibit ikB activity being critical for NF-kB pathway involved in progressing of cancer. Similarly inn another experiment, virtual docking has predicted the inhibitory activity of about 1400 FDA approved drug in against to *Pseudomonas aeruginosa* showing inhibitory activity against the various virulence gene expression (Álvarez-Machancoses & Fernández-Martínez, 2019).Zheng et AL., in 2019 gave the drug by repurposing of drug molecule by development of a tool named as QD repurposing tool used automatically for the repurposing of drugs of Addison disease and Parkinson disease. Similarly, telmisartan was provided to be the most effective repurposed drug for Parkinson disease formed by the scanning of literature and involvement of artificial intelligence and machine learning process in drug development (Usmani et al., 2018).

EXAMPLES OF THE USE OF AI IN DRUG REPURPOSING AND DISCOVERY PROCESS

Atom wise is used by Biopharma for the identification and prediction of the small structures in 3D basis now a days. The atomwise has used this technique for the identification of active molecules in the case of Ebola virus (Díaz et al., 2019). Using Artificial Intelligence Company has developed two different drugs which are more effective against Ebola virus as compared to medications which are existed before. Although the method proves to be promising but the companies need to provide the safety and other consideration overview using a peer review or other methods(Zhu, 2020).It integrates with two-structural based approaches which include protein ligand binding pharmacophores search and docking and another four structural based approaches which include vector regression affinity based prediction, SVM binary classifications, three dimensional similarity search function and neighboring affinity prediction (Torres-Carrión, 2019). In the virtual screen of structure based prediction, RF score has been found and applied subsequently for the prediction if accurate targets. RF-score VS is actually an enhanced level scoring which are trained on the directions of full decoy datasets (Feala et al., 2010). The integration of AI in suture based virtual screening is found to be a promising approach and has been used for improvement of the post processing after the structural based virtual screening by reconsideration of the virtual score calculated with docking algorithms using machine learning models without any consensus scoring (Kumar, Das, & Ghosh, 2017). As for examples Auto dock can also be integrated with RF score virtual screening in order to get better performance in VS. Integration of advanced learning and machine based methods is helpful in the prediction of potential ligands (Shahbaaz et al., 2019). Hence the involvement of AI and ML in drug discovery has resulted in bringing down the value of false negative and false positive predictions in term of drug discovery process and in future it will also consider the physicochemical properties and structural information of predicted protein (Chan et al., 2019). (Wang et al., 2019). We recently employed VirtualKinomeProfiler which is an efficient platform for distinguishing of chemical similarity of kinome, thus speeding up the drug repurposing process for accurate identification prediction of inhibitors (Green et al., 2018). SVM sequence vector machine algorithm has enabled the prediction of greater than 30M kinase compounds using which we carried out in silico predictions of 150k compounds in term of drug repurposing and optimization of lead compounds. Experimental testing provided the validation of about 15 targets out of 50leading to 1.5% increase in precision and decrease of false negative activity to about 1.3% (Bender & Cortes-Ciriano, 2021).

CONCLUSION

With the emergence of the field, the scientists are in search of new drugs, therapies or treatments having more efficiencies as compared to existing ones. By understanding the underlying mechanism in the progression of disease and the effect of already discovered drug and unrevealing of their genetic codes can lead to the new and precision drug therapies which in turn will improve both the health and life of patients. Classical methods used for the discovery of the drugs are found to be time consuming, having more false negative results. In comparison using computational approaches having AI, one can identify the drug more quickly. A number of researches has shown the impact of the drugs on various targets and many of them are in the process of discovery now. In addition to identification of targeted drug or protein, repurposing of drugs provide new molecular targets which can be further used based on their properties also for the prediction of new drug molecule using AI based tools in field of bioinformatics. In future there are expectations that bioinformatics will play a more significant role in the analyzing of data using AI and ML approaches in order to save time and resources at the same time. It will in turn also accelerate the discoveries in the field of biomedical, biological sciences and robotic surgeries.

REFERENCES

Álvarez-Machancoses, Ó., & Fernández-Martínez, J. L. (2019). Using artificial intelligence methods to speed up drug discovery. *Expert Opinion on Drug Discovery*, *14*(8), 769–777. doi:10.1080/17460441.2019.1621284 PMID:31140873

Bajorath, J. R. (2020). *Artificial intelligence in drug discovery: Into the great wide open*. ACS Publications.

Bender, A., & Cortes-Ciriano, I. (2021). Artificial intelligence in drug discovery: what is realistic, what are illusions? Part 2: A discussion of chemical and biological data used for AI in drug discovery. *Drug Discovery Today*, *26*(4), 1040–1052. doi:10.1016/j.drudis.2020.11.037

Bülow, R. D. (2021). How will artificial intelligence and bioinformatics change our understanding of IgA in the next decade? In *Seminars in Immunopathology*. Springer. doi:10.100700281-021-00847-y

Cavalli, A., Spitaleri, A., Saladino, G., & Gervasio, F. L. (2015). Investigating drug–target association and dissociation mechanisms using metadynamics-based algorithms. *Accounts of Chemical Research*, *48*(2), 277–285. doi:10.1021/ar500356n PMID:25496113

Chan, H. S., Shan, H., Dahoun, T., Vogel, H., & Yuan, S. (2019). Advancing drug discovery via artificial intelligence. *Trends in Pharmacological Sciences*, *40*(8), 592–604. doi:10.1016/j.tips.2019.06.004 PMID:31320117

Chen, S. H., Jakeman, A. J., & Norton, J. P. (2008). Artificial intelligence techniques: An introduction to their use for modelling environmental systems. *Mathematics and Computers in Simulation*, *78*(2-3), 379–400. doi:10.1016/j.matcom.2008.01.028

Daniel, O. O., Kolawole, J. A., & Kolawole, J. A. (2017). In-vitro and In-silico Drug-Food Interaction: An Evaluation of Metformin and Green Tea Interactions. *Novel Approaches in Drug Designing & Development*, *2*(2), 34–39.

Díaz, Ó., Dalton, J. A., & Giraldo, J. (2019). Artificial intelligence: A novel approach for drug discovery. *Trends in Pharmacological Sciences*, *40*(8), 550–551. doi:10.1016/j.tips.2019.06.005 PMID:31279568

Doniger, S., Hofmann, T., & Yeh, J. (2002). Predicting CNS permeability of drug molecules: Comparison of neural network and support vector machine algorithms. *Journal of Computational Biology*, *9*(6), 849–864. doi:10.1089/10665270260518317 PMID:12614551

Ezziane, Z. (2006). Applications of artificial intelligence in bioinformatics: A review. *Expert Systems with Applications*, *30*(1), 2–10. doi:10.1016/j.eswa.2005.09.042

Fang, J. (2020). A critical review of five machine learning-based algorithms for predicting protein stability changes upon mutation. *Briefings in Bioinformatics*, *21*(4), 1285–1292. doi:10.1093/bib/bbz071 PMID:31273374

Feala, J. D., Cortes, J., Duxbury, P. M., Piermarocchi, C., McCulloch, A. D., & Paternostro, G. (2010). Systems approaches and algorithms for discovery of combinatorial therapies. *Wiley Interdisciplinary Reviews. Systems Biology and Medicine*, *2*(2), 181–193. doi:10.1002/wsbm.51 PMID:20836021

Fethi, M. D., & Pasiouras, F. (2010). Assessing bank efficiency and performance with operational research and artificial intelligence techniques: A survey. *European Journal of Operational Research*, *204*(2), 189–198. doi:10.1016/j.ejor.2009.08.003

Gore, M., & Desai, N. S. (2014). Computer-aided drug designing. In *Clinical Bioinformatics* (pp. 313–321). Springer. doi:10.1007/978-1-4939-0847-9_18

Green, C. P., Engkvist, O., & Pairaudeau, G. (2018). *The convergence of artificial intelligence and chemistry for improved drug discovery.* Future Science. doi:10.4155/fmc-2018-0161

Henson, A. B., Gromski, P. S., & Cronin, L. (2018). Designing algorithms to aid discovery by chemical robots. *ACS Central Science*, *4*(7), 793–804. doi:10.1021/acscentsci.8b00176 PMID:30062108

Hoq, M. (2019). *In silico drug designing against Klebsiella pneumoniae adhesin protein*. Brac University.

Jiménez-Luna, J., Grisoni, F., & Schneider, G. (2020). Drug discovery with explainable artificial intelligence. *Nature Machine Intelligence*, *2*(10), 573–584. doi:10.103842256-020-00236-4

Kohli, A., Mahajan, V., Seals, K., Kohli, A., & Jha, S. (2019). Concepts in US Food and Drug Administration regulation of artificial intelligence for medical imaging. *AJR. American Journal of Roentgenology*, *213*(4), 886–888. doi:10.2214/AJR.18.20410 PMID:31166758

Koromina, M., Pandi, M.-T., & Patrinos, G. P. (2019). Rethinking drug repositioning and development with artificial intelligence, machine learning, and omics. *OMICS: A Journal of Integrative Biology*, *23*(11), 539–548. doi:10.1089/omi.2019.0151 PMID:31651216

Kumar, P., Das, G., & Ghosh, I. (2017). Critical assessment of contribution from Indian publications: The role of in silico designing methods leading to drugs or drug-like compounds using text based mining and association. *J Proteins Proteom*, *8*, 133–148.

Kumar, R., Sharma, A., Siddiqui, M. H., & Tiwari, R. K. (2017). Prediction of human intestinal absorption of compounds using artificial intelligence techniques. *Current Drug Discovery Technologies*, *14*(4), 244–254. doi:10.2174/1570163814666170404160911 PMID:28382857

Kumar, R., Sharma, A., Siddiqui, M. H., & Tiwari, R. K. (2018). Prediction of drug-plasma protein binding using artificial intelligence based algorithms. *Combinatorial Chemistry & High Throughput Screening*, *21*(1), 57–64. doi:10.2174/1386207321666171218121557 PMID:29256344

Lamberti, M. J., Wilkinson, M., Donzanti, B. A., Wohlhieter, G. E., Parikh, S., Wilkins, R. G., & Getz, K. (2019). A study on the application and use of artificial intelligence to support drug development. *Clinical Therapeutics*, *41*(8), 1414–1426. doi:10.1016/j.clinthera.2019.05.018 PMID:31248680

Laughton, M. (1997). *Artificial intelligence techniques in power systems*. Academic Press.

LaValle, S. M. (2006). *Planning algorithms*. Cambridge university press. doi:10.1017/CBO9780511546877

Martinez-Romero, M. (2010). Artificial intelligence techniques for colorectal cancer drug metabolism: Ontologies and complex networks. *Current Drug Metabolism, 11*(4), 347–368. doi:10.2174/138920010791514289 PMID:20446907

Mellit, A., & Kalogirou, S. A. (2008). Artificial intelligence techniques for photovoltaic applications: A review. *Progress in Energy and Combustion Science, 34*(5), 574–632. doi:10.1016/j.pecs.2008.01.001

Mellit, A., Kalogirou, S. A., Hontoria, L., & Shaari, S. (2009). Artificial intelligence techniques for sizing photovoltaic systems: A review. *Renewable & Sustainable Energy Reviews, 13*(2), 406–419. doi:10.1016/j.rser.2008.01.006

Mitra, S. (2005). Computational intelligence in bioinformatics. In *Transactions on Rough Sets III* (pp. 134–152). Springer. doi:10.1007/11427834_6

Narayanan, A., Keedwell, E. C., & Olsson, B. (2002). Artificial intelligence techniques for bioinformatics. *Applied Bioinformatics, 1*, 191–222. PMID:15130837

Nicolas, J. (2020). Artificial intelligence and bioinformatics. In *A Guided Tour of Artificial Intelligence Research* (pp. 209–264). Springer. doi:10.1007/978-3-030-06170-8_7

Quazi & Jangi. (2021). *Artificial intelligence and machine learning in medicinal chemistry and validation of emerging drug targets*. Academic Press.

Quazi, S. (2021). Vaccine in response to COVID-19: Recent developments, challenges, and a way out. *Biomedical and Biotechnology Research Journal, 5*(2), 105. doi:10.4103/bbrj.bbrj_166_20

Rahmanifard, H., & Plaksina, T. (2019). Application of artificial intelligence techniques in the petroleum industry: A review. *Artificial Intelligence Review, 52*(4), 2295–2318. doi:10.100710462-018-9612-8

Sfetsos, A., & Coonick, A. (2000). Univariate and multivariate forecasting of hourly solar radiation with artificial intelligence techniques. *Solar Energy, 68*(2), 169–178. doi:10.1016/S0038-092X(99)00064-X

Shahbaaz, M., Nkaule, A., & Christoffels, A. (2019). Designing novel possible kinase inhibitor derivatives as therapeutics against Mycobacterium tuberculosis: An in silico study. *Scientific Reports, 9*(1), 1–12. doi:10.103841598-019-40621-7 PMID:30867456

Sharma, A., & Rani, R. (2020). Ensembled machine learning framework for drug sensitivity prediction. *IET Systems Biology*, *14*(1), 39–46. doi:10.1049/iet-syb.2018.5094 PMID:31931480

Sharma, V., & Sarkar, I. N. (2013). Bioinformatics opportunities for identification and study of medicinal plants. *Briefings in Bioinformatics*, *14*(2), 238–250. doi:10.1093/bib/bbs021 PMID:22589384

Singh, D. B., & Pathak, R. K. (2020). Computational approaches in drug designing and their applications. In *Experimental protocols in biotechnology* (pp. 95–117). Springer. doi:10.1007/978-1-0716-0607-0_6

Singh, V. (2019). Ligand-Based Designing of Natural Products. In Bioactive Natural Products for the Management of Cancer: From Bench to Bedside. Springer. doi:10.1007/978-981-13-7607-8_8

Singla, D., Dhanda, S. K., Chauhan, J. S., Bhardwaj, A., Brahmachari, S. K., Consortium, O. S. D. D., & Raghava, G. P. S. (2013). Open source software and web services for designing therapeutic molecules. *Current Topics in Medicinal Chemistry*, *13*(10), 1172–1191. doi:10.2174/1568026611313100005 PMID:23647540

Torres-Carrión, P. (2019). Application of techniques based on Artificial Intelligence for predicting the consumption of drugs and substances. A Systematic Mapping Review. In *International Conference on Applied Technologies*. Springer.

Tripathi, A., & Misra, K. (2017). Molecular docking: A structure-based drug designing approach. *JSM Chemistry*, *5*(2), 1042–1047.

Usmani, S. S., Kumar, R., Bhalla, S., Kumar, V., & Raghava, G. P. S. (2018). In silico tools and databases for designing peptide-based vaccine and drugs. *Advances in Protein Chemistry and Structural Biology*, *112*, 221–263. doi:10.1016/bs.apcsb.2018.01.006 PMID:29680238

Wang, L., Ding, J., Pan, L., Cao, D., Jiang, H., & Ding, X. (2019). Artificial intelligence facilitates drug design in the big data era. *Chemometrics and Intelligent Laboratory Systems*, *194*, 103850. doi:10.1016/j.chemolab.2019.103850

Weinstein, J. N., Myers, T., Buolamwini, J., Raghavan, K., Van Osdol, W., Licht, J., Viswanadhan, V. N., Kohn, K. W., Rubinstein, L. V., Koutsoukos, A. D., Monks, A., Scudiero, D. A., Zaharevitz, D., Chabner, B. A., Anderson, N. L., Grever, M. R., & Paull, K. D. (1994). Predictive statistics and artificial intelligence in the US National Cancer Institute's drug discovery program for cancer and AIDS. *Stem Cells (Dayton, Ohio)*, *12*(1), 13–22. doi:10.1002tem.5530120106 PMID:8142917

Yang, X., Wang, Y., Byrne, R., Schneider, G., & Yang, S. (2019). Concepts of artificial intelligence for computer-assisted drug discovery. *Chemical Reviews, 119*(18), 10520–10594. doi:10.1021/acs.chemrev.8b00728 PMID:31294972

Zhavoronkov, A. (2020). Medicinal Chemists versus Machines Challenge: What Will It Take to Adopt and Advance Artificial Intelligence for Drug Discovery? *Journal of Chemical Information and Modeling, 60*(6), 2657–2659. doi:10.1021/acs.jcim.0c00435 PMID:32469509

Zhavoronkov, A., Vanhaelen, Q., & Oprea, T. I. (2020). Will Artificial Intelligence for Drug Discovery Impact Clinical Pharmacology? *Clinical Pharmacology and Therapeutics, 107*(4), 780–785. doi:10.1002/cpt.1795 PMID:31957003

Zhu, H. (2020). Big data and artificial intelligence modeling for drug discovery. *Annual Review of Pharmacology and Toxicology, 60*(1), 573–589. doi:10.1146/annurev-pharmtox-010919-023324 PMID:31518513

Chapter 10
Structural and Functional Data Processing in Bio-Computing and Deep Learning

Karthigai Selvi S.
The Gandhigram Rural Institute (Deemed), India

ABSTRACT

The goal of new biocomputing research is to comprehend bio molecules' structures and functions via the lens of biofuturistic technologies. The amount of data generated every day is tremendous, and data bases are growing exponentially. A majority of computational researchers have been using machine learning for the analysis of bio-informatics data sets. This chapter explores the relationship between deep learning algorithms and the fundamental biological concepts of protein structure, phenotypes and genotype, proteins and protein levels, and the similarities and differences between popular deep learning models. This chapter offers a useful outlook for further research into its theory, algorithms, and applications in computational biology and bioinformatics. Understanding the structural aspects of cellular contact networks helps to comprehend the interdependencies, causal chains, and fundamental functional capabilities that exist across the entire network.

INTRODUCTION

The massive amounts of biological data from genomics, proteomics, metabolomics, transcriptomics, drug development, and other fields need to be supported by mathematical and computational models. Biological challenges like alignment of gene sequence, gene discovery, assembly of gene, prediction of protein structure,

DOI: 10.4018/978-1-6684-6523-3.ch010

gene expression analysis, protein-protein connections, and the modelling of evolution have all been solved using computational biology. By studying the order of biological molecules like DNA and proteins, functional and morphological information, computational tools and software for the evaluation of bioinformatics sought to solve biological puzzles (Chou et al., 2004).

In microbiology, understanding the structural aspects of cellular contact networks helps us to comprehend the interdependencies, causal chains, and fundamental functional capabilities that exist across the entire network (Klamt et al., 2006). Advances in molecular biology and imaging techniques such as X-ray, electron microscopy and Nuclear Magnetic Resonance (NMR) have led to a revolution in structural biology. Thus permit us to see the complex three-dimensional shapes of protein structures and their functions such as interaction with other proteins and ligands. The growing technological advancements in imaging techniques are visualizing the exact structure of individual-atom in 2-Dimension and 3-Dimenstion, protein molecules, other body organ structures and blood flow in veins (functional MR Image) (Sljoka et al., 2022).

The computational models explain the various biological processes that are carried out by specific nucleic acid, result in a specific phenotype changes in gene series or protein expression or localization result in a specific disease, and how modifications to cell organisation affect cell behaviour. It is also known as "bioinformatics" the bioinformatics data sets are holding the information. In order to create models for various types of experimental data, such as concentrations, sequences, images, molecules, cells, tissues, and organs, etc., computational biology employs techniques from a broad range of mathematical and computational fields, including complexity theory, algorithms, machine learning, robotics, etc.

COMPUTATIONAL METHODS

Computing scientists must be able to identify computational methods and techniques that can be used to address problems that may arise in unfamiliar fields. The necessary biological concepts will be used to describe the problems. The typical stages of computational processing include data pre-processing, model selection, model validation, hyper parameter adjustment, and performance evaluation. Recent works employs machine learning for all the works. The remaining chapter describes the machine learning models and recent research works employed machine learning for structural and functional analysis.

Artificial Neural Network (ANN)

ANN is the imitation of human brain and a network made up of computational concepts. It includes several layers with ascends of neurons. The neurons are connected with other neurons in the same layer and with neurons in different layers. Three kinds of layers such as input layer, hidden layer and output layer compiled as common. Each neuron performs computation on the input data with additionally added weight value. Usually, two stages of processes carried out in ANN that are known as training stage and testing stage. The weight value of a connection determination is the primary work in the training stage. The weighted sum of all inputs is passed to the activation function. The activation function plays a role as threshold detection that finalize the node to fire or not. There are distinctive activation functions available. They are,

- Logistic sigmoid function
- Hyperbolic tangent function
- Softmax function
- Rectified Linear Unit (ReLU) function
- Parametric ReLU function
- Exponential linear function
- Leaky ReLU

Logistic Sigmoid Function: this function is used in logistic regression algorithms. It takes numerical value as input and results the values between 0 to 1

$$f\left(x\right) = \frac{1}{1 + e^{-ax}} \tag{1}$$

where f(x) represents output value, x is the input and a is a constant.

Hyperbolic Tangent Function: It is known as Tanh and similar to sigmoid activation function. It takes the numerical real values. the output value between -1 to 1. It is mainly used for two class classification.

$$f\left(x\right) = \frac{e^{x} - e^{-x}}{e^{x} + e^{-x}} \tag{2}$$

Softmax Function: It is used for multi class classification work. The summation output of the softmax function will be 1.

$$f(x) = \frac{e^x}{\sum e^x} \tag{3}$$

To soften the data Binhu Tang (2019) suggested to use

$$f(\alpha_k) = \frac{e^{\frac{\alpha_k}{T}}}{\sum_k e^{\frac{\alpha_k}{T}}} \tag{4}$$

Rectified Linear Unit (ReLU) function: Frequently used activation function especially in CNN and deep learning

$$f(x) = \begin{cases} 0 \ for \ x < 0 \\ x \ for \ x \geq 0 \end{cases} \tag{5}$$

The output of ReLU function depends on the input. For negative input value, it returns 0, otherwise it returns the same input value

Parametric ReLU function: A constant 'a' is multiplied with the input data x.

$$f(x) = \begin{cases} ax \ for \ x < 0 \\ x \ for \ x \geq 0 \end{cases} \tag{6}$$

Exponential Linear function: It is different from other function. It contains an α value which should be in positive. It works faster and produce accurate result.

Leaky ReLU function: It accounts on zero constant like $\alpha = 0.01$

$$f(x) = \begin{cases} x, x > 0 \\ \propto x, x \leq 0 \end{cases} \tag{7}$$

Types of ANN

As given in Figure 1, neural networks (NN) might be divided into different networks such as feed-forward neural networks (FNN), recurrent NN (RNN), radial basis function NN (RBNN), Kohonen self-organizing NN, and modular neural networks.

Data in FNN moves from the input layer via the hidden layer to the output layer in a single path.

In an RNN, a layer's output serves as the input for the following layer by creating a feed back loop. Thus, enables the network to remember past states and utilize those memories to affect the present output. RNNs are capable to process a series of input values and generating a series of outputs.

The RBNN includes input, hidden, and output layers as other models. Hidden layer utilizes radial basis function and each node of that layer serves as the cluster centre. The cluster centre learns by the assigned input, the output layer unites the outputs of the radial basis function and weight parameters supplied by the learning.

The Kohonen self-organizing network practices unsupervised learning phenomena that adjusts the network model by the input data. Kohenen self-organizing network is made up of an input layer and an output layer that are completely connected. The output layer is structured as a grid in two dimensions. It does not use any activation function and computes the weights of each node by its position in the two-dimensional grid of the output layer. The Euclidean distance played an important role to define the nodes in a class. The distance between the input node and the position of the output node in respect of its weight determines the closeness of nodes. The closeness of nodes and position of the node in the output layer determines the output. If the network size is large that are divided into smaller, independent neural network modules using modular neural networks. The smaller networks carry out particular tasks that are eventually integrated to generate the network's overall output as a whole.

In ANN-based model of gene regulation, each neuron in the network represents a specific gene. The connections between the neurons in the network stand in for regulatory interactions. Here, the output of a neuron at time 't' may be determined from the level of gene expression at time 't'. The advantages of this model include its continuous nature. The use of a transfer function changes the inputs into a form like that of natural processes, and the exclusion of artificial elements. DNA can now be used as novel covert channels in steganography. Ho Bae et al. (2018) suggested a method that learns the inherent distribution of coding and non-coding sequences. In the genomic research, the hidden messages find out by taking distributional variations among the nodes of a layer. The framework uses deep recurrent neural networks (RNNs) to predict whether a sequence will be a coding sequence or not in order to identify the distribution variances.

Deep Learning Neural Network

Deep learning Neural Network constructed by increasing the nodes and layer counts. The ANN gets outfitted with DNN. The following DNN models are much familiar in the field of Bioinformatics.

1. Sparse Autoencoders
2. Convolutional Neural Network (CNN)
3. Restrictive Boltzmann Machine (RBM)
4. Long Short Term Memory (LSTM)

Sparse Autoencoders

In order to reduce dimensionality of the original data set, the autoencoder plays a vital role. Sparse Autoencoders utilizes the unsupervised approach to train the representations in the given data set. It adopts back propagation learning approach to learn the representation. The concept of principal component analysis (PCA) is expanded by Autoencoders. It generalise PCA to carry out dimensionality of feature reduction and eventually regenerate the original data using encoder and decoder blocks placed in the non-linear hidden layers. The lower density of nodes in the hidden layer or every other layer of the two-layer blocks is frequently cited as the cause of this. However, even if the hidden layer has a greater number of nodes, a sparsity constraint can be imposed on the hidden units to keep interesting lower dimension input representations. In order to achieve sparsity, some nodes are prohibited from joining the ring which means that the output is set to a value near to zero. Sparse Autoencoders used with RBM to find the likelihoods.

The Role of Sparse Autoencoders in Biocomputing

Generally, gene expression profiles are in high dimension. Danaee et al. (2017) utilized stacked denoising autoencoder (SDA) to take out functional features from the profiles. Abdolhosseini et al. (2019) used an autoencoder with 30 latent variables which were connected to different biological aspects of the cell to detect the transcriptomics using genes. Another work obtained the latent variable from variational autoencoder (VAE) for the analysis of cancer type detection from TCGA pancancer RNA sequences data (Way et al. 2017). Subsequently, sparsely connected autoencoders and variational autoencoders employed to project gene level in blood cells that predict the severity of breast cancer (Maxwell P., 2019). A four encoding and decoding layer with 128, 64 and 128 dimensional hidden layers proposed to denoise a single cell RAN sequence data. This network utilizes Poisson negative log-likelihood loss function to remove the noise (Kinalis, 2019). The Gene Ontology project (GO) is a bioinformatics initiative to characterize all the important features of genes and gene products within a cell. Qi Wei et al. (2021) utilized the VAE as the pre-processing tool for analyzing the chemotherapy drug response for several cancers such as colon, pancreatic, bladder, breast and sarcoma. In the work, tumor transcriptome profile data are used as input, the data reduction carried out using

VAE and the drug responses are predicted by employing gradient boosted decision trees. Chen et al. (2018) and Maxwell et al. (2019) tested several available methods to predict the drug sensitivity of cancer cell. They found the results provided by the autoencoders are not consistent. Since, in each trial, the encoder function is not identical. Based on their report several research is going on to explore the fitted activation function, acceptable hyper parameters and the way to regularize the consistency without compromise the accuracy.

Convolution Neural Network (CNN)

The CNN is one of the ANN models which deals image processing tasks such as segmentation, computer vision, video analysis and speech analysis. It takes significant role in the technologically updated and fast-growing society. CNN consists of input layer, hidden layer and an output layer. The hidden layer is not a single layer, and it holds several convolutional filters which is known as convolutional layer. As given in Fig. 3 convolution layer, sub-sampling layers are connected to a fully connected layer which utilizes softmax function. Moving from input to output layers, a series of several convolution layers extracts features with increasing fineness at each layer. The convolution layers are followed by fully linked layers that carry out classification. Every convolution layer is frequently followed by a sub-sampling or pooling layer. Each layer is made up of clusters of 2D neurons known as kernels or filters. Unlike other neural networks, a 2D n × n pixel image is given as the input for CNN at a time. The neurons assembled in the feature extraction layer of the network are not joined to the neurons to the nearby levels. Rather, they are only connected to the spatially mapped neurons which are in fixed size, The preceding layer contains partially overlapped neurons. Sometimes, the area of input is known as Local Receptive Field (LRF). The fewer connections take less training time and have a smaller likelihood of over-fitting. All neurons in a filter must have the same order of weights and biases and must be coupled to the equal number of neurons in the preceding input layer (or feature map). These elements accelerate learning and lower the network's memory needs. As a result, the neuron in a particular filter searches for the similar pattern in several locations within the given image. The network's size is decreased by the sub-sampling layers. The neuron size is minimized by the sub-sampling layer in which max or mean pooling, or averaging filters are supporting to get sub-sampling. The fully connected layers are performing the actual classification works. The neurons in the layers are connected with other layers as given in Fig. 2. The layer strength of CNN highly supports to provide excellent results in the job of classification.

Table 1. Parameters of ResNet

Parameters	Values
Rotation	-180° to 180°
Translation	0.1 times of image height and width
Scaling	0.9 times image height and 1.1. times image width
Shear	-5° to 5°
Normalization with mean	0.485, 0.456, 0,406
Normalization with standard deviation	0.229, 0.224, 0.225

Role of CNN in Biocomputing

CNN is most suitable for the job of pattern recognition or object detection in image analysis. Predominantly, the CNN is frequently applying in the field of medical diagnosis research. The recent updated versions of CNN are ResNet and InceptionNet. These networks include transfer learning by using random affine transformation with the parameters of rotation, translation, scaling, shearing and normalization. The ResNet parameters are listed in Table 1.

DenseNet-161 with ADAM optimizer operated by ReLU activation function with above mentioned transfer learning was utilized to detect single cell from whole slide datasets (Santosh, 2022). Jai Hao et al. (2020) detected different survival rates among people by using CNN called PAGE-Net that combines the genomic data and histopathological images of a patient. The model improves the prediction of survival period of patients. A strategic method introduced in max-pooling of CNN called deep max-pooling CNN was employed in the process of mitosis detection from histological images of breast cancer patients (Ciresan D.C., 2013). Survival Convolutional Neural Networks (SCNNs) was proposed in the diagnosis of survival outcomes of cancer patients (Mobadersany P., 2018). SCNN identifies morphological pattern of tumor by using high-power field from tumor region. Another work predicted survival period of a cancer patient called Whole Slide Histopathological Images Survival Analysis framework (WSISA) which involved Deep Convolutional Survival (DeepConvSur) models for learning process (Zhu et al, 2017). Genomic survival convolutional neural networks (GSCNN) proposed to detect the survival period of glioma patient by using pathological images and genomic biomarkers.

Restricted Boltzmann Machine

RBM is a crucial component of deep learning and it was used in deep belief networks (DBNs) (Hinton, 2006) and deep boltzmann machines (DBMs) (Salakhutdinov

R, 2009). Among the deep learning models, Boltzman machine is unsupervised model. All nodes of this network are connected to each other, and the connections are undirected as given in Fig.4. Hence, it is functioning as stochastic or generative model. In this model, the nodes which can do measures are known as visible nodes and others are called hidden nodes as given in Fig. 3. Each node acts as a single system. Like other deep learning models, when receiving the training data, the machine stimulates the process of weight adjustment. A distribution function called Boltzman distribution function determines the states of the system. The Boltzman distribution function shares the energy of the system. The energy level of the node determines the stability.

The Role of Restricted Boltzmann Machine

In the job of constructing deep belief nets, RBM is considered as best learning modules (Arel et al, 2010; Bengio, 2009). The network has been successfully employed for dimensionality reduction in computational biology (Eickholt & Cheng, 2012). RBM model can encode variety information though it received from various sources. It is employed to encode the drug-target interaction (DTI) to predict relationships among the drug and targeted activities and mode of actions (Wang & Zeng, 2013). A user friendly and user control machine is required to model RNA and Protein sequence. adabmDCA is such a RBM equipped machine that allows to initialize parameter, regularize and decimate the traning during training period. Further, the adabmDCA with Monte Carlo Markov Chain sampling used to ensure the equilibrium in training (Muntoni et al., 2021). A recent work proposed RBM to characterize coevolution patterns between amino acids in protein sequences and utilizing for scheming new sequences (Tubiana, 2019).

Long Short-Term Memory (LSTM)

Hochreiter et al. (1997) proposed LSTM at first which includes RNN. LSTM delivers state awareness and it requires memory or state awareness. This work differs from the feed forward network that was previously defined. The previously stated networks do not hold the gradients value for long time. To avoid the issues, the network structure redefined with the utilization of memory cells called LSTM which includes input, forget, and output gates, as provided in the in Fig 5.

Role of LSTM in Biocomputing

Wang (2019) implemented LSTM in the prediction of a gene expression called L-GEPM which captures the nonlinear features which are affecting gene expression.

In the model, the learned features are using to predict the target genes. Lysine succinylation is a typical protein that takes vital role in the regulation of cellular processes. The detection of succinylation sites is a primary task to explore its functions. Many computational methods were involved to deal with this challenge, LSTM and CNN used together to form a deep learning for the prediction of succinylation site by Huang et al. (2021). The molecular-level interactions between the virus and their host play a vital role in the understanding of infection method and the manner of development of a disease (pathogenesis). Mei et al. (2017) used transfer learning-based technique which includes three different classifiers. In their model, each classifier was trained by gene ontology (GO)-based features. At the end of the method, ensemble process is employed by using weighting probability outputs of individual classifiers that provides final result. Generally, Histopathology is considered as a tool to derive diagnosis and prognosis mainly in cancer disease. It allows clinicians to make precise decisions on therapies, whereas high-throughput genomic data have been investigated to dissect the genetic mechanisms of cancers. Now-a-days, most of above mentioned works are done with the help of LSTM.

SUMMARY

The uses of neural networks (NN) in bioinformatics are compiled in this paper and a few literatures are listed in Table 2. This chapter demonstrates how several NN-based applications are created and put into use to make predictions about a range of protein-related information, including structure, binding locations, and localization. Although other architectures like RBF and recurrent NNs are frequently employed, the most common architecture in these methods is a straightforward three-layer feed forward NN. Some protein bioinformatics applications use multilayered designs, which combine the usage of two (or more) NNs. The most commonly used applications include the prediction of binding sites, the detection of secondary structure of proteins, relative solvent accessibility and protein secondary structure. Several research works derived conclusions that the quantity and calibre of NN-based applications yields reliable and beneficial outcomes for the bioinformatics community. We acknowledge a number of additional helpful publications that go over the uses of a wider spectrum of machine learning methods in bioinformatics. None of these contributions focus only on NNs, however some of them cover NNs alongside other related techniques. According to the poll, CNN is a popular technique for extracting local features, particularly in the context of image processing. It has excellent segmentation applicability, and RBM enhances the precision of structural predictions when used directly or as an input for more sophisticated deep learning supervised algorithms. The following key points regarding deep learning were extracted from the previous research work.

(1) The structural predictions' accuracy whether used directly or as an input to more sophisticated deep learning supervised procedures (Xu J, 2019; Senior A W, 2020). (Yang, 2020) (2) the ability to produce synthetic sequences that fold similarly to their natural counterparts (Russ et al., 2020) (3) the capacity to anticipate the impact of mutations (Hopf, 2017). RBM's performance was compared in a study to that of other common representation learning techniques, such as principal or independent component analysis (PCA, ICA), AE, VAE, and their sparse variations. In comparison to deterministic approaches like PCA or ICA, the RBMs are much more robust with respect to sample size and better capture the underlying interactions in the system due to the stochastic mapping between data configurations and representations (Tubiana, 2019). It was used in denoising of single cell data, imputation of missing values, and dimensionality reduction of feature vectors in biocomputing. A family of neural networks, namely autoencoders, facilitates the detection of missing values and dimensionality reduction.

CONCLUSION

As the big data era begins, deep learning is becoming more and more popular, driven by international academic and business interests. In the discipline of bioinformatics, where conventional machine learning techniques have already made substantial progress, deep learning is likewise projected to produce outstanding results. This chapter presented an in-depth analysis of deep learning-based bioinformatics research, looking at input data, research objectives, and characteristics of prominent deep learning architectures. Deep learning, despite it appears to be tremendously promising, is not a cure-all and cannot deliver outstanding results when used alone to bioinformatics. There are still a lot of considerations to be made, including choosing the best architecture and its hyperparameters, interpreting the results of deep learning, and dealing with data of limited size and class imbalance. In order to fully harness the potential of deep learning, multi-modality and acceleration of deep learning are the appealing areas for further research. Therefore, according to researchers, the effectiveness of such research depends on thorough planning in connection to the issues covered in the study. Scholars that are interested in incorporating deep learning into their bioinformatics research may find this review to be enlightening and useful as a starting point.

Table 2. Deep Leaning Methods and Application Areas

Network	Authors	Method	Function of the Network
Sparse Autoencoders	Padideh Danaee et al. (2017)	Stacked Denoising Autoencoder (SDA)	Reduce the feature set of gene expression prediction
	Abdolhosseini et al. (2019)	Autoencoder with 30 latent variables	Detect the transcriptomics using genes
	Way et al. 2017	Variational autoencoder (VAE)	Analysis of cancer type detection from TCGA pancancer RNA sequences data
	Maxwell P., 2019	Sparsely-connected autoencoders and variational autoencoders	Predict the breast cancer using gene level in blood cells
	Savvas Kinalis, 2019	Poisson negative log-likelihood loss function	Denoise a single cell RAN sequence data
	Wei et al., 2021	Gene Ontology project	Characterize all the important features of genes
	Qi Wei et al. 2021	VAE	Analyzing the chemotherapy drug response in cancer treatment
	Chen et al. (2018) and Maxwell et al. (2019)	Different Autoencoders	Analyse the activation function to predict the drug sensitivity of cancer cell
Convolution Neural Network (CNN)	Santosh, 2022	DenseNet-161 with ADAM optimizer	Detect single cell from whole slide datasets
	Jai Hao et al. 2020	PAGE-Net	Detect the survival period of patients by using genomic data
	Ciresan D.C., 2013	Deep max-pooling CNN	Process of mitosis detection from histological images of breast cancer patients
	Mobadersany P., 2018	Survival Convolutional Neural Networks (SCNNs)	Diagnosis of survival outcomes of cancer patients
	Zhu et al, 2017	Deep Convolutional Survival (DeepConvSur)	Predicted survival period of a cancer patient
	Unknown	Detect the survival period of glioma patient	Genomic survival convolutional neural networks (gscnn)
Restricted Boltzmann Machine	Arel *et al*, 2010; Bengio, 2009	Deep belief nets	Using RBM in the construction of deep belief net
	Fickholt and Cheng, 2012	RBM	Dimensionality reduction
	Yuhao Wang and Jianyang Zeng, 2013	RBM	Predict relationships among the drug and targeted activities
	Muntoni, A.P et al., 2021	AdabmDCA	Initialize parameter, regularize and decimate the traning
	Muntoni, A.P et al., 2021	AdabmDCA with Monte Carlo Markov Chain	Scheming new sequences
Long Short-Term memory	Huiqing Wang, 2019	L-GEPM	Prediction of gene sequence
	Guohua Huang et al. 2021	LSTM and CNN	Prediction of succinylation site
	Mei et al. 2017	Transfer learning-based technique	Gene ontology

REFERENCES

Abdolhosseini, F. (2019). Cell Identity Codes: Understanding Cell Identity from Gene

Expression Profiles using Deep Neural Networks. *Scientific Reports, 9*(1), 2342.

Arel, I., Rose, D. C., & Karnowski, T. P. (2010). Deep machine learning-a new frontier in artificial intelligence research. *IEEE Computational Intelligence Magazine, 5*(4), 13–18. doi:10.1109/MCI.2010.938364

Bengio, Y. (2009). Learning deep architectures for AI. *Foundations and Trends in Machine Learning, 2*(1), 1–127. doi:10.1561/2200000006

Tang, B., Pan, Z., Yin, K., & Khateeb, A. (2019). Recemt advamces of deep learning in bioinformatics and computational biology. *Frontiers in Genetics, 10*, 214. doi:10.3389/fgene.2019.00214 PMID:30972100

Chou, K. C. (2004). Structural bioinformatics and its impact to biomedical science. *Current Medicinal Chemistry, 11*(16), 2105–2134. doi:10.2174/0929867043364667 PMID:15279552

Ciresan, D. C. (2013). Mitosis Detection in Breast Cancer Histology Images with Deep Neural Networks. In Medical Image Computing and Computer-Assisted Intervention – MICCAI 2013.

Eickholt, J., & Cheng, J. (2012). Predicting protein residue-residue contacts using deep networks & boosting. *Bioinformatics (Oxford, England), 28*(23), 3066–3072. doi:10.1093/bioinformatics/bts598 PMID:23047561

Huang, G., Shen, Q., Zhang, G., Wang, P., & Yu, Z.-G. (2021). LSTMCNNsucc: A Bidirectional LSTM and CNN-Based Deep Learning Method for Predicting Lysine Succinylation Sites. *BioMed Research International, Article ID, 9923112*, 10. doi:10.1155/2021/9923112 PMID:34159204

Hinton, G. E., Osindero, S., & Teh, Y.-W. (2006). A fast learning algorithm for deep belief nets. *Neural Computation, 18*(7), 1527–1554. doi:10.1162/neco.2006.18.7.1527 PMID:16764513

Bae, H., Lee, B., Kwon, S., & Yoon, S. (2018). DNA Steganalysis Using Deep Recurrent Neural Networks. *Biocomputing,* 88-99. doi:10.1142/9789813279827_0009

Hopf, T.A., Ingraham, J.B.., Poelwijk, F.J., Schärfe C.P., Springer M., Sander C., &Marks D.S. (2017). Mutation effects predicted from sequence co-variation. *Nat Biotechnol. 35*(2):128. doi:. 3769. doi:10.1038/nbt

Wang, H., Li, C., Zhang, J., Wang, J., Ma, Y., & Lian, Y. (2019) . A new LSTM-based gene expression prediction model, *L-GEPM, Journal of Bioinformatics & Computational Biology.*

Tubiana, J., Cocco, S., & Monasson, R. (2019). Learning Compositional Representations of Interacting Systems with Restricted Boltzmann Machines, Comparative Study of Lattice Proteins. *Neural Computation*, *31*(8), 1671–1717. doi:10.1162/neco_a_01210 PMID:31260391

Hao, J. (2020). Sai Chandra Kosaraju, Nelson Zange Tsaku, Dae Hyun Song & Mingon Kang. PAGE-Net: Interpretable and Integrative deep learning for survival analysis using Histopathological images and genomic data. *Pasific Symposium on Biocomputing*, (355-366). World Scientific publishing company.

Maxwell, P. G., LeNail, A., & Fraenkel, E. (2018). Shallow Sparsely-Connected Autoencoders for Gene Set Projection. *Pacific Symposium on Biocomputing*, *2019*, 374–385. PMID:30963076

Mei, S., Flemington, E. K., & Zhang, K. (2017). A computational framework for distinguishing direct versus indirect interactions in human functional protein–protein interaction networks. *Integrative Biology*, *9*(7), 595–606. doi:10.1039/c7ib00013h PMID:28524201

Mobadersany, P., Yousefi, S., Amgad, M., Gutman, D. A., Barnholtz-Sloan, J. S., Velázquez Vega, J. E., Brat, D. J., & Cooper, L. A. D. (2018). Predicting cancer outcomes from histology and genomics using convolutional networks. *Proceedings of the National Academy of Sciences of the United States of America*, *115*(13), E2970. doi:10.1073/pnas.1717139115 PMID:29531073

Muntoni, A. P., Pagnani, A., Weigt, M., & Zamponi, F. (2021). adaptive Boltzmann machine learning for biological sequences. *BMC Bioinformatics*, *22*(1), 528. doi:10.118612859-021-04441-9 PMID:34715775

Wei, Q., & Stephen, A. (2021, September 22). Ramsey. (2021) Predicting chemotherapy response using a variational autoencoder approach. *BMC Bioinformatics*, *22*(1), 453. doi:10.118612859-021-04339-6 PMID:34551729

Russ, W.P., Figliuzzi, M., Stocker, C., Barrat-Charlaix, P., Socolich, M., Kast, P., Hilvert, D., Monasson, R., Cocco, S., Weigt, M., & Ranganathan, R. (2020). An evolution-based model for designing chorismate mutase enzymes. Science, *369*(6502):440–5.

Salakhutdinov, R., & Hinton, G. E. (2009). Deep boltzmann machines. In *International Conference on Artificial Intelligence and statistics*, (pp. 448–455). IEEE.

Santosh, K. C., Das, N., & Ghosh, S. (2022). Cytology image analysis. In KC Santosh, Nibaran Das, Swarnendu Ghosh (eds). Primers in Biomedical Imaging Devices and Systems, Deep Learning Models for Medical Imaging, Academic Press. 99-123. doi:10.1016/B978-0-12-823504-1.00014-3

Kinalis, S., Nielsen, F. C., Winther, O., & Bagger, F. O. (2019) Deconvolution of autoencoders to learn biological regulatory modules from single cell mRNA sequencing data. *BMC Bioinformatics, 20*, 379.

Senior, A. W., Evans, R., Jumper, J., Kirkpatrick, J., Sifre, L., Green, T., Qin, C., Žídek, A., Nelson, A. W., Bridgland, A., Penedones, H., Petersen, S., Simonyan, K., Crossan, S., Kohli, P., Jones, D. T., Silver, D., Kavukcuoglu, K., & Hassabis, D. (2020). Improved protein structure prediction using potentials from deep learning. *Nature, 577*(7792), 706–710. doi:10.103841586-019-1923-7 PMID:31942072

Sljoka, A. (2022). Structural and Functional Analysis of Proteins Using Rigidity Theory. Sublinear Computation Paradigm. Springer. doi:10.1007/978-981-16-4095-7_14

Klamt, S., Saez-Rodriguez, J., Lindquist, J. A., Simeoni, L., & Gilles, E. D. (2006). A methodology for the structural and functional analysis of signalling and regulatory networks. *BMC Bioinformatics, 7*(1), 56. doi:10.1186/1471-2105-7-56 PMID:16464248

Way, G. P., & Casey, S. Greene. (2017). Extracting a biologically relevant latent space from cancer transcriptomes with variational autoencoders. *bioRxiv*, ●●●, 174474.

Xu. J.(2019). Distance-based protein folding powered by deep learning. *Proc Natl Acad Sci., 116*(34), 16856–65.

Yang . J, Anishchenko .I, Park. H, Peng .Z, Ovchinnikov. S & Baker. D.(2020). Improved protein structure prediction using predicted interresidue orientations. *Proc Natl Acad Sci, 117*(3), 1496–503.

Wang, Y., & Zeng, J. (2013). Predicting drug-target interactions using restricted Boltzmann machines. *Bioinformatics (Oxford, England), 29*(13), i126–i134. doi:10.1093/bioinformatics/btt234 PMID:23812976

Zhu, X., Yao, J., Zhu, F., & Huang, J. (2017). WSISA: Making Survival Prediction from Whole Slide Histopathological Images. *2017 IEEE Conference on Computer Vision and Pattern Recognition (CVPR)*. IEEE. 10.1109/CVPR.2017.725

APPENDIX

Figure 1. Types of Neural Networks which include Feed Forward, Recurrent, Radial basis function, Kohen self organizing map and Modular neural networks.

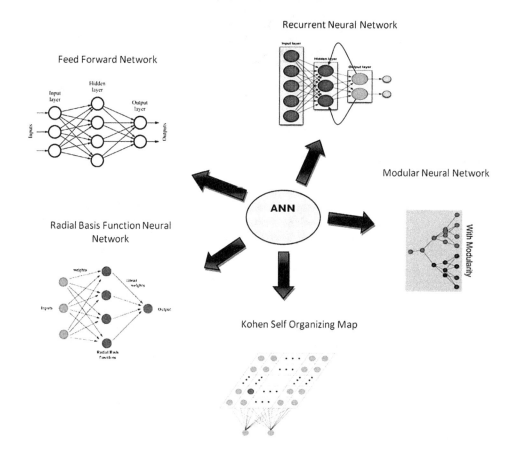

Figure 2. Sparse Autoencoder

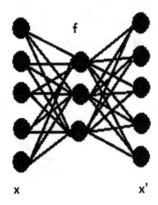

Figure 3. Structure of Convolution Neural Network.

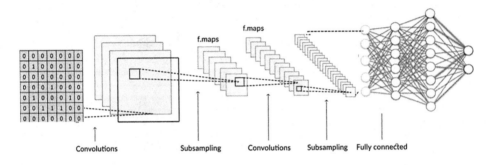

Figure 4. Restricted Boltzman machine

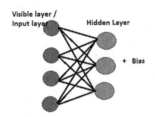

Figure 5. LSTM structure

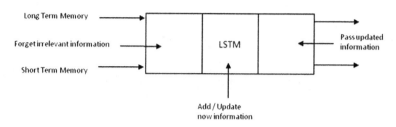

Compilation of References

Abbas, M.M. & Abdelsamea, M.M. (2020). *Classification of COVID-19 in chest X-ray images* using DeTraC deep convolutional neural network. Springer.

Abdolhosseini, F. (2019). Cell Identity Codes: Understanding Cell Identity from Gene Expression Profiles using Deep Neural Networks. Scientific Reports, 9(1), 2342.

Abouelhoda, M. (2014). Extracting Maximal Exact Matches on GPU. IEEE 28th International Parallel & Distributed Processing Symposium *Workshops, pp. 1417–1426.* IEEE.

Agarwal, R. K., Raman, B., & Mittal, A. (2015). Hand gesture recognition using discrete wavelet transform and support vector machine. 2nd International Confer*ence on Signal* Processing and Integrated Networks (SPIN). 10.1109/SPIN.2015.7095326

Ahmad, N. (2005). The vertical transmission of human immunodeficiency virus type 1: Molecular and bio*logical properties of the virus.* Critical Reviews in Clinical Laboratory Sciences, 42(1), 1–34. doi:10.1080/10408360490512520 PMID:15697169

Alazab, M., Awajan, A., Mesleh, A., Abraham, A., Jatana, V., & Alhyari, S. (2020). COVID-19 prediction and detection using deep learning. Int J Comput Information Syst Indus Manage Appl, 12, 168–181. doi:10.1016/*j.chaos.2020.1103*38

Albahli, S. (2020). Efficient GAN-based Chest Radiographs (CXR) augmentation to diagnose coronavirus disease pneumonia. International Journal of Medical Sciences, 17, 1439–1448. doi:10.7150/ijms.46*684*

Albahli, S., & Albattah, W. (2020). Detection of coronavirus disease from X-ray images using deep learning and transfer learning algorithms. Journal of X-Ray Science and Technology, 28, 841–850. do*i:10.3233/XST-200720*

*Alharthi, A. S., Yunas, S. U., & Ozanyan, K. B. (2019). Deep lea*rning for monitoring of human gait: A review. IEEE Sensors Journal, 19(21), 9575–9591. doi:10.1109/JSEN.2019.2928777

Allaoui, M., Ahiod, B., & El Yafrani, M. (2018). *A hybrid crow search algorithm for solving the DNA f*ragment assembly problem. Expert Systems with Applications, 102, 44–56. doi:10.1016/j. eswa.*2018.02.018*

Alsharman, N., & Jawarneh, I. (2020). GoogleNet CNN neural network towards chest CT-coronavirus medical image classification. Journal of Computational Science, 16, 620–625. doi:10.3844/jcssp.2020.620.*625*

*Altan, A., & Karasu, S. (2020). Recognition of COVID-19 dise*ase from X-ray images by hybrid model consisting of 2D curvelet transform, chaotic salp swarm algorithm and deep l*earning techniqu*e. Chaos, Solitons, and Fractals, 140, 110071. doi:10.1016/j.chaos.2020.110071

Altschul, S. F., Madden, T. L., Schäffer*, A. A., Zhang, J., Zhang, Z., M*iller, W., & Lipman, D. J. (1997). Gapped BLAST and PSI-BLAST: A new generation of protein database search program*s*. *Nucleic Aci*ds *R*esearch, 25(17), 3389–3402. doi:10.1093/nar/25.17.3389 PMID:9254694

Ancin, H., Roysam, B., Dufresne, T. E., Chestnut, M. M., Ridder, G. M., Szarowski, D. H., & Turner, J. N. (*1996, November 1). Advances in automat*ed *3*-D image analyses of cell populations imaged by confocal microscopy. Cytometry, 25(3), 221–234. doi:10.1002/(SICI)1097-0320(19961101)25:3<221::AID-CYTO3>3.0.CO;2-I PMID:8914819

Angwin, J., & Stecklow*, S. (2010). 'Scrapers' dig deep for* data on Web. The Wall Street Journal. https://www.wsj.com/articles/SB10001424052748703358504575544 381288117888

Anwar, A. R., Yu, H., & Vassallo, M. 2018. An automatic gait feature extraction method for identifying gait asymmetry *using wearabl*e *se*nsors. Sensors, 18(2), 676.

Apostolopoulos, I.D. & Mpesiana, T.A. (2020). Covid-19: automatic detection from X-ray images utilizing transfer l*earning with convolution*al *n*eural networks. Phys. Eng. Sci. Med. 1–8.

Ardakani, A., Acharya, U. R., Habibollahi, S., & Mohammadi, A. (2020). COVIDiag: A clinical CAD system to diagnose COVID-19 pneumonia based o*n CT findings. European Radiology,* 31, 1–10. doi:10.100700330-020-07087-y

Arel, I., Rose, D. C., & Karnowski, T. P. (2010). Deep *machine learning-a new frontier in artificial i*ntelligence research. IEEE Computational Intelligence Magazine, 5(4), 13–18. doi:10.1109/MCI.2010.938364

Arian, R., Hariri, A., Mehridehnavi, A., Fassihi, A., & Ghasemi, F. (2020). Protein kinase inhibitors' classification using *K-Nearest neighbor algorithm. Computational Biology and Chemistry, 86, 107269. do*i:10.1016/j.compbiolchem.2020.107269 PMID:32413830

Atalan, A. (2020). Is the lockdown important to prevent the COVID-19 pandemic? Effects on psychology, environment and economy-perspective. Annals of Medicine and Surgery (London), 56, 38–42. doi:10.10*16/j.amsu.2020.06.010*

Babu, M. M., van der Lee, R., de Groot, N. S., & Gsponer, J. (2011). Intrinsically disordered proteins: Regulation and disease. Current Opinion in Structural Biology, 21(3), 432–440. doi:10.1016/j.sbi.2011.03.011 P*MID:21514144*

Badea, M. S., Felea, I. I., Florea, L. M., & Vertan, C. (2016). The use of deep learning in image segmentation, classification, and detection. arXiv preprint arXiv:1605.09612.

Bae, H., Lee, B., *Kwon, S., & Yoo*n, S. (2018). DNA Steganalysis Using Deep Recurrent Neural Networks. Biocomputing, 88-99. doi:10.1142/9789813279827_0009

Bai, X., Niwas, *S. I., Lin, W., Ju, B. F.*, Kwoh, C. K., Wang, L., ... Chew, P. T. (2016). Learning ECOC code matrix for multiclass classification with application to gl*aucoma diagnosis. Journal of Medical Systems, 40(4), 1–10.*

Bajorath, J. R. (2020). Artificial intelligence in drug discovery: Into the great wide open. ACS Publications.

Ballesteros, J. A., & Weinstein, H. (1995). Integrated methods for *the construction of three-dimen*sional models and computational probing of structure-function relations in G protein-coupled receptors. In Methods in neur*osciences (Vol. 25, pp. 366–428).* Academic Press.

Bartels, P.H., Bibbo, M., Graham, A., Paplanus, S., Shoemaker, R.L., & Thompson, D. (1989). Image understanding system for histopathology. Analytical Cellular Pathology, 1(4), 195-214.

Belien, J. A., Baak, J. P., van Diest, P. J., & van Ginkel, A. H. (1997, June 1). *Counting mitoses by imag*e processing in Feulgen stained breast cancer sections: The influence of resolution. Cytometry, 28, 135–140. doi:10.10*02/(SICI)1097-0320(19970601)28:2<135::*AID-CYTO6>3.0.CO;2-E PMID:9181303

Bender, A., & Cortes-Ciriano, I. (2021). Artificial intelligence in drug discovery: what is realistic, what are illusions? Part 2: A discussion of chemical and biolog*ical data used for AI in drug discov*ery. Drug Discovery Today, 26(4), 1040–1052. doi:10.1016/j.drudis.2020.11.037

*Bengio, Y. (2009). Learning deep architectures for AI. Foundations a*nd Trends in Machine Learning, 2(1), 1–127. doi:10.1561/2200000006

Bhavani, S., Nagargadde, A., Thawani, A., Sridhar, V*., & Chandra, N. (2006). Substructure-based* support vector machine classifiers for prediction of adverse effects in diverse classes of drugs. Journal of Chemical Information and Modeling, 46(6), 2478–2486. doi:10.1021*/ci0601281 PMID:17125188*

Bibbo, M., Kim, D. H., Pfeifer, T., Dytch, H. E., Galera-Davidson, H., & Bartels, P. H. (1991, February). Histometric features for the grading of pr*ostatic carcinoma. Analytical and Q*uantitative Cytology and H*is*tology, 13, 61–68. PMID:2025375

Bilgin, C., Demir, C., Nagi, C., & Yener, B. (2007). Cell-graph mining for breast tissue modeling and classification. Proc. 29th Annu. Int. Conf. IEEE Eng. Med. Biol. Soc. (EMBS 2007), 531–5*34. 10.1109/IEMBS.2007.4353540*

*Birla, D. (2019). Ba*sics of Autoencoders. The Medium. https://medium.com/@birla.deepak26/autoencoders-76bb49ae6a8f

Boudrioua M. S. and Boudri*oua A. (2020). Predicting the COVID-19 epidemic i*n Algeria using the SIR model. medRxiv.

Bou Ezzeddine, A. (2014). Applying the Firefly Approach to the DNA Fragments Assembly Problem. Annales Univ. *Sci. Budapest. Sec*t. Comp., 42, 69–81.

Breton, R., Clews, G., Metcalfe, L., Milliken, N., Payne, C., Winton, J., & Woods, A. (2015). Research indices using web scraped data. Office for National Statistics.

Bridge, J., Meng, Y., *Zhao, Y., Du, Y., Zhao, M., & Sun, R. (2020). Introducing the GEV activation function* for highly unbalanced data to develop COVID-19 diagnostic models. IEEE Journal of Biomedical and Health Informatics, 24, 1–10. doi:10.1109/JBHI.*2020.3012383*

Brooks-Wilson, A., Marcil, M., Clee, S. M., Zhang, L. H., Roomp, K., van Dam, M., Yu, L., Brewer, C., Collins, J. A., Molhuizen, H. O. F., Loubser, O., Ouelette, B. F. F., Fichter, K., *Ashbourne-Excoffon, K. J. D., Sensen, C. W.,* Scherer, S., Mott, S., Denis, M., Martindale, D., & Hayden, M. R. (1999). Mutations in ABC1 in Tan*gier disease and familial high-de*nsity lipoprotein deficiency. Nature Genetics, 22(4), 336–345. doi:1*0.1038/11905 PMID:10431236*

Bukhari, S.U.K., Bukhari, S.S.K., Syed, A., & Shah, S. S. H. (2020. The diagnostic evaluation of Convolutional Neural Network (CNN) for the assessment of chest X-ray of patients infected with COVID-19. MedRxiv.

Butt, C., Gill, J., Chun, D., & Babu, B. A. (2020). Deep learning system to screen coronavirus disease 2019 pneumonia. Applied Intelligence, 6, 1–7. doi:10.100710489-020-01714-3

Byun, J. Y., *Verardo, M. R., Sumengen, B., L*ewis, G. P., Manjunath, B. S., & Fisher, S. K. (2006, August 16). Automated tool for the detection of cell nuclei in digital microscopic image*s: Application to retinal image*s. Molecular Vision, 12(105–107), 949–960. PMID:16943767

Bülow, R. D. (2021). How will artificial intelligence and bioinformatics change our understanding of IgA in the next decade? In Seminars in Immunopathology. Springer. doi:10.100700281-021-00847-y

Cai, L., & Wang, J. (2019). Liquid biopsy for lung cancer immunoth*erapy (Review). Oncology Letters, 17(6), 4751–4760. doi:10.3892/ol.2019.10166 PMID:31186680*

Caldas, R., Mundt, M., Potthast, W., *Buarque de Lima Neto, F., & Markert, B. (2017). A systematic review of gait a*nalysis methods based on inertial sensors and adaptive algorithms. Gait & Posture, 57, 204–210. doi:10.1016/j.gaitpost.2017.06.019 PMID:28666178

Castiglioni, I., Rundo, L., Codari, M., Di Leo, G., Salvatore, C., Int*erlenghi, M.,* & Sardanelli, F. (2021). AI applications to medical images: From machine learning to deep learning. Physica Medica, 83, 9–24.

Cavalli, A., Spitaleri, A., Saladino, G., & Gervasio, F. L. (2015). Investigating drug–target association and dissociation mechanisms using metadynamics-based algorithms. Accounts of Chemical *Research, 48(2), 277–285. doi:10.1021/ar5*00356n PMID:25496113

CDC. (2021). COVID Data Tracker. CDC. https://covid.cdc.gov/COVID-data-tracker

Celik, Y., Talo, M., Yildirim, O., Karabatak, M., & Acharya, U. R. (2020). *Automated invasive ductal carcinoma detection ba*sed using deep transfer learning with whole-slide images. Pattern Recognition Letters, 133, 232–239. https://doi.org/10.1016/j.patrec.2020.03.011

Chan, H. S., Shan, H., Dahoun, T., Vogel, H., & Yuan, S. (2019). Advancing drug discovery via artifi*cial intelligence. Trends in* Pharmacological Sciences, 40(8), 592–604. doi:10.1016/j. tips.2019.06.004 PMID:31320117

Chandra, N. (2009). Support Vector Machine Classifier for Predicting Drug Binding to P-glycoprotein, 136.

Chang, Y., & Sahinidis, N. V. (2011). An integer programming approach to DNA sequence assembly. Computational Biology and Chemistry, *35(4), 251–258. doi:10.10*16/j.compbiolchem.2011.06.001 PMID:21864794

Chauhan, N. B. (2003). Membrane dynamics, cholesterol homeostasis, and Alzheimer's disease. Journal of Lipid Research, *44(11), 2019–2029. doi:*10.1194/jlr.R300010-JLR200 PMID:12951356

Chen, H., Dou, Q., Yu, L., *Qin, J., & Heng, P. A. (2018). VoxResNet: Deep voxelwise residual networks for brain segmentation from 3D M*R images. NeuroImage, 170, 446–455. doi:10.1016/j. neuroimage.2017.04.041 PMID:28445774

Chen, S. H., Jakeman, A. J., & Norton, J. P. (2008). Artificial intelligence techniques: An i*ntroduction to the*ir *u*se for modelling environmental systems. Mathematics and Computers in Simulation, 78(2-3), 379–400. doi:10.1016/j.matcom.2008.01.028

Chen, T., Peng, L., Yin, X., Ron*g, J., Yang, J., & Cong, G. (2020). Analysis of us*er *s*atisfaction with online education platforms in China during the COVID-19 pandemic. Health Care. doi:10 doi:.3390/healthcare8030200

Cherezov, V., Rosenbaum, D. M., Hanson, M. A., Rasmussen, *S. G., Thian, F. S., Kobilka, T.* S., & Stevens, R. C. (2007). High-resolution crystal structure of an engineered human β2-adrenergic G protein–coupled receptor. science, 3*18(5854), 1258-1265.*

*Chial, H. (2008). DNA seq*uencing technologies key to the Human Genome Project. Nature Education, 1(1), 219.

Chou, K. C. (2004). Structural bioinformatics and its impact to biomed*ical science. Current Medicinal Chemistry, 11(16), 2105–2134. doi:10.2174/0929867043364667* PMID:15279552

Cillekens, M. J., Beliën, J. A. M., van der Valk, P., Faes, T. J. C., van Diest, P. J., Broeckaert, M. A. M., Kralendonk, J. H., & Kamphorst, W. (2000, January). A Histo*pathological Contributi*on *to* Supratentorial Glioma Grading, Definition of Mixed Gliomas *and Recognition of Low Grade Glioma With Rosen*thal Fibers. Journal of Neuro-Oncology, 46(1), 23–43. doi:10.1023/A:1006496328729 PMID:10896203

Ciresan, D. C. (2013). Mitosis Detection in Breast Cancer Histology *Images with* Deep Neural Networks. In Medical Image Computing and Computer-Assisted Intervention – MICCAI 2013.

Cohen, J. P., Morrison, *P., & Dao, L. (2020). COVID-19 Image Data Collection. https://arxiv. org/abs/*2003.11597.

Currie, G., Hawk, K. E., Rohren, E., Vial, A., & Klein, R. (2019). Machine learning and deep learning in medical imaging: Inte*lligent imaging. Journal of Medical Imagi*ng *a*nd Radiation Sciences, 50(4), 477–487.

Daniel, O. O., Kolawole, J. A., & Kolawole, J. A. (2017). In-vitro and In-silico Drug-Food Interaction: An Evaluation of Metformin and *Green Tea Interactions. Nov*el Approaches in Drug Designing & Development, 2(2), 34–39.

Deb, S., & Yang, X.-S. (2010). Engineering optimization by Cuckoo search. International Journal of Mathematical Modeling and Numerical Optimization, 1(4), 330–343. doi:10.1504/IJMMNO.2010.035430

Delgado-Escano, R., Castro, F. M., *Cózar, J. R., Marín-Jiménez, M. J., & Guil, N. (2018). An end-*to-end multi-task and fusion CNN for inertial-based gait recognition. IEEE Access: Practical Innovations, Open Solutions, 7, 1897–1908. doi:10.1109/ACCESS.2018.2886899

De Solorzano, C. O., Malladi, R., Lelievre, S. A., & Lockett, S. J. (2001, March). Segmentation of *nuclei and cells using membrane related pr*otein markers. J. Microsc. Oxford, 201(3), 404–415. doi:10.1046/j.1365-2818.2001.00854.x PMID:11240857

Devos, D., & Valencia, A. (2000). Practical limits of function predicti*on. Proteins, 41(1)*, 98–107. doi:10.1002/1097-0134(20001001)41:1<98::AID-PROT120>3.0.CO;2-S PMID:10944397

Dey, N., Rajinikanth, V., Fong, S. J., Kaiser, M. S., & Mahmud, M. (2020). Social group optimization-assisted Kapur's entropy and morphological segmentati*on for automated detection of COVID-19 in*fection from computed tomography images. Cognitive Computation, 12, 1–13. doi:10.20944/preprints202005.0052.v1

Dollár, K. H. G. G. P., & Girshick, *R. (2017, April). Mask r-cnn. In Pro*ceedings of the IEEE international conference on computer vision (pp. 2961-2969). IEEE.

Dong, E., Du, H., & Gardner, L. (2020). An interactive web-based dashboard to track COVID-19 in real time. The Lancet Infectious Diseases, 20, 533–534. doi:10.1016/S1473-3099(20)*30120-1*

*Doniger, S., Ho*fmann, T., & Yeh, J. (2002). Predicting CNS permeability of drug molecules: Comparison of neural network and support vector machine algorithms. Journal of Computational Biology, 9(6), 849–864. doi:10.1089/10665270260518317 PMID:12614551

Díaz, Ó., Da*lton, J. A., & Giraldo, J. (2019). Artificial intelligence: A novel app*roach for drug discovery. Trends in Pharmacological Sciences, 40(8), 550–551. doi:10.1016/j.tips.2019.06.005 PMID:31279568

Eickholt, J., & Cheng, J. (2012). Predicting protein residue-residue conta*cts using deep networks & boosting.* Bioinformatics (Oxford, England), 28(23), 3066–3072. doi:10.1093/bioinformatics/bts598 PMID:23047561

El Asnaoui, K., & Chawki, Y. (2020). Using X-ray images and deep learning for automated detection of coronavirus disease. Journal of Biomolecular Structure & Dynamics, 1–12. doi:10.1080/07391102.2020.1767212

Elloumi, M., & Kaabi, S. (1999). Exact and approximation algorithms for the DNA sequence assembly problem. SCI in Biology and Medicine, 8, 24.

Ezziane, Z. (2006). Applications of artificial intelligence in bioinformatics: A review. Expert Systems with Applications, 30(1), 2–10. doi:10.1016/j.eswa.2005.09.042

Fang, C., Li, G., Pan, C., Li, Y., & Yu, Y. (2019, October). Globally guided progressive fusion network for 3D pancreas segmentation. In International conference on medical image computing and computer-assisted intervention (pp. 210-218). Springer.

Fang, J. (2020). A critical review of five machine learning-based algorithms for predicting protein stability changes upon mutation. Briefings in Bioinformatics, 21(4), 1285–1292. doi:10.1093/bib/bbz071 PMID:31273374

Fatakdawala, H., Xu, J., Basavanhally, A., Bhanot, G., Ganesan, S., Feldman, M., Tomaszewski, J. E., & Anant, M. (2010, July). (EMaGACOR): Application to Lymphocyte Segmentation on Breast Cancer Histopathology. IEEE Transactions on Biomedical Engineering, 57(7), 1676–1689. doi:10.1109/TBME.2010.2041232 PMID:20172780

Feala, J. D., Cortes, J., Duxbury, P. M., Piermarocchi, C., McCulloch, A. D., & Paternostro, G. (2010). Systems approaches and algorithms for discovery of combinatorial therapies. Wiley Interdisciplinary Reviews. Systems Biology and Medicine, 2(2), 181–193. doi:10.1002/wsbm.51 PMID:20836021

Fethi, M. D., & Pasiouras, F. (2010). Assessing bank efficiency and performance with operational research and artificial intelligence techniques: A survey. European Journal of Operational Research, 204(2), 189–198. doi:10.1016/j.ejor.2009.08.003

Firoz, J. S., Rahman, M. S., & Saha, T. K. (2012). Bee algorithms for solving DNA fragment assembly problem with noisy and noiseless data. In Proceedings of the 14th annual conference on Genetic and evolutionary computation, (pp. 201-208). ACM. 10.1145/2330163.2330192

Fu, B., Wang, Y., Campbell, A., Li, Y., Zhang, B., Yin, S., Xing, Z., & Jin, X. (2017). Comparison of object-based and pixel-based Random Forest algorithm for wetland vegetation mapping using high spatial resolution GF-1 and SAR data. Ecological Indicators, 73, 105–117. doi:10.1016/j.ecolind.2016.09.029

Fu, G. S., Levin-Schwartz, Y., Lin, Q. H., & Zhang, D. (2019). Machine learning for medical imaging. Journal of Healthcare Engineering.

Gerlt, J. A., & Babbitt, P. C., (2000). Can sequence determine function?. Genome Biology, 1(5).

Gonzalez, C., Resano, J., Plaza, A., & Mozos, D. (2012). FPGA implementation of abundance estimation for spectral unmixing *of hyperspectral da*ta *u*sing the image space reconstruction algorithm. IEEE Journal of Selected Topics in Applied Earth Observations and Remote Sensing, 5(1), 248–261. doi:10.1109/JSTARS.2011.2171673

Gore, M., & Desai, N. S. (2014). Computer-aided *drug designing. In Clinical Bioinformatics (pp. 31*3–321). Springer. doi:10.1007/978-1-4939-0847-9_18

Green, C. P., Engkvist, O., & Pairaudeau, G. (2018). The convergence of artificial intelligence and chemistry for improved drug discovery. Future *Science. doi:10.4155/fmc-2018-0161*

Groves, P., Kayyali, B., Knott, D., & Kuiken, S. V. (2016). The big data revolution in healthcare: Accelerating value and innovation. McKinsey.

Gu, H., Guo, Y., Gu, L., Wei, A., *Xie, S., Ye, Z., ... Hong, J. (2020). Deep learning for identifying* corneal diseases from ocular surface slit-lamp photographs. Scientific Reports, 10(1), 1–11.

Gudla, P. R., Nandy, K., Collins, J., Meaburn, K. J., Misteli, T., & Lockett, S. J. (2008, May). A high-throughput system for segmenting nuclei using multiscale tech*niques. Cytometry. Part A, 73(5), 451–466. doi:10.1002/cy*to.a.20550 PMID:18338778

Gulshan, V., Peng, L., Coram, M., Stumpe, M. C., Wu, D., Narayanaswamy, A., & Webster, D. R. (2016). Development and val*idation of a dee*p *le*arning algorithm for detection of diabetic retinopathy in retinal fundus photog*raphs. Journal of th*e American Medical Association, 316(22), 2402–2410.

Guyon, I., & Elisseeff, A. (2003). An introduction to variable and feature selection. Journal of Machine Learning Research, 3, 1*157–1182.*

Hao, J. (2020). Sai Chandra Kosaraju, Nelson Zange Tsaku, Dae Hyun Song & Mingon Kang. PAGE-Net: Interpretable and Integrative deep learning for survival analysis using Histopathological images and genomic data. Pasific Symposi*um on Biocomputing, (355-366). World S*cientific publishing company.

Hassija, V., Ratnakumar, R., Chamola, V., Agarwal, S., Mehra, A., Kanhere, S. S., & Binh, H. T. T. (2022). A machine learning and blockchain ba*sed secure and cost*-ef*f*ective framework for minor medical consultations. Sustainable Computing: Informatics and Systems, 35, 100651. doi:10.1016/j.suscom.2021.100651

Havaei, M., Davy, A., Warde-Farley, D., Biard, A., Courville, A., Bengio, Y., Pal, C., Jodoin, P.-M., & Laro*chelle, H. (2017). Brain tumor segmen*tation with deep neural networks. Medical Image Analysis, 35, 18–31. doi:10.1016/j.media.2016.05.004 PMID:27310171

Hedberg, H., Kristensen, F., & Öwall, V. (2007). Implementation of a Labeling Alg*orithm based on Contour Tracing with Feature Extr*action. IEEE International Symposium on Circuits and Systems. 10.1109/ISCAS.2007.378202

Hemdan, E. E.-D., Shouman, M. A., & Karar, M. E. (2020). COVIDX-Net: A Framework of Deep Learning Classifiers to Diagnose COVID-19 in X-Ray Images. https://arxiv.org/abs/2003.11055

Henson, A. B., Gromski, P. S., & Cronin, L. (2018). Designing algorithms to aid discovery by chemical robots. ACS Central Science, 4(7), 793–804. doi:10.1021/acscentsci.8b00176 PMID:30062108

Hesamian, M. H., Jia, W., He, X., & Kennedy, P. (2019). Deep learning techniques for medical image segmentation: Achievements and challenges. Journal of Digital Imaging, 32(4), 582–596.

Higgins, C. F. (1992). ABC transporters: From microorganisms to man. Annual Review of Cell Biology, 8(1), 67–113. doi:10.1146/annurev.cb.08.110192.000435 PMID:1282354

Hinton, G. E., Osindero, S., & Teh, Y.-W. (2006). A fast learning algorithm for deep belief nets. Neural Computation, 18(7), 1527–1554. doi:10.1162/neco.2006.18.7.1527 PMID:16764513

Hnatiuc, M., Geman, O., Avram, A. G., Gupta, D., & Shankar, K. (2021). Human signature identification using IoT technology and gait recognition. Electronics (Basel), 10(7), 852. doi:10.3390/electronics10070852

Hopf, T.A., Ingraham, J.B.., Poelwijk, F.J., Schärfe C.P., Springer M., Sander C., &Marks D.S. (2017). Mutation effects predicted from sequence co-variation. Nat Biotechnol. 35(2):128. doi:. 3769. doi:10.1038/nbt

Hoq, M. (2019). In silico drug designing against Klebsiella pneumoniae adhesin protein. Brac University.

Hore, A., & Ziou, D. (2010) Image quality metrics: PSNR vs. SSIM. In Pattern Recognition (ICPR), 20th International Conference on (pp. 2366-2369). IEEE.

Horry, M.J., Chakraborty, S., Paul, M., Ulhaq, A., Pradhan, B. (2007). X-Ray Image based COVID-19 Detection using Pre-trained Deep Learning Models.

Hu, J., Shen, L., & Sun, G. (2018). Squeeze-and-excitation networks. In Proceedings of the IEEE conference on computer vision and pattern recognition (pp. 7132-7141). IEEE.

Huang, G., Liu, Z., Van Der Maaten, L., & Weinberger, K. Q. (2017). Densely connected convolutional networks. In Proceedings of the IEEE conference on computer vision and pattern recognition (pp. 4700-4708). IEEE.

Huang, G., Shen, Q., Zhang, G., Wang, P., & Yu, Z.-G. (2021). LSTMCNNsucc: A Bidirectional LSTM and CNN-Based Deep Learning Method for Predicting Lysine Succinylation Sites. BioMed Research International, Article ID, 9923112, 10. doi:10.1155/2021/9923112 PMID:34159204

Huang, K. W., Chen, J. L., Yang, C.-S., & Tsai, C.-W. (2015). A memetic particle swarm optimization algorithm for solving the DNA fragment assembly problem. Neural Computing & Applications, 26(3), 495–506. doi:10.100700521-014-1659-0

Hunkapiller, T., Kaiser, R., & Hood, L. (1991). Large-scale DNA sequencing. Current Opinion in Biotechnology, 2(1), 92–101. doi:10.1016/0958-1669(91)90066-E PMID:1367715

Ihm, H., Jang, K., Lee, K., Jang, G., Seo, M.-G., Han, K., & Myaeng, S.-H. (2017). Multi-source food hazard event extraction for public health. 2017 IEEE International Conference on Big Data and Smart Computing *(BigCo*mp), (pp. 414-417). doi:10.1109/BIGCOMP.2017.7881747

Indumathy, R., & Maheswari, S. U. M. a, & Subashini, G. (2015). Nature-inspired novel Cuckoo Search Algorithm. Springer India, 40, 1–14.

Islam, M.Z., Islam, *M.M., & As*raf, A. (2020). A Combined Deep CNN-LSTM Network for the Detection of Novel Coron*avirus (COVID-19) Us*- ing X-ray Images, 1–20.

Janosi, W. (1988). Steinbrunn, M. Pfisterer, and R. Detrano, "UCI machine learning r*epository-heart disease data set. School Inf. Comput. Sci., Univ.*

Jarmul, K., & Lawson, R. (2017). Python Web Scraping (2nd ed.). Packt Publishing.

Jia, Z., Huang, X., Eric, I., Chang, C., & Xu, Y. (2017). Constr*ained deep weak supervision for* his*t*opathology image segmentation. IEEE Transactions on Medical Imaging, 36(11), 2376–2388. doi:10.1109/TMI.2017.2724070 PMID:28692971

Jiménez-Luna, J., Grisoni, F., & Schneider, G. (2020). Drug discovery with explainable *artificial intelligence. Nature Machine Intelligen*ce, 2(10), 573–584. doi:10.103842256-020-00236-4

Joyseeree, R., Abou Sabha, R., & Mueller, H. (2015). Applying machine learning to gait analysis data for disease identifica*tion. In Digital Healthcare Empowe*ring Europeans (pp. 850–854). IOS Press.

Kanne, J. P., Little, B. P., Chung, J. H., Elicker, B. M., & Ketai, L. H. (2020). Essentials for radiolo*gists on COVID-19: an update—radiology scien*tific expert panel. Radiological Society of North America.

Kececi, A., Yildirak, A., Ozyazici, K., Ayluctarhan, G., Agbulut, O., & Zincir, I. (2020). Implementation of machine learning algorithms for gait recognition. Engineering Science and Technolo*gy, an International Journal, 23(4), 931-937.*

Kermany, D., Zhang, K., & Goldbaum, M. (2018). Labeled optical coherence tomography (OCT) and Chest X-Ray images for classification. Mendeley Data, 2. doi:10.17632/RSCBJBR9SJ.2

Khan, A.I., Sha*h, J.L., Bhat, M. (2020). CoroNet: A Deep Neural Network for* Detection and Diagnosis of Covid-19 from Chest Xray Images. Computer Methods and Programs in Biomedicine.

Khan, M. A., Kadry, S., Parwekar, P., Damaševičius, R., Mehmood, A., Khan, J. A., & Naqvi, S. R. (2021). Human gait analysis for osteoarthritis prediction: A framework *of deep learning a*nd kernel extreme learning machine. Complex & Intelligent Systems.

Kim, J., Hong, J., & Park, H. (2018). Prospects of deep learning for medical imaging. Precision and Future Medicine, 2(2), 37–52.

Kim, M., Yun, J., Cho, Y., Shin, K., Jang, R., Bae, H. J., & Kim, N. (2019). Deep learning in medical imaging. Neurospine, 16(4), 657.

Kim, Y. J., Romeike, B. F., Uszkoreit, J., & Feiden, W. *(2006, March-April). Automated nuclea*r segmentation in the determination of the Ki-67 labeling index in meningiomas. Clinical Neuropathology, 25, 67–73. PMID:16550739

Kinalis, S., Nielsen, F. C., Winther, O., & Bagger, F. O. *(2019) Deconvolution of a*utoencoders to learn biological regulatory modules from single cell mRNA sequencing data. BMC Bioinformatics, 20, 379.

King, R. D., Karwa*th, A., Clare, A., & Dehaspe, L. (2000).* Accurate prediction of protein functional class from sequence in the Mycobacterium tuberculosis and Escherichia coli genomes using data mining. Yeast (Chichester, England), 17(4), 283–293. doi:10.*1155/2000/107461 PMID:11119305*

King, R. D., Karwath, A., Clare, A., & Dehaspe, L. (2001). The utility of different representations of protein sequence for predicting functional class. Bioinformatics (Oxf*ord, England), 17(5), 445–454. doi:10.1093/bioinformatics/17.5.445 PMID:11331239*

Klamt, S., Saez-Rodriguez, J., Lindquist, J. A., Simeoni, L., & Gilles, E. D. (2006). A methodology for the structural and functional analysis of signalling and regulatory networks. BMC Bioinformatic*s, 7(1), 56. doi:10.1186/1471-2105-7-56 PMID:16464248*

Klang, E. (2018). Deep learning and medical imaging. Journal of Thoracic Disease, 10(3), 1325.

Kohli, A., Mahajan, V., Seals, K., Kohli, A., & Jha, S. (2019). Concepts in US Food and Drug Administration regulation of artificial intelligence for medical imaging. AJR. American Journal of Roentgenology, 213(4), 886–888. doi:10.2214/AJR.18.20410 PMID:31166758

Koromina, M., Pandi, M.-T., & Patrinos, G. P. (2019). Rethinking drug r*epositioning and develo*pment with artificial intelligence, machine learning, and omics. OMICS: A Journal of Integrative Biology, 23(11), 539–548. doi:10.*1089/omi.2019.015*1 *P*MID:31651216

Kumar, P., & Kumari, S. (2020). Detection of coronavirus Disease (COVID-19) based on Deep Features. Https://Www.Preprints.Org/Manuscript/202003.0300/V1.

Kumar, P., Das, G., & Ghosh, I. (2017). Critical assessment *of contribution from Indian publications: The r*ole of in silico designing methods leading to drugs or drug-like compounds using text based mining and association. J Proteins Proteom, 8, 133–148.

Kumar, R., Sharma, A., Siddiqui, M. H., & *Tiwari, R. K. (2017). P*rediction of human intestinal absorption of compounds using artificial intelligence te*chniques. Current Drug Discove*ry Technologies, 14(4), 244–254. doi:10.2174/1570163814666170404160911 PMID:28382857

Kumar, R., Sharma, A., Siddiqui, M. H., & *Tiwari, R. K. (2018). Prediction of drug-plasma protein binding using a*rtificial intelligence based algorithms. Combinatorial Chemistry & High Throughput Screening, 21(1), 57–64. doi:10.2174/1386207321666171218121557 PMID:29256344

La, V.-P., Pham, T.-H., Ho, M.-T., Nguye*n, M.-H., Nguyen, K.-L. P., Vuong, T.-T., & Vuong,* Q.-*H.* (2020). Policy response social media and science journalism for the sustainability of the public health system amid the COVID-19 outbreak: The Vietnam lessons. Sustainability, 12. doi:10.3390u12072931

Lamberti, M. J., Wilkinson, M., Donzanti, B. *A., Wohlhieter, G. E., Parikh, S., Wilkins, R. G., & Getz, K. (2019). A study on the appl*ication and use of artificial intelligence to support drug development. Clinical Therapeutics, 41(8), 1414–1426. doi:10.1016/j.clinthera.2019.05.018 PMID:31248680

Laughton, M. (19*97). Artificial in*telligence techniques in power systems. Academic Press.

LaValle, S. M. (2006). Planning algorithms. Cambridge university press. doi:10.1017/CBO9780511546877

Law, H., & Deng, J. (2018). Cornernet: Detecting objects as paired keypoint*s. In Proceedings of* the European conference on computer vision (ECCV) (pp. 734-750). Academic Press.

Lawler, E., Rinnooy-Kan, A*., & Shmo*ys, D. (1985). The Travelling Salesman Problem, p. 463. John Wiley and Sons.

Li, G., Liu, T. M., Nie, J. X., Guo, L., Malicki, J., Mara, A., Holley, S. A., Xia, W. M., & Wong, S. T. *C. (2007, October). Detecti*on of blob objects in microscopic zebrafish images based on gradient vector diffusion. Cytometry. Part A, 71A(10), 835–845. doi:10.*1002/cyto.a.20436 PMID:17654652*

Li, L., Qi*n,* L., Xu, Z., Yin, Y., Wang, X., & Kong, B.. (2020). Using artificial intelligence to detect COVID-19 and community-acquired pneumonia based on pulmonary CT: Evaluation of the diagnostic accuracy. Radio*logy, 296, E65–E71. doi:10.1148/radiol.*2020200905

Li, Y., Zhao, J., Lv, Z., & Li, J. (2021). Medical image fusion method by deep learning. International Journal of Cognitive Computing in Engineering, 2, 21–29.

Li, Z., Zhang, S., Zhang, J., Huang, *K., Wang, Y., & Yu, Y.* (2019, October). MVP-Net: multi-view FPN with position-aware attention for deep universal lesion detection. In International Conference on Medical Image Computing and Comput*er-Assisted Intervention (p*p. 13-21). Springer.

Lin, G., Chawla, M. K., Olson, K., Barnes, C. A., Guzowski, J. F., Bjornsson, C., Shain, W., & Roysam, B. (2007, Septe*mber). A multi-model approach to simultaneous segmentation and classifica*tion of heterogeneous populations of cell nuclei in 3D confocal microscope images. Cytometry. Part A, 71(9), 724–736. doi:10.1002/cyto.a.20430 PMID:17654650

Liu, J*., Zhao, G., Fei, Y., Zhang, M., Wang, Y., & Yu, Y. (2019). Align, attend and locate*: Chest x-ray diagnosis via contrast induced attention network with limited supervision. In Proceedings of the IEEE/CVF International Conference on Computer Vision (pp. 10632-10641). IEEE.

Liu, W., Anguelov, D., Erhan, *D., Szegedy, C., Ree*d, S., Fu, C. Y., & Berg, A. C. (2016, October). Ssd: Single shot multibox d*etector. In European conference on computer vision* (pp. 21-37). Springer.

Liu, X., Song, L., Liu, S., & Zhang, Y. (2021). A review of deep-learning-based medical image segmentation methods. Sustainability, 13(3), 1224.

Liu, Y., Zhang, F., Zhang, Q., Wang, S., Wang, Y., & Yu, Y. (2020). Cross-view *correspondence reasoning based on bipartite grap*h convolutional network for mammogram mass detection. In *Proceedings of the IEEE/CVF Conference on Computer Vision and Pattern Recognition (pp. 3812-3822)*. IEEE.

Lo, S. C., Lou, S. L., Lin, J. S., Freedman, M. T., Chien, M. V., & Mun, S. K. (1995). Artificial convolution neural network techniques *and applications for* lung nodule detection. IEEE Transactions on Medical Imaging, 14(4), 711–718.

Loey, M., Smarandache, F., & Khalifa, N. E. M. (2020). Within the l*ack of chest COVID-19 X-ray dataset: A novel detectio*n model based on GAN and deep transfer learning. Symmetry, 12.

Lu, L., Zheng, Y., Carneiro, G., & Yang, L. (2017). Deep learning and convolutional neural networks for medical image computing. A*dvances in Computer Vision and Pattern Recogniti*on, 10, 978-3.

Luz, E., Silva, P. L., Silva, R., Silva, L., Moreira, G., & Menotti, D. (2020). Towards an Effective and Efficient Deep Learning Model for COVID-19 Pat*terns Detection in X-ray Images, 1–10*.

Ma, X., Niu, Y., Gu, L., Wang, Y., Zhao, Y., Bailey, J., & Lu, F. (2021). Understanding adversarial attacks on deep learning based medical image analysis systems. Pattern Recognition, *110, 107332*.

Mahmud, T., Rahman, M. A., & Fattah, S. A. (2020). CovXNet: A multi-dilation convolutional neural network for automatic COVID-19 and other pneumonia detection from chest X-*ray images with tran*sfer*able multi-receptive feature optimization. Computers in Biology and Medicine, 122, 103869.

Majumder, M. S., Santillana, M., Mekaru, S. R., McGinnis, D. P., Khan, K., & Brown*stein, J. S. (2016). Utilizing no*ntraditional data sources for near real-time estimation of transmission dynamics during the 2015–2016 Colombian Zika virus disease outbreak. JMIR Public Health and Surveillance, 2. doi:10.2196/publichealth.5814

Mallén-Fullerton, G. M., & *Fernandez-Anaya, G. (2013). D*NA *fr*agment assembly using optimization. In 2013 IEEE Congress on Evolutionary Computation, pp. 1570-1577. IEEE. 10.1109/CEC.2013.6557749

Mannini, A., Trojaniello, D., Cereatti, A., & Sabatini, A. M.. (2016). A machine learning framewor*k for gait classificati*on using inertial sensors: Application to elderly, post-stroke and Huntington's disease patients. Sensors, 16(1), 134.

Markiewicz, T., *Osowski, S., Patera,* J., & Kozlowski, W. (2006, October). Image processing for accurate cell recognition and count on histologic slides. Analytical and Quantitative Cytology and Histology, 28, 281–291. PMID:17067010

Martinez-Romero, M. (*2010). Arti*ficial intelligence techniques for colorectal cancer drug metabolism: Ontologies and complex networks. Current Drug Metabolism, 11(4), 347–368. doi:10.2174/138920010791514289 *PMID:20446907*

Maxwell, P. G., LeNail, A., & Fraenkel, E. (2018). Shallow Sparsely-Connected Autoencoders for Gene Set Projection. Pacific Symposium on Biocomputing, 2019, 374–385. *PMID:30963076*

*Me*i, S., Flemington, E. K., & Zhang, K. (2017). A computational framework for distinguishing direct versus indirect interactions in human functional protein–protein in*teraction networks*. *Integrative Biology, 9(7),* 595–606. doi:10.1039/c7ib00013h PMID:28524201

Mellit, A., & Kalogirou, S. A. (2008). Artificial intelligence techniques for photovoltaic applications: A review. Progress in Energy and Combus*tion Science, 34(5), 574–632. doi:10.1016/j.* pecs.2008.01.001

Mellit, A., Kalogirou, S. A., Hontoria, L., & Shaari, S. (2009). Artificial intelligence techniques for sizing photovoltaic systems: A review. Renewable & Sustainable Energy Review*s, 13(2), 406–419. doi:10.1016/j.rser.2008.01.006*

Midelfart, H., Komorowski, J., Nørsett, K., Yadetie, F., Sandovik, A. K., & Lægreid, A. (2002). Learning rough set classifiers from gene expressions and clinical *data. Fundamenta Informaticae, 53(2), 155–*183.

Milletari, F., Ahmadi, S. A., Kroll, C., Plate, A., Rozanski, V., Maiostre, J., & Navab, N. (2017). Hough-CNN: Deep learning for segmentation of deep brain regions in MRI and ultrasound. Compute*r Vision and Image Understandin*g, 164, 92–102.

Minaee, S., Kafieh, R., Sonka, M., Yazdani, S., & Soufi, G. J. (2020). Deep-covid: Predi*cting covid-19* from chest x-ray images using deep transfer learning. arXiv preprint arXiv:2004.09363.

Minaee, S., Kafieh, R., Sonka, M., Yazdani, S., Soufi, G. J. (2020). Deep-COVID: Predicting COVID-19 From Chest X-Ray Images Using Deep Transfer Learning. *Medical Image Analysis.*

Minetti, G., & Alba, E. (2010). Metaheuristic assemblers of DNA strands: Noiseless and noisy case*s. In IEEE Congress on Evolutionary Comput*ation, pp. 1-8. IEEE. 10.1109/CEC.2010.5586524

Mitchell, R. (2018). Web Scraping with Python (2nd ed.). O'Reilly Media, Inc.

Mitra, S. (2005). Computational intelligence in bioinformatics. In Transactions on Rough Sets III (pp. 134–*152). Springer. doi:10.1007/11427834_6*

*Mit*tal, M., Arora, M., Pandey, T., & Goyal, L. M. (2020). Image segmentation using deep learning techn*iques in me*dical images. In Advancement of machine intelligence in interactive medical image analysis (pp. 41–63). Springer.

Mobadersany, P., Yousefi, S., Amgad, M., Gutman, D. A*., Barnh*oltz-Sloan, J. S., Velázquez Vega, J. E., Brat, D. J., & Cooper, L. A. D. (2018). Predicting cance*r outcomes from histology and genomics u*sing convolutional networks. Proceedings of the National Academy of Sciences of the United States of America, 115(13), E2970. doi:10.1073/pnas.1717139115 PMID:29531073

Muhammad, L. J., Islam, M. M., Usman, S. *S., & Ayon, S. I. (2020). Predictive Data Mining Mo*dels for Novel Coronavirus (COVID-19) Infected Patients' Recovery, SN. Computer Science, 1, 206.

Muntoni, A. P., Pagnani, A., Weigt, M., & Zamponi, F. (2021). adaptive Boltzmann machine learning for biological sequences. BMC Bioinformatics, 22(1), 528. doi:10.118612859-021-04441-9 PMID:34715775

Narayanan, A., Keedwell, E. C., & Olsson, B. (2002). Artificial intelligence techniques for bioinformatics. Applied Bioinformatics, 1, 191–222. PMID:15130837

Narin, A. Kaya, C., & Pamuk, Z. (2020). Automatic Detectrion of Coronavirus Disease Using x-ray images and deep convolutional neural networks. ArXiv2003.10849.

Narin, C. K. & Pamuk, Z. (2016). Automatic detection of coronavirus disease (covid-19) using x-ray images and deep convolutional neural networks. arXiv preprint arXiv:2003.10849.

Nicolas, J. (2020). Artificial *intelligence and bio*informatics. In A Guided Tour of Artificial Intelligence Research (pp. 209–264). Springer. doi:10.1007/978-3-030-06170-8_7

Niyaz, U., & Sambyal, A. S. (2018, December). Advances in deep learning techniques for medical im*age analysis.* In 2018 Fifth International Conference on Parallel, Distributed and Grid Compu*ting (PDGC) (pp. 271-277).* IEEE.

Norris, M., Anderson, R., & Kenny, I. C. (2014). Method analysis of accelerometers and gyroscopes in running gait: A systematic review. Proceedings of the Institution of Mechanical Engineers. Part P, Journal of Spor*ts Engineering and Technolo*gy, 228(1), 1, 3–15. doi:10.1177/1754337113502472

Oram, J. F. (2002). Molecular basis of cholesterol homeostasis: Lessons from Tangier disease and ABCA1. Trends in Molecular Medicine, 8(4), 168–173. doi:10.1016/S1471-4914(02)02289-X PMID:11927274

Ortiz de S*olorzano, C., Garcia Rodrigue*z, E., Jones, A., Pinkel, D., Gray, J. W., Sudar, D., & Lockett, S. J. (1999, March). Segmentation of confocal microscope images of cell nuclei in thick tissue sections. Journal of Microscopy, 193(3), 212–226. *doi:10.1046/j.*1365-2818.1999.00463.x PMID:10199001

Ozturk, T., Talo, M., Yildirim, E. A., Baloglu, U. B., Yildirim, O., & Acharya, U. R. (2020). Automated detection of COVID-19 cases using deep neural networks with X-ray images. Computers in Bi*ology and M*edicine, p. 103792.

Paila, Y. D., & Chattopadhyay, A. (2010). Membrane cholesterol in the function and organization of G-protein coupled receptors. Cholesterol Binding and Cholesterol Transport Proteins:, 439-466.

Patibandla, R. L., Narayana, V. L., Gopi, A. P., & Ra*o*, B. T. (2021). Comparative Study on Analysis of Medical Images Using Deep Learning Techniques. In Deep *Learning for Biomedical Applic*ations (pp. 329–345). CRC Press.

Pau, M., Corona, F., Pili, R., Casula, C., Guicciardi, M., Cossu, G., & Murgia, M. (2018). Quantitative assessment of gait parameters in people with Parkinson's disease in the laboratory and clinical setting: Are the measures interchangeable. Neurology *International, 10(2), 69–73.* d*o*i:10.4081/ni.2018.7729 PMID:30069292

Pawar, N., Rajeswari, K., & Joshi, A. (2016). Implementation of an efficient Web crawler to search medicinal plants and relevant diseases. International Conference o*n Computing Communication Control and automation (*ICCUBEA), (pp. 1-4). doi:10.1109/ICCUBEA.2016.7860006

Pawlak, Z. (1996). Rough sets and data analysis, Fuzzy Systems Symposium. Soft Computing in Intelligent Systems and Information Processing, 1-6.

Pazos, F., & Bang, J. W. (2006). Computational prediction of functionally important *regions in proteins.* Current Bioinformatics, 1(1), 15–23. doi:10.2174/157489306775330633

Pearson, J., & Havill, D. C. (1988). The effect of hypoxia and sulphide on culture-grown *wetland and non-wetland plant*s: *Π*. Metabolic and physiological changes. Journal of Experimental Botany, 39(4), 431–439. doi:10.1093/jxb/39.4.431

Persson, E. (2019). Evaluating tools and t*echniques for web scraping. [M.S. Th*esis, Kth Royal Institute Of Technology, Sweden].

Pollett, S., Althouse, B. M., Forshey, B., Rutherford, G. W., & Jarman, R. G. (2017). Internet-based biosurveillance methods for vector-b*orne diseases: Are they novel public health* tools or just novelties? PLoS Neglected Tropical Diseases, 11. doi:10.1371/journal.pntd.0005871

Pospichal, P., & Jaros, J., (2009). GPU-based acceleration of the genetic algorithm. GECCO competition.

Punn, N. S., & Agarwal, S. (2020). Automated diagnosis of COVID-19 with lim*ited posteroanterior ch*e*st* X-ray images using fine-tuned deep neural networks. https://arxiv.org/abs/2004.11676

Quazi & Jangi. (202*1). Artificial intelligence and machine learning in medicinal chemistry a*nd validation of emerging drug targets. Academic Press.

Quazi, S. (2021). Vaccine in response to *COVID-19: Recent developments, chall*enges, and a way out. Biomedical and Biotechnology Research Journal, 5(2), 105. doi:10.4103/bbrj.bbrj_166_20

Rahimzadeh, M., Attar, A. (2020). New Modified Deep Convolutional Neural Network for Detecting COVID-19 from X-ray Imag*es. Informatics in Medicine Unlo*cked, 19.

Rahmanifard, H., & Plaksina, T. (2019). Application of artificial intelligence techniques in the petroleum industry: A review. Artificial Intelligence Review, 52(4), 2295–2318. doi:10.100710462-018-9612-8

Raj, R. J. S., *Shobana, S. J., Pus*t*okhi*na, I. V., Pustokhin, D. A., Gupta, D., & Shankar, K. J. I. A. (2020). Optimal feature selection-based medical im*age classification using deep learning model in internet of medical things. IEEE Access:* Practical Innovations, Open Solutions, 8, 58006–58017.

Ratnakumar, R., & Nanda, S. J. (2016, May). A FSM *based approach for efficient* implementation of K-means algorithm. In 2016 20th International Symposium on VLSI Design and Test (VDAT) (pp. 1-6). IEEE.

Ratnakumar, R., & Nanda, S. J. (2019a). A lo*w complexity hardw*are architecture of K-means algorithm for real-time satellite image segmentation. Multimedia Tools and Applications, 78(9), 11949–11981. doi:10.100711042-018-6726-6

Ratnakumar, R., & Nanda, S. J. (2019b). A hard*ware architecture based* on genetic clustering for color image segmentation. In Soft Computing for Problem Solving (pp. 863–876). Springer. doi:10.1007/978-981-13-1592-3_69

Ratnakumar, R., & Nanda, S. J. (2021a, January). An *improved genetic* clustering architecture for real-time satellite image segmentation. In 2021 International Conference on Advances in Technology, Management & Education (ICATME) (pp. 123-128). IEEE. 10.1109/ICATME50232.2021.9732768

Ratnakumar, R., & Nanda, S. J. (2021b). A high speed roller dung beetles clustering algorithm and its architecture for real-time image segmentation. *Applied Intelligence, 51(7), 4682–4713.* d*oi:10.1*00710489-020-02067-7

Ratnakumar, R., Chaitanya, P. V., & Gurunarayanan, S. (2019, November). An Energy Efficient Multilevel Reconfigurable parallel Cache Architecture for Embedded Multicore *Processors. In 2019 International Conference on Electrical, Electronics and* Computer Engineering (UPCON) (pp. 1-6). IEEE. 10.1109/UPCON47278.2019.8980197

Redmon, J., Divva*la, S., Girshick, R., & Farhadi, A. (2016). You only look once: Unified, real-time object detection. In* Proceedings of the IEEE conf*erence on computer vision and pattern recognition (pp. 779-788). IEEE.*

Rekha Hanumanthu, S. (2020). Role of intelligent computing in COVID-19 prognosis: A state-of-t*he-art review. Chao*s, Solitons, and Fractals, 138, 109947. doi:10.1016/j.chaos.2020.109947

Ren, S., He, K., Girshick, R., & Sun, J. (2015). Faster r-cnn: Towards real-time object d*etection with region proposal networ*ks. Advances in Neural Information Processing Systems, 28.

Rennie, S., Buchbinder, M., Juengst, E., Brinkley-Rubinstein, L., Blue, C., & Rosen, D. L. (2020). Scraping the Web for public health gai*ns: Ethical considerations from a 'big* data' research project on HIV and incarceration. Public Health Ethics, 13, 111–121. doi:10.1093/phe/phaa006

Revathy, S., Parvaathavarthini, B., & Rajathi, S. (2015). Futuristic validation method for rough fuzzy clustering. Indian Journal of Science and Technology, 8(2), 120–127. doi:10.17485/ijst/2015/v8i2/58943

Richardson, L. (2018). Beautiful Soup Documentation. Crummy. https://www.crummy.*com/software/BeautifulSoup/bs4/doc/*

Rost, B., Liu, J., Nair, R., Wrzeszczynski, K. O., & Ofran, Y. (2003). Automatic prediction of protein function. Cellular and Molecular Life Sciences CMLS, 60(12), 2637–2650. *doi:10.1*00700018-003-3114-8 PMID:14685688

Roth, H. R., Shen, C., Oda, H., Oda, M., Hayashi, Y., Misawa, K., & Mori, K. (2018). Deep learning and its application to medical image s*egmentation. Medical Imaging Technology, 36(2)*, 63–71.

Rothan, H. A., & Byrareddy, S. N. (2020). The epidemiology and pathogenesis of coronavirus disea*se (COVID-19) outbreak. Journal of Autoimmunity, 109, 102433. doi:10.1016/j.jaut.2020.102433*

Rout, S. B., Mishra, S., & Mishra, S. (2016). Fuzzy Applications in Protein Structure Prediction: A New Era to Bioinformatics. Structure, 5(4).

Rupanagudi, S. R., Ranjani, B., Bhat, V. G., Surabhi, K., & Reshma, P. (2015). A h*igh speed algorithm fo*r identifying hand gestures for an ATM input system for the blind. IEEE Bombay Section Symposium (IBSS). 10.1109/IBSS.2015.7456642

Russ, W.P., Figliuzzi, M., Stocker, C., Barrat-Charlaix, P*., Socolich, M., Kas*t, P., Hilvert, D., Monasson, R., Cocco, S., Weigt, M., & Ranganathan, R. (2020). An evolution-based model for designing chorismate mutase enzymes. Science, 369(6502):440–5.

RVest. (n.d.). Easily harvest (scrape) web pages. Tidyverse. https://rvest.tidyverse.org

Saboor, T. Kask, A. Kuusik, M. M. Alam, Y. Le Moullec, I. K. Niazi, A. Zoha and R. Ahmad. (2021). Latest research trends in gait analysis using wearable sensors and machine learning: A systematic re*view. IEEE Acce*ss: Practical Innovations, Open Solutions, 8, 167830–167864.

Salakhutdinov, R., & Hinton, G. E. (2009). Deep boltzmann machines. In International Conference on Artificial Intelligence and statistics, (pp. 448–455). IEEE.

Santos, B. *S., Silva, I.,* Ribeiro-Dantas, M. d., Alves, G., Endo, P. T., & Lima, L. (2020). COVID-19: A scholarly production dataset report for research analysis. Data in Brief, 32. doi:10.1016/j.dib.2020.106178

Santosh, K. C., Das, N*., & Ghos*h, S. (2022). Cytology image analysis. In KC Santosh, Nibaran Das, Swarnendu Ghosh (eds*). Primers in Biomedical Imaging Devices and Systems, Deep Learning Models for Medical Imaging, Academ*ic Press. 99-123. doi:10.1016/B978-0-12-823504-1.00014-3

Sasson, S. (2006). Expression of interleukin (IL)-2 and IL-7 receptors discriminates between human regulatory and activated T cells. The Journal of Experimental Medicine, 203(7), 1693–1700. d*oi:10.1084/jem.20060468 PMID:16818676*

Saurkar, A. V., Pathare, K. G., & Gode, S. A. (2018). An Overview on Web Scraping Techniques and Tools. International Journal on Future Revolution in Computer Science & Communication Engineering, 4, 363–367.

Schatz, M. C. (2009). Cloudburst: Highly sensitive read m*apping with mapreduce. Bioinformatic*s (Oxford, England), 25(11), 1363–1369. doi:10.1093/bioinformatics/btp236 PMID:19357099

Schwartz, M. H., Rozumalski, A., Truong, W., & Novacheck, T. F. (2013). Predicting the outcome of intramuscular psoas lengthening in children with cerebral palsy usi*ng preopera*tive gait data and the random forest algorithm. Gait & Posture, 37(4), 473–479. doi:10.1016/j.gaitpost.2012.08.016 PMID:2307958*6*

*Senior, A. W., Evans, R., Jumpe*r, *J.,* Kirkpatrick, J., Sifre, L., Green, T., Qin, C., Žídek, A., Nelson, A. W., Bridgland, A., Penedones, H., Petersen, S., Simonyan, K., Crossan, S., Kohli, P., Jones, D. T., Silver, D., Kavukcuoglu, K., & Hassabis, *D. (2020). Improved* protein structure prediction using potentials from deep learning. Nature, 577(7792), 706–710. doi:10.103841586-019-1923-7 PMID:31942072

Setubal, J., & Meidanis, J. (1999). Introduction to Computational Molecular Biology. *International Thomson Publishing.*

Sfetsos, A., & Coonick, A. (2000). Univariate and multivariate forecasting of hourly solar radiation with artificial intelligence techniques. Solar Energy, 68(2), 169–178. doi:10.1016/S0038-092X(99)00064-X

Sha, D., Liu, Y., Liu, Q., Li, Y., Tian, Y., Beaini, F., & Yang, C. (2021). A spatiotemporal data collection of viral cases for COVID-19 rapid response. Big Earth Data, 5, 90–111. doi:10.1080/20964471.2020.1844934

Shahbaaz, M., Nkaule, A., & Christoffels, A. (2019). Designing novel possible kinase inhibitor derivatives as therapeutics against Mycobacterium tuberculosis: An in silico study. *Scientific Reports*, 9(1), 1–12. doi:10.103841598-019-40621-7 PMID:30867456

Shaiket, H. A., Anisuzzaman, D. M., & Saif, A. S. (2019). Data analysis and visualization of continental cancer situation by Twitter scraping. International Journal of Modern Education and Computer Science, 11, 23–31. doi:10.5815/ijmecs.2019.07.03

Sharma, A., & Rani, R. (2020). Ensembled machine learning framework for drug sensitivity prediction. IET Systems Biology, 14(1), 39–46. doi:10.1049/iet-syb.2018.5094 PMID:31931480

Sharma, V., & Sarkar, I. N. (2013). Bioinformatics opportunities for identification and study of medicinal plants. Briefings in Bioinformatics, 14(2), 238–250. doi:10.1093/bib/bbs021 PMID:22589384

Shi, F., Wang, J., Shi, J., Wu, Z., Wang, Q., Tang, Z., He, K., Shi, Y., & Shen, D. (2020). Review of artificial intelligence techniques in imaging data acquisition, segmentation and diagnosis for COVID-19. IEEE Reviews in Biomedical Engineering.

Shi, Y., & Eberhart, R. (1998). A modified particle swarm optimizer. In Evolutionary Computation Proceedings, IEEE World Congress on Computational Intelligence, pp. 69-73. IEEE.

Shi H., Han X., Jiang N., Cao Y., Alwalid O., Gu J. (2020). Radiological findings from 81 patients with COVID-19 pneumonia in Wuhan, China: a descriptive study. The Lancet Infectious Diseases. pmid:32105637

Sikandar, A., Anwar, W., Bajwa, U. I., Wang, X., Sikandar, M., Yao, L., Jiang, Z. L., & Chunkai, Z. (2018). Decision tree based approaches for detecting protein complex in protein protein interaction network (PPI) via link and sequence analysis. IEEE Access: Practical Innovations, Open Solutions, 6, 22108–22120. doi:10.1109/ACCESS.2018.2807811

Singh, D. B., & Pathak, R. K. (2020). Computational approaches in drug designing and their applications. In Experimental protocols in biotechnology (pp. 95–117). Springer. doi:10.1007/978-1-0716-0607-0_6

Singh, M., Jakhar, A. K., & Pandey, S. (2021). Sentiment analysis on the impact of coronavirus in social life using the BERT model. Social Network Analysis and Mining, 11. doi:10.100713278-021-00737-z

Singh, S. P., Wang, L., Gupta, S., Goli, H., Padmanabhan, P., & Gulyás, B. (2020). 3D deep learning on medical images: A review. Sensors (Basel), 20(18), 5097.

Singh, V. (2019). Ligand-Based Designing of Natural Products. In Bioactive Natural Products for *the Management of Cancer: From* Bench to Bedside. Springer. doi:10.1007/978-981-13-7607-8_8

Singla, D., Dhanda, S. K., Chauhan, J. S., Bhardwaj, A., Brahmachari, S. K., Consortium, O. S. D. D., & Raghava, G. P. S. (2013). *Open source software and web services for designing therapeutic molecules. Curre*nt Topics in Medicinal Chemistry, 13(10), 1172–1191. doi:10.2174/1568026611313100005 PMID:23647540

Singrodia, V., Mitra, *A., & Paul, S. (2019). A Review on Web Scrapping and its Applic*ations. International Confer*ence on Computer Communication and Informatics (I*CCCI), (pp. 1-6). doi:10.1109/ICCCI.2019.8821809

Sirisuriya, D. S. (2015). A Comparative Study on Web Scraping. Proceedings of 8th International Research Conference.

Sljoka, A. (2022). Structural and Functional Analysis of Proteins Using Rigidity Theory. Sublinear *Computation Paradigm. Springer. d*oi:10.1007/978-981-16-4095-7_14

Sont, J. K., De Boer, W. I., van Schadew*ijk, W. A., Grunberg, K., van Krieken, J. H., Hiemstra, P. S., & Sterk, P. J. (2003, June 1). Fully automated assessme*nt of inflammatory cell counts and cytokine expression in bronchial tissue. American Journal of Respiratory and Critical Care Medicine, 167(11), 1496–1503. do*i:10.1164/rccm.2205003 PMID:12770855*

Staab, W., Hottowitz, R., Sohns, C., Sohns, J. M., Gilbert, F., Menke, J., & Lotz, J. (2014). Accelerometer and *gyroscope-based gait analysi*s *usi*ng spectral analysis of patients with osteoarthritis of the knee. Journal of Physical Therapy Science, 26(7), 997–1002. doi:10.1589/jpts.26.997 PMID:25140082

Suzuki, K. (2017). Overview of deep learning in medical imaging. Radiological Physics and Technology, 10(3), *257–273. doi:10.1007*12194-017-0406-5 PMID:28689314

Tahir, N. M., & Manap, H. H. (2012). Parkinson disease gait classification based on machine learning approach. Journal of *Applied Sciences, 12(2), 180–185. doi:10.*3923/jas.2012.180.185

Tang, B., Pan, Z., Yin, K., & Khateeb, A. (2019). Recemt advamces of deep learning *in bio*informatics and computational biology. Frontiers in Genetics, 10, 214. doi:10.3389/fgene.2019.00214 PMID:30972100

Ting, D. S. W., Cheung, C. Y. L., Lim, G., Tan, G. S. W., Quan*g, N. D., Gan, A., ... Wo*ng, T. Y. (2017). Development and validation of a deep learning system for diabetic retinopathy and related eye diseases using retinal images from multiethnic populations with diabetes. Journal o*f the American Medical Ass*ociation, 318(22), 2211–2223.

Torres-Carrión, P. (2019). Application of techniques based on Artificial Intelligence for predicting the consump*tion of dr*ugs and substances. A Systematic Mapping Review. In International Conference on Applied Technologies. Springer.

Tripathi, A., & Misra, K. (2017). Molecular docking: A structure-based drug designing approach. JSM Chemistry, 5(2), 1042–1047.

Tripathy, R., Mishra, D., & Konkimalla, V. B. (2015). A novel fuzzy C-means approach for uncovering cholesterol consensus motif from human G-protein coupled receptors (GPCR). Karbala International Journal of Modern Science, 1(4), 212–224. doi:10.1016/j.kijoms.2015.11.006

Tripathy, R., Mishra, D., & Konkimalla, V. B. (2016). A hybridized clustering approach based on rough set and fuzzy c-means to mine cholesterol sequence from ABC family. Indian Journal of Science and Technology, 9(22). doi:10.17485/ijst/2016/v9i22/94237

Tubiana, J., Cocco, S., & Monasson, R. (2019). Learning Compositional Representations of Interacting Systems with Restricted Boltzmann Machines, Comparative Study of Lattice Proteins. Neural Computation, 31(8), 1671–1717. doi:10.1162/neco_a_01210 PMID:31260391

UniProt Consortium. (2007). The universal protein re- source (UniProt). Nucleic Acids Research, 36, D190–D195. doi:10.1093/nar/gkm895 PMID:18045787

Usmani, S. S., Kumar, R., Bhalla, S., Kumar, V., & Raghava, G. P. S. (2018). In silico tools and databases for designing peptide-based vaccine and drugs. Advances in Protein Chemistry and Structural Biology, 112, 221–263. doi:10.1016/bs.apcsb.2018.01.006 PMID:29680238

Vargiu, E., & Urru, M. (2013). Exploiting web scraping in a collaborative filtering- based approach to web advertising. Artificial Intelligence Review, 2, 44–54. doi:10.5430/air.v2n1p44

Wang, C. R., Zhang, F., Yu, Y., & Wang, Y. (2020, October). BR-GAN: bilateral residual generating adversarial network for mammogram classification. In International Conference on Medical Image Computing and Computer-Assisted Intervention (pp. 657-666). Springer.

Wang, H., Li, C., Zhang, J., Wang, J., Ma, Y., & Lian, Y. (2019) . A new LSTM-based gene expression prediction model, L-GEPM, Journal of Bioinformatics & Computational Biology.

Wang, J., Yang, C., Min, Z., & Wang, C. (2009). Implementation of Otsu's thresholding process based on FPGA. 2009 4th IEEE Conference on Industrial Electronics and Applications, 479-483.

Wang, L., Ding, J., Pan, L., Cao, D., Jiang, H., & Ding, X. (2019). Artificial intelligence facilitates drug design in the big data era. Chemometrics and Intelligent Laboratory Systems, 194, 103850. doi:10.1016/j.chemolab.2019.103850

Wang, L., Wong, A. (2020). COVID-Net: A Tailored Deep Convolutional Neural Network Design for Detection of COVID-19 Cases from Chest X-Ray Images. Scientific Reports.

Wang, W., Liang, D., Chen, Q., Iwamoto, Y., Han, X. H., Zhang, Q., & Chen, Y. W. (2020). Medical image classification using deep learning. In Deep learning in healthcare (pp. 33–51). Springer.

Wang, Y., & Zeng, J. (2013). Predicting drug-target interactions using restricted Boltzmann machines. Bioinformatics (Oxford, England), 29(13), i126–i134. doi:10.1093/bioinformatics/btt234 PMID:23812976

Wang, Z., Bovik, A. C., Sheikh, H. R., & Simoncelli, E. P. (2004). Image quality assessment: From error visibility to structural similarity. IEEE Transactions on Image Processing, 13(4), 600–612. doi:10.1109/TIP.2003.819861 PMID:15376593

Wang, Z., Chen, Y., Liang, H., Bender, A., Glen, R. C., & Yan, A. (2011). P-glycoprotein substrate models using support vector machines based on a comprehensive data set. Journal of Chemical Information and Modeling, 51(6), 1447–1456. doi:10.1021/ci2001583 PMID:21604677

Watanabe, Y., & Kimura, M. (2020). Gait identification and authentication using LSTM based on 3-axis accelerations of the smartphone. Procedia Computer Science, 176, 3873–3880. doi:10.1016/j.procs.2020.09.001

Way, G. P., & Casey, S. Greene. (2017). Extracting a biologically relevant latent space from cancer transcriptomes with variational autoencoders. bioRxiv, •••, 174474.

Wei, Q., & Stephen, A. (2021, September 22). Ramsey. (2021) Predicting chemotherapy response using a variational autoencoder approach. BMC Bioinformatics, 22(1), 453. doi:10.118612859-021-04339-6 PMID:34551729

Weinstein, J. N., Myers, T., Buolamwini, J., Raghavan, K., Van Osdol, W., Licht, J., Viswanadhan, V. N., Kohn, K. W., Rubinstein, L. V., Koutsoukos, A. D., Monks, A., Scudiero, D. A., Zaharevitz, D., Chabner, B. A., Anderson, N. L., Grever, M. R., & Paull, K. D. (1994). Predictive statistics and artificial intelligence in the US National Cancer Institute's drug discovery program for cancer and AIDS. Stem Cells (Dayton, Ohio), 12(1), 13–22. doi:10.1002tem.5530120106 PMID:8142917

Weng, Y., Wang, X., Hua, J., Wang, H., Kang, M., & Wang, F.-Y. (2019). Forecasting horticultural products price using ARIMA model and neural network based on a large-scale data set collected by Web crawler. IEEE Transactions on Computational Social Systems, 6, 547–553. doi:10.1109/TCSS.2019.2914499

Wiki, A. I. (2020). A Beginner's Guide to Important Topics in AI, Machine Learning, and Deep Learning. https://wiki.pathmind.com/restricted-boltzmann-machine

Wong, H. L., Bendayan, R., Rauth, A. M., Xue, H. Y., Babakhanian, K., & Wu, X. Y. (2006). A mechanistic study of enhanced doxorubicin uptake and retention in multidrug resistant breast cancer cells using a polymer-lipid hybrid nanoparticle system. The Journal of Pharmacology and Experimental Therapeutics, 317(3), 1372–1381. doi:10.1124/jpet.106.101154 PMID:16547167

Wong, S. L., Rual, J. F., Venkatesan, K., Hao, T., Hirozane-Kishikawa, T., Dricot, A., Li, N., & Klitgord, N. (2005). Towards a proteome-scale map of the human protein–protein interaction network. Nature, 437(7062), 1173–1178. doi:10.1038/nature04209 PMID:16189514

Xiao, L. H., Chen, P. R., Gou, Z. P., Li, Y. Z., Li, M., Xiang, L. C., & Feng, P. (2017). Prostate cancer prediction using the random forest algorithm that takes into account transrectal ultrasound findings, age, and serum levels of prostate-specific antigen. Asian Journal of Andrology, 19(5), 586. doi:10.4103/1008-682X.186884 PMID:27586028

Xu, Q., Shen, Z., Shah, N., Cuomo, R., Cai, M., Brown, M., ... Mackey, T. (2020). Characterizing Weibo social media posts from Wuhan China during the early stages of the *COVID-19 pandemic: Qualitative content analysis. JMIR Publ*ic Health and Surveillance, 6. doi:10.2196/24125

Xu. J.(2019). Distance-based protein folding powered by deep learning. Proc Natl Acad Sci., 116(34), *16856–65.*

Yadav, S., Mehra, A., Rohmetra, H., Ratnakumar, R., & Narang, P. (2021). DerainGAN: Single image deraining using *wasserstein GAN. Multimedia Too*ls and Applications, 80(30), 36491–36507. doi:10.100711042-021-11442-6

Yadav, S. S., & Jadhav, S. M. (2019). Deep convolutional neural network based medical image classification for disease diagnosis. Journal of Big Data, 6(1), 1–18.

Yang, *C., Sha, D., Liu, Q., Li, Y., Lan, H., Guan,* W. W., & Ding, A. (2020). Taking the pulse of COVID-19: A spatiotemporal perspective. International Journal of Digital Earth, 13, 1186–1211. doi:10.1080/17538947.2020.1809723

Yang, L., Mee*r, P., & Foran, D. J. (2005, S*eptember). Unsupervised Segmentation Based on Robust Estimation and Color Active Contour Models. IEEE Transactions on Information Technology in Biomedicine, 9(3), 475–486. doi:10.1109/TITB.200*5.847515 PMI*D:16167702

Yang, X., Wang, Y., Byrne, R., Schneider, G., & Yang, S. (2019). Concepts of artificial intelligence for computer-assisted drug discov*ery. Chemical Revi*ews, 119(18), 10520–10594. doi:10.1021/acs.chemrev.8b00728 PMID:31294972

Yang . J, Anishchenko .I, Park. H, Peng .Z, Ovchinnikov. S & Baker. D.(2020). Improved protein structure prediction using predicted interresidue orientations. Proc Natl Acad Sci, 117(3), 1496–*503.*

Ye, C., Wang, W., Zhang, S., & Wang, K. (2019). Multi-depth fusion network for whole-heart CT image segmentation. IEEE Access: Practical Innovations, Open Solutions, 7, 23421–23429.

Zhang, S., Xu, J., Chen, Y. C., Ma, J., Li, Z., Wang, Y., & Yu, Y. (2020, October). Revisiting 3D context modeling with supervised pre-training for universal lesion detection in CT slices. In International Conference on Medical Image Computing and Computer-Assisted Intervention (pp. 542-551). Springer.

Zhang, Y., DeVries, *M. E., & Skolnick, J. (2006).* Structure modeling of all identified G protein–coupled receptors in the human genome. PLoS Computational Biology, 2(2), e13. *doi:10.1371/journal.pc*bi.0020013 PMID:16485037

Zhavoronkov, A. (2020). Medicinal Chemists versus Machines Challenge: What Will It Take to Adopt and Advance Artificial Intelligence for Drug Discovery? Journal of Chemical Information and Modeling, 60(6), 2657–*2659. doi:10.1021/acs.jcim.0c00435* PMID:32469509

Zhavoronkov, A., Vanhaelen, Q., & Oprea, T. I. (2020). Will Artificial Intelligence for Drug Discovery Impact Clinical Pharmacology? Clinical Pharmacology and Therapeu*tics, 107(4), 780–785.* doi:10.1002/cpt.1795 PMID:31957003

Compilation of References

Zhou, X., Yamada, K., Kojima, T., Takayama, R., Wang, S., Zhou, X., & Fujita, H. (2018, February). Performance evalua*tion of 2D and 3D deep learning approa*ches for automatic segmentation of multiple organs on CT images. In Medical Imaging 2018: Computer-Aided Diagnosis (Vol. 10575, pp. 520-525). Spie.

Zhu, H. (2020). Big data and artificial *intelligence modeling for* drug discovery. Annual Review of Pharmacology and Toxicology, 60(1), 573–589. doi:10.1146/annurev-pharmtox-010919-023324 PMID:31518513

Zhu, X., Yao, J., Zhu, F., & Huang, J. (2017). WSISA: Making Survival Prediction from Whole Slide Histopathological Images. 2017 IEEE Conference on Computer Vision and Pattern Recognition (CVPR). IEEE. 10.1109/CVPR.2017.725

Zou, Q., Wang, Y., Wang, Q., Zhao, Y., & Li, Q. (2020). Deep learning-based gait recognition using smartphones in the wild. IEE*E Transactions on Information Forensics and Security, 15, 3197–3212.*

Zu, Z. Y., Jiang, M. D., Xu, P. P., Chen, W., Ni, Q. Q., & Lu, G. M. (2020). Coronavirus disease 2019 (COVID-19): a perspective from China. Radiology, p. *200490.*

Álvarez-Machancoses, Ó., & Fernández-Martínez, J. L. (2019). Using artificial intelligence methods to speed up drug discovery. Expert Opinion on Drug Discovery, 14(8), 769–777. doi:1 0.1080/17460441.2019.1621284 PMID:31140873

About the Contributors

U. Vignesh is currently an Associate Professor in Information Technology Department, Vel Tech Rangarajan Dr. Sagunthala R&D Institute of Science and Technology, Chennai, Tamilnadu, Previously he was working as Senior Assistant Professor at Manipal Institute of Technology, Manipal. Prior to his recent appointments, he was a Post-Doctoral Fellow in National Institute of Technology (NIT), Trichy – India. Dr. Vignesh received his undergraduate degree in B.Tech (IT) as well as his M.Tech (IT) degree from Anna University - Chennai, and his PhD in Computer Science and Engineering from VIT University - Chennai. Dr. Vignesh published several papers in preferred Journals, patents and chapters in books, and participated in a range of forums on computer science, social science, etc. He also presented various academic as well as research-based papers at several national and international conferences. His research activities are currently twofold: while the first research activity is set to explore the developmental role that society needs with technology such as, Artificial Intelligence; the second major research theme that he is pursuing is focused on the bioinformatics and data mining.

R. Parvathi is an Associate Professor of School of Computing Science and Engineering at VIT University, Chennai since 2011. She received the Doctoral degree in the field of spatial data mining in the same year. Her teaching experience in the area of computer science includes more than two decades and her research interests include data mining, big data and computational biology.

Ricardo Goncalves holds a PhD degree and received his habilitation (Agregação) in Industrial Information Systems by the NOVA University of Lisbon (UNL). He is Full Professor at the New University of Lisbon, Faculty of Sciences and Technology, and a Principal Investigator at UNINOVA – Instituto de Desenvolvimento de Novas Tecnologia. He has graduated in Computer Science, with MSc in Operational Research and Systems Engineering. His research activities have been focused on Interoperability of Complex Systems. He has been researching in European Commission funded projects during the last 30 years, with more than 200 papers published in conferences, journals and books. He directs GRIS (GRupo para a investigação em Interoperabilidade de Sistemas; Group for Research in Interoperability of Systems) at UNINOVA (Instituto para o Desenvolvimento de Novas Tecnologias), CTS (Centro para as Tecnologias e Sistemas). He has a relevant standardization activity acting as member of the Planning and Policy Committee and project leader in ISO TC184/SC4.

* * *

Parth Birthare is a dedicated and quick learner, and he likes to engage in areas that lead to innovation and welfare. He has marked his presence by making open source contributions and participating in events and activities where he used his technical skills to solve the problems faced by social-good organizations. Having strong technological intellect and empathy, he strives to build next-generation solutions to existing problems.

Shreya Birthare is an assiduous and optimistic person. Being an innovative thinker, she likes to use her prowess and technological expertise to solve advanced problems and find optimal solutions and unique approaches. Moreover, she is a virtuous person and has strong leadership capabilities. She has worked with the most brilliant minds while contributing to numerous technological innovations and solving countless challenging problems in the world.

Carol Hargreaves is an associate professor and Director of Data Analytics Consulting Centre at the Department of Statistics and Data Science, at National University of Singapore

Shilpa K. is currently working as a Junior Pharmacovigilance Associate, ADR Monitoring Center, Pharmacovigilance Programme of India (PvPI, MoHFW, Govt. of India), Department of Pharmacology Government Medical College, Kozhikode. She has completed her Doctor of Pharmacy (Pharm D) from Al-Shifa college of Pharmacy, Perinthalmanna, Malappuram, Kerala, affiliated to KUHAS University, Kerala.

Chitra P. has completed her Doctoral Degree in Computer Science and Applications in 2019 and she has also finished her PDF in the year 2021. She is a vibrant researcher in the field of Image compression, Machine learning and deep learning. She has a good number of publications in journals, Book chapters, and National and international conferences. She is currently working on AI-based techniques.

Maheswari R. is a Professor at the School of Computing Science and Engineering, VIT Chennai. She has published seven patents in her research domain and has received awards like Outstanding FOSSEE Contributor Award from IIT Bombay & MHRD, Govt. of India, Best Faculty Award, Best achiever award, Best researcher award, Best paper and Excellent paper awards, Best Club Coordinator award. She has published more than 40 papers in various International peer-reviewed journals (IEEE, ACM, etc.) and conferences. She has created her own footprint by contributing her work in FOSSEE (Free and Open Source Software for Education) such as esim, Scilab. She actively coordinated Institution accreditation activities like NBA, ISO certification, NAAC, ABET. She has successfully completed various consultancy project works like an Exhibition hall proposal at the Gujarat Institute of Disaster Management in collaboration with NID (National Institute of Design) Gujarat, Microsoft internship projects, etc. Currently pursuing consultancy work with fundboon technologies. She visited various countries namely Hong Kong, Singapore, Malaysia, etc. for presenting her research contributions as well as to give keynote addresses. Acted as a resource person, panel member, chief guest, and guest of honor and gave a plenary talk in various seminars, workshops, and international conferences. She has been an active reviewer in various International journals like International Journal of High Performance Computing and Networking- Inderscience, Journal of Electrical Engineering & Technology, Journal of Services Technology and Management- Inderscience and various International Conferences. Her teaching and research expertise covers a wide range of subject areas including Big data analytics, Machine Learning, Block Chain technology, Embedded Systems, Processor level architecture, High-Performance Computing, Reconfigurable Computing, IoT, etc.

A. Saleem Raja is a part of the IT Department at the University of Technology and Applied Sciences Shinas, Sultanate of Oman.

Ganesan Ramachandran is Professor and Dean in School of Computer Science and Engineering at Vellore Institute of Technology Chennai Campus, Tamil Nadu, India. He has acted as an Assistant Director for Office of International Relations from the year 2018 to 2021 and as an Assistant Director for Outreach Programs from the year 2018 to 2019. He was a program chair for B.Tech. Computer Science and Engineering during the year 2013–2017. Earlier, he was an Associate Professor and Head of the Department at Computer Science Department, PSG College of Arts and Science, Coimbatore, Tamil Nadu, India from 1998 to 2012. He is having more than 24 years of teaching experience. He has obtained his Doctor of Philosophy in Computer Science from Bharathiar University, Coimbatore, Tamil Nadu, India in the year 2011. His area of research work is Information Security and Network Security. Under his supervision, 7 researh scholars have successfully completed their PhD in Computer Science and one research scholar is pursuing PhD. He has published several research papers in the peer reviewed National and International Level Journals and he had delivered various guest lectures in the field of Information Security. He is a reviewer for various national and international journals. Also, certified ISO internal auditor by TUV Rheinland (India) Pvt. Ltd. in the year 2007.

Siva Shankar Ramasamy got a Masters and Doctorate from Gandhigram Rural University (MHRD-India), Tamil Nadu, India. He worked in the National Institute of Technology-Trichy., and Madanapalle Institute of Technology & Science, India. He is a Life Member of "Computer Society of India" and "International Association of Engineers". He is currently working in the International College of Digital Innovation-Chiang Mai University, Thailand. He possesses 3 Research Patents and more than 20 Research articles. His research areas are Sustainable Development, Medical Image Segmentation, IoT, Rural Reconstruction, Cross Border Commerce and Blue Economy.

Vijayalakshmi S. received her bachelor's degree in Computer Science in 1995 and Master of Computer Application degree in 1998 from Bharathidasan University, Trichy, India. She completed her Master of Philosophy in 2006. Mother Teresa Women's University, Kodaikanal, TN, India, awarded her with a Ph.D. degree in 2014. She has served as an Assistant Professor from 1998 to 2013 in the Department of Computer Science and Applications, Gandhigram Rural Institute – Deemed University, TN, India, and in the School of Computing Science and Engineering, Galgotias University, Greater Noida, UP from 2013 to 2021. She is currently working as an Associate Professor in the Data Science Department in CHRIST (Deemed to be University), Pune, Lavasa Campus. She is having many academic portfolios associated with her current position. Her research area is on Image Processing and IoT. She has contributed to many international and national level conferences and reputed journals. She has published many book chapters and a few books are under process. She is also a member of many academic bodies such as IFERP. Other than teaching she is guiding the students in their research as well as academic-related activities.

Gayathri S. P. finished Ph.D. in the Department of Computer Science and Applications in Gandhigram Rural Institute (DU), Dindigul, TN, India and currently working as a Guest Teacher in the same department. She has 13 years of teaching experience in the field of computer science. She has published many research articles in reputed journals and contributed book chapters. Her research interest is Digital and Medical Image Processing.

Pattabiraman Venkatasubbu obtained his Bachelor's from Madras University and Master's degree from Bharathidasan University. He completed his PhD from Bharathiar University, India. He has a total Professional experience of more than 16 years working in various prestigious institutions. He has published more than 30 papers in various National and International peer reviewed journals and conferences. He visited various countries namely few China, Singapore, Malaysia, Thailand and South Africa etc. for presenting his research contributions as well as to giving key note address. He is currently an Associate Professor and Program-Chair for Master's Programme at VIT University-Chennai Campus, India. His teaching and research expertise covers a wide range of subject area including Data Structures, Knowledge Discovery and Data mining, Database echnologies, Big Data Analytics, Networks and Information Security, etc.

Index

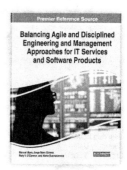

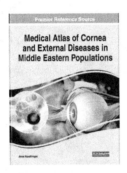

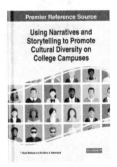

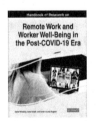

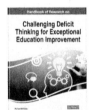